The Sacred and the Psychic

The Sacred and the Psychic

Parapsychology and Christian Theology

John J. Heaney

Paulist Press New York/Ramsey

Library of Congress
Catalog Card Number: 83-82015

ISBN: 0-8091-2594-3

Published by Paulist Press
545 Island Road, Ramsey, N.J. 07446

Printed and bound in the
United States of America

Contents

Acknowledgements

I wish to express my gratitude to The Parapsychology Foundation for the grant which facilitated the completion of this book. In particular, I owe a debt of gratitude to Mrs. Eileen Coly, president of The Parapsychology Foundation, for her kind support. Also I want to thank Fr. John Shea of Fordham University for his careful and critical reading of the manuscript. Dr. Karlis Osis of The American Society for Psychical Research for his warm charity and encouragement, and lastly my wife, Pat, for her many important and clarifying comments and for her continual support.

To Pat

Preface

George Tyrrell once likened man to a bird born in a cage which does not know what to do with its wings. Theologians, I suppose, are professional wing-watchers. This has become especially true today when theology has taken up seriously the dialogue with the human sciences. In this dialogue, theologians do not commence as God-watchers but as wing-watchers. But theologians are not alone in claiming to perceive these wings. Spiritual people of all beliefs claim to be able to see them. Even secular humanists who claimed to be atheists, like Erich Fromm and Abraham Maslow, have also glimpsed these wings of self-transcendence. Ordinary people, caught up in the so-called "consciousness explosion," are trying out these wings awkwardly in efforts at self-transcendence.

But this characteristic of "wing-watcher" often generates a certain wariness among parapsychologists when a theologian enters their edifice to observe what is transpiring. The parapsychologist's glance is often sidelong and cautious when this stranger enters. He feels uneasy with this wing-watcher just as he does with the individual who claims to be able to see an aura around people. He is afraid that the theologian may embarrass his science by seeing spiritual wings where no such things are observable to "the eyes of the crow and the eye of the camera," as Auden put it.

On the other hand, the theologian's own peers may also cast a glance at their colleague when he enters this strange edifice. "Is he or she making parapsychology into a religion? Does he or she feel that faith is not enough? With what new works is he or she trying to justify man?" The late Cardinal Franz König of Vienna summarized this view in a speech at the University of Chicago in 1974, "Those unable to find their way to traditional religious faith will seek an outlet in occultism, clairvoyance, parapsychology or astrology, right down to the various forms of primitive superstition."[1]

The justification for the theologian's visit to this strange land will, I trust, become clear in the course of this book. For the moment, the only justification that can be offered is the search for truth. As St. Augustine put it in *Praedestinatione Sanctorum,* "But everybody who believes thinks—both thinks in believing and believes in thinking."

I write for truth-seekers. I hope this epithet includes not only my readers but also myself. By a "truth-seeker" I wish to exclude the debater. A debater is one who wishes to win rather than to find the true. In the course of our study, we will meet parapsychologists, theologians and critics who seem unconsciously to fall into the trap of desiring to win (debating) rather than to walk the road of truth-seeking.

However, many genuine truth-seekers who are deeply religious may feel they cannot profit from the discussions which follow. If they read along, they will have learned something, namely that they do not take to this type of study. Others, some equally religious, and some very puzzled or even agnostic, may find some value here. This is particularly true of those who are deeply influenced by the still persisting residue of eighteenth century Enlightenment thought. These suffering believers have unknowingly taken on the posture of people living in a box, lined with physical phenomena, and whose vision is limited to our five senses. The "eyes of the crow and the eye of the camera" become their only criteria. While one may postulate a super-world "out there," still all postulates are suspect. Such postulates often originate in wishful thinking in the Freudian sense. The result, even for orthodox believers, can be at times a sense of frustration or else a kind of schizophrenia, here the box, so tangible and visible, out there the super-world, God.

The result of a study on the implications of parapsychology for theology may be a very humble one. It may be seen in a prosaic way or it may come as a "blik"—"ah! the box is gone" or "there is no box!" If we are still bound in today, the boundaries have changed. There is a strange numinous or mystical element in the world which transcends man's powers as we have known them.

For many people today, however, the implications brought out in the following pages have deep significance for theology. I am one of those people. I am not by profession a psychical investigator but a Catholic theologian who specializes in fundamental theology. I hope to present a balanced view of the implications of parapsychology for theology, and especially for fundamental theology. As I use this term, it refers first to the study of the experience and doctrine of the foundational Christian category, revelation, and, second, to the study of the presuppositions and assumptions, both conscious and unconscious, which are involved in the commitment to Christian revelation.

This edifice is built upon the labors of those who have gone before us, parapsychologists and theologians. I am sure that those who follow us will find here much to question, clarify, deepen or correct. New syntheses will be achieved by the theological giants of the future. But giants, if they sit on others' shoulders, can see further than giants alone.

Chapter I

Telepathy and Clairvoyance

Parapsychology is not a synonym for the occult movement. The word "occult" means hidden or mysterious. The occult movement is based on claims to knowledge about supernatural agencies or mysterious events which are inscrutable to humans in general but which are available to the initiated. The basis of this claim tends to be "dogmatic." That is, it seems to the observer to be overly *a priori,* esoteric, and not sufficiently related to critical study. Critical study may be either historical, philosophical-religious or scientific. However, it must be admitted that some occultists do make a serious effort to use critical investigation in the pursuit of their subject. Insofar as they do, they are approaching parapsychology.

I would define parapsychology as the attempt to apply scientific method and/or critical investigation to phenomena which are "paranormal." Paranormal here means whatever is outside the normal paradigms of science and critical reasoning. As we will see, parapsychology either will attempt to show how certain phenomena can be explained by the traditional paradigms or it will finally come to challenge these very paradigms. By "paradigm" I mean a set of generally accepted assumptions and rules regarding the nature of the problems in a given discipline and the appropriate means of addressing them.[1] Paradigms are like windows through which we see reality. Paradigms are very important because they usually decide what we can observe. Perspective determines what can be seen.

What parapsychology studies is often called Psi. This is the general term for extra-sensory perception and extra-sensory motor activity. "Extra-sensory" here means not necessarily beyond all our senses but beyond their known activities, or outside our present paradigms. Also, the term does not necessarily mean "spiritual." After all, there seems to be such a thing as animal telepathy and clairvoyance (Anpsi).

Psi includes many areas which we will discuss later. For the moment let us confine ourselves to three: telepathy, clairvoyance and psychokinesis. *Telepathy:* the knowledge of another's mental activities beyond any known means. *Clairvoyance:* the knowledge of objects or objective events at a distance beyond any known means. *Psychokinesis* (PK): the direct influence of mind on matter beyond any known medium.

Kinds of Evidence

There are three basic types of evidence involved in parapsychological research. (a) *Anecdotal evidence:* the stories of ordinary witnesses about paranormal events. This is usually uncritical and has the tendency to become embroidered with the passing of time. However, without the anecdotal tradition, there would be no critical study of the paranormal. Furthermore, the anecdotal tradition through the sheer weight of the convergence of witnesses can at times be a solid base for study. (b) *Controlled experimental evidence:* this is the type of evidence which has been studied under controlled laboratory conditions. Also systematic efforts have been made to replicate or reduplicate the experiment. (c) *Spontaneous experimental evidence:* this consists of data which cannot be strictly controlled, e.g., an apparition or a poltergeist display. However, it is called "experimental" because at least one trained observer or investigator is present.

In the present study I will place a great deal of emphasis on the experimental evidence. However, I cannot do full justice to the empirical studies in a work of this size and in a study which is theologically oriented. Accordingly, the reader is referred for further investigation to the histories of parapsychology listed in the notes.

A Brief Sketch of the Historical Background

As we begin, we must set the questions with which we will be dealing in an historical and psychological context of some length. Modern parapsychology did not begin with the scientific investigation of telepathy and clairvoyance. At least in its Anglo-Saxon form, it began with an attempt to assess the evidence for survival beyond bodily death. This investigation, particularly with regard to apparitions, began roughly in the last quarter of the nineteenth century and during the first years of this century. The Society for Psychical Research (S.P.R.) was founded in London in 1882, and the American Society (A.S.P.R.), first organized in 1885, later became a branch of the S.P.R. Finally it became an independent organization in 1906, with James Hyslop, formerly professor at Columbia University, as its secretary, and with William James as a distinguished member.

For the purpose of brevity, I will center mainly on the British scene. The last half of the nineteenth century was a time when the "higher" biblical criticism coming from Germany was beginning to weaken the traditional Protestant faith of the intellectual classes in Britain. Many conservative Christians were appalled at the work of exegetes dedicated to the understanding of Holy Scripture. Faced then with both the higher criticism as well as the recent influence of evolutionary thought, these Christians tended to resort to ridicule and abuse as weapons of defense.

Some Christian intellectuals were disturbed by such a response. Of these I am principally concerned with Henry Sidgwick, Frederic Myers and Edmund Gurney. Henry Sidgwick (1838–1900), who was to become the first president of the S.P.R. as well as a distinguished professor of moral philosophy at Cambridge, about 1861 began to pursue historical studies on the origins of Christianity. He visited Germany and spent a good portion of three years studying Hebrew and Arabic. But by 1864 he had come to the conclusion that these efforts would not solve for him the difficulties he now felt. These concerned the incarnation, the Gospel miracles, the resurrection and eternal life. Subsequently, he threw himself into the study not only of moral philosophy but also of the question of survival beyond death. Sidgwick, who was a member of the Church of England, never resolved his doubts. As Alan Gauld puts it: "He continued for the rest of his life to lean somewhat hesitantly towards theism," principally because of an inescapable sense of duty, though he could come to no definite conclusion about the existence of an afterlife.[2]

Henry Sidgwick and Frederic W.H. Myers (1843–1901) perhaps may stand as representative symbols of two types of minds. Sidgwick had one of the most subtle minds of his time. He also possessed a keen sense of the quest for "objectivity," a passion for the weighing of evidence, and he was certainly a man of great candor.

Frederic Myers, on the other hand, had a very powerful and passionate personality. As a child he was noticeably precocious, openly religious and deeply sensitive about, among other things, death. Near death from pneumonia in 1869, Myers realized that he was no longer a Christian. Bogged down in an agnosticism which caused him great unhappiness, he turned to Sidgwick as a guide. Sidgwick, who shrank from the possibility of dominating anyone through guidance, would help or teach only those whose "bent or choice is to search after ultimate truth."[3] Sidgwick saw in Myers one who, as Gauld puts it, "preferred Truth, however grim, to illusion, however soothing. . . ." Myers, however, had a keen zest for life and a love of experience for its own sake. He could not understand how anyone could help but find the thought of personal extinction dreadful. It seemed not only to threaten his love for life, but to rob life itself of all point and purpose. Furthermore, annihilation held dire implications for Myers' deep love for Annie Marshall, which love persisted after her suicide in 1875 until his death. Myers was an outstanding classical scholar, and despite his tendency toward an unrestrained expression of feeling and despite his dramatic personality (which contributed to his unpopularity outside the circle of his friends), he was an authentic member of the band of truth seekers. What he wrote in the Proceedings of the Society for Psychical Research in 1900 was a genuine expression of his cherished striving:

We must recognise that we have more in common with those who may criticise or attack our work with competent diligence than with those who may acclaim and exaggerate it without adding thereto any careful work of their own. We must experiment unweariedly; we must continue to demolish fiction as well as to accumulate truth; we must make no terms with any hollow mysticism, any half-conscious deceit.[4]

Edmund Gurney (1847–1888) was the first Honorary Secretary of the S.P.R. A man of great speculative ability, wit and cool judgment, he was also a musician, and extremely sensitive to the suffering he saw in the world. This latter characteristic undoubtedly accounts in part for Gurney's joining in the work of the S.P.R. For this Society, he labored with incredible industry until his mysterious death from a perhaps accidental overdose of a drug.

Gurney, Sidgwick and Myers joined in a prodigious effort of research on paranormal phenomena, the latter two from about 1874 until their deaths in 1900 and 1901 respectively. By the end of their lives a vast amount of data had been investigated by the first members of the S.P.R.: table rapping, apparitions, automatic script writing, and verbal messages from séances as well as ectoplastic materialization phenomena. A breakthrough which resulted from their work was that an open-minded scientist could no longer interpret all paranormal phenomena, in particular those connected with apparent afterlife, as simply fraudulent. Furthermore, these phenomena could not be dismissed as capable of explanation according to any assured tenet of science.

The work of these early researchers, however, came in for a good deal of criticism, the main thrust of which greatly disturbed them. It was because of this that Gurney, who had uncovered a large amount of inexplicable phenomena, in exasperation neatly penned a parody on some of the critiques he received: "The fact is so improbable that extremely good evidence is needed to make us believe it; and this evidence is not good, for how can you trust people who believe in such absurdities."

The interpretation of the data, however, still was uncertain. The early members of the S.P.R. themselves differed in their conclusions. Henry Sidgwick had doubts whether the phenomena investigated pointed without doubt to human survival of bodily death; so, too, Walter Leaf (1852–1927), a Fellow of Trinity, classical scholar and banker; Edmund Gurney, a most careful investigator, was unable to reach a state of certainty; Myers and the hard-headed Australian investigator, Richard Hodgson (1885–1905), who later guided the A.S.P.R., both arrived at the conviction of human survival beyond death. Eleanor Sidgwick, the wife of Henry, also believed that the evidence pointed toward the survival hypothesis. The intelligent lady has impressed most of the commentators as a meticulous investigator and as one of the most brilliant women of her time in England.

However, it seems that most of the original members of the S.P.R. (including Gladstone, Arthur Balfour, Lord Rayleigh, Oliver Lodge, Tennyson and Ruskin) had not actually anticipated reaching a scientific state of certainty on the survival question. Rather they hoped only to find some good grounds for keeping the options open in the face of the contemporary closed-universe materialism, and in this most were abundantly satisfied. (Here it might be mentioned in passing that William James, one of the early members of the A.S.P.R., also was left unable to reach a conviction about personal survival though he felt rather favorable toward the evidence.)

The ambivalence about the meaning of survival phenomena among the early members of the S.P.R. should not, however, obscure certain advances which were made. Gurney, for example, clearly demonstrated the impossibility of explaining all apparitions as fraudulent.[5] Secondly, a plausible case was made for the hypothesis that "crisis" apparitions, those appearing for example on the occasion of a death, were telepathic messages from the dying person. Furthermore, collective apparitions, where several people at the same time see the figure and actions of a deceased person, were and still remain extremely puzzling phenomena. Lastly, some of the accurate evidence obtained from mediums, either through verbal communication ("clairaudi-ence") or through automatic writing, had (and has) as yet no adequate scientific explanation. The highly challenging séances of Mrs. Lenora E. Piper, the Boston medium, tested both by the S.P.R. and William James, produced turns of phrase, personality characteristics and intimate details of lives of deceased persons not known to the medium. These phenomena caused many people at the time to wonder whether the experiments done with her did not mark "the dawn of a new era in man's knowl-edge of the Universe."[6]. However, it was the very impasse reached in the early work of these researchers that led to the modern scientific investigation of telepathy and clairvoyance. The need was felt to put the study of the paranormal on a more firm scientific footing and thus Joseph Rhine began his famous studies at Duke.

Experimental Evidence for Telepathy and Clairvoyance

Dr. Joseph Rhine (1895–1980) published his famous work, *Extra-Sensory Perception* in 1935. For his tests Rhine used Zener cards. These cards have five symbols, a star, a circle, a plus sign, parallel wavy lines and a rectangle. In a pack of 25 cards, each symbol appears 5 times. The person who was guessing would guess in runs of 25 cards. He would not see the cards after each guess. The experimenter also did not see the symbols on the cards as they were picked. If he saw them, the test could have been a test for telepathy. As he did not see them, this was a test for clairvoyance. In the telepathy experiments the experimenter simply imaged in his mind one of the five symbols. Details of these experiments may be found in the many books and the reader might check some of these experiments for the systems of control which were used.[7]

In 1931 a Duke undergraduate, A.J. Linzmayer, achieved 238 hits in 600 trials. The expected average for each 25 cards is 5. Linzmayer first averaged 9.9. Later, for example, he averaged 6.5 in October 1931 and 6.7 in March 1932. Statistically these results are beyond a trillion to 1 against chance. In 1932 Rhine worked with a ministerial student, Hubert Pearce, Jr. After scoring only at chance level, in 2250 subsequent calls Pearce averaged 9.7. By April 1933, in 11,250 trials he had an average of 8.9 for each 25 cards. The odds against chance as the cause are astronomical.

J.G. Pratt (1910–1979), Rhine's assistant, tested Pearce who was over 100 yards away from the cards. In 300 calls he averaged 9.5 per 25 cards. The odds here are 10^{22}-1 against chance. In 1939 Pratt tested J.L. Woodruff. In 2,400 runs he had 489 hits above chance, or 500,000-1 against chance.

At the University of London, S.G. Soal set out to disprove Rhine. At first, while testing Basil Shackleton, nothing paranormal was detected. But it was noticed Shackleton was guessing cards which would turn up one or two calls later. Shackleton seemed to have precognitive power. The results of these tests were ten million to one against chance. Soal also tested two Welch boys. However, they were caught cheating, and even though they may have had some ESP power, the results were rejected. Mrs. G. Stewart was also tested by Soal. In 3,200 trials she had 759 direct hits. This was over two million to one against chance. These brief samplings which I have listed need filling out from other sources, but they serve to give us a sense of the excitement of those early days.

The Critics

Following the publication of these experiments, many scientific investigators pointed out that the controls were not up to scientific standards. The backs of the cards might have contained clue marks, fraud was not sufficiently excluded, etc. Rhine tightened up his controls and after that the results were much more modest. The critics claimed that this demonstrated that no ESP was involved. Rhine and his colleagues, however, used as evidence an unusual fact which they had noticed. It is called "the decline factor." In card guessing experiments, subjects who began with a high scoring level fell into a gradual, uniform decline in their scores. This pattern seemed not to be due to pure chance. Rhine and his colleagues said that this was due to boredom, not only in the subject but also in the investigator. If this is true, then boredom affects ESP.

Such a position infuriated, and still infuriates, some of the critics. How can one run controlled studies with so subjective an element involved. Today, parapsychologists have added to the list of subjective factors which influence ESP performance. There is very strong probability that relaxation states, alpha states (in which the brain waves have slowed down to about 8 to 13 cycles per second), the kind of experiment, the personality of the experimenter as well as the personality of the one undergoing the experiment, all have impact on the final score. How can one make a controlled study in such an uncontrollable situation? Many critics believe that these subjective variances are really part of an *ad hoc* theory put together as a means of escape from scientific study.

Modern Studies

A large number of statistically significant experiments have been run since those early days. The cumulative evidence now seems to point overwhelmingly to the existence of telepathy and clairvoyance. Here, I can do no more than briefly present a few examples of such experiments. In 1963 and 1968, teams led by J.G. Pratt in Prague and by Ian Stevenson at the University of Virginia tested the Czech, Pavel Stepanek. The combined results for three major experiments in these studies were 10,000,000 to 1 against chance.[8] In 1976 James Terry and Charles Honorton reported statistically significant results with eighteen St. John's University undergraduates while employing sensory deprivation techniques.[9] In 1976 Charles Tart of the University of California at Davis in a telepathic test with gifted students reported results which were greater than a billion to one against chance.

Charles Honorton, presently director of The Psychophysical Research Laboratories at The Princeton Forrestal Center, Princeton, N.J., claims that parapsychology is actually in a better position vis-à-vis replication than many other areas of behavioral research. For example, of the experiments reported at one convention, 73 percent were replications with significant confirmation of earlier findings in 43 percent of the cases.[10]

Statistics and the Critics

Some critics of parapsychological conclusions, instead of claiming fraud or poor experimentation, hold the conviction that there must be some "fluke" in the statistics that we do not understand. Nevertheless, insurance companies and gambling casinos continue to make their profits, the surety of which is based on statistical methods. Stan Gooch in *The Paranormal* graphically shows both the relativity of statistical conclusions in gambling, for example, and the limits of this relativity. In a study of a roulette wheel which has the numbers 0 to 36 on it, the highest number of times that a given number has been repeated is six. The chances of this happening are 37^6. Gooch says that, while it is hard to set an upper limit for a given number to appear successively that would rule out all chance, still one could say that 50 times would be impossible. But what of 12 times? Gooch, however, believes one can get close to a limit.

Most parapsychological scientists believe that with choice subjects the chance barrier has often been surpassed. In 1937, the American Institute of Mathematical Statistics agreed that Rhine's results had shown non-chance factors, and that the ESP debate should be conducted on other than mathematical grounds. Statisticians must make the final decisions in this area. But the reader should be aware of what we will discuss in Chapter II, that statistics alone are not the sole crucial factor in deciding whether a given event is paranormal. If all the statistics were deceptive, one would still have to account for certain psychokinetic events, such as bending a metal bar in a jar without any physical contact. What are the chances of doing this? One in a billion? No. It is normally impossible. The evidence for the paranormal, then, must be seen as a whole. If PK is a fact, the overwhelming probability about the conclusions from statistical evidence seems to me to be also strengthened.

"Proof"

This seems to be an appropriate place to make a few remarks on the relationship between science and parapsychology. Science looks for proof. A rough definition of *hard* scientific proof might be as follows: a conclusion, resulting from the gathering and testing of data, that a *given explanation* is the only *working hypothesis at present* which will explain the data, and in which the experiments can be tested by any capable individual. This last aspect is called "replicability" or repeatability. That is, the certitude can become socially assimilable through repeated experimentation.

Scientists who analyze ESP according to this norm seem to forget that such "proof" is rarely attainable, even in *hard* science, especially where a vast amount of data and a large vision of the process of life or energy is involved, for example, in relativity theory, in evolutionary processes, and in questions of astronomy. In more limited experiments, such as whether aspirin prevents the clotting of blood, hard scientific proof often is attained. But when the issue is of a larger and broader perspective, such as the nature of man or the origin of the universe, science itself becomes "soft." The soft sciences, like psychology, sociology and history, are usually based rather on strong, very strong or almost overwhelming probability. In science itself, the broad lines of the theory of evolution seem to be almost overwhelmingly probable. Yet a small group of people, some of them scientists, do not find the theory replicable in their "experiments" with the data. Simply because the theory of evolution (I am not speaking here of the details or of the exact processes) has not gained universal acceptance from all intelligent people does not allow us to wash our hands of the theory and conclude, as so many undergraduate essays or various similar topics conclude, with a shrug of the shoulders and an exclamation, "Who knows!"

When we turn to the parapsychological area, the same point needs to be made. When consistent experiments point to the same conclusion, one cannot simply assert, "But it has not been scientifically proven." Parapsychology, if it is capable of being a science, belongs to the area of the soft or probabilistic sciences.

If we reach conclusions which are only highly probable, strongly probable or almost overwhelmingly probable, one cannot wash one's hands of the subject while saying, "But it has not been scientifically proven." In my judgment, parapsychology has reached the point with regard to telepathy and clairvoyance (as we will shortly see) at which it can say, "Telepathy and clairvoyance exist as paranormal powers beyond any reasonable doubt, but not beyond all possible doubt." In this sense, there is "proof" in some areas of parapsychology.

Paradigms and Reality

On the other hand, the parapsychologist or theologian may say to the hard scientist, "Look, you have us locked in a room with a sliding panel window which is only partially opened. The perspective seen through this window is that of hard science. But is this view the only road to truth and certainty? It is a fairly sure road to temporary certainty but it is not the only road to meaning. Science is surely a great gift from the northwestern sector of the globe to the world but never forget that it is also a limited view. Why can't we open that window wider?" Reaction to such statements has, at times, been strongly negative on the part of some famous scientists. This is the result of what Michael Mahoney in *Scientist as Subject* (1978) calls "paradigm passion." "Through your window," the parapsychologist and theologian might continue, "I see a human being who in the 1940's was seen as reducible to 79¢ worth of chemicals in a vial, and recently, because of inflation and because of the discovery of endorphins and like substances in the brain, this chemical composite has become worth millions of dollars. But your partially opened window reveals sparks and strange anomalies around this human being which reach out beyond the window's perspective. These strange anomalies cannot be ridiculed simply because they do not seem to fit into your *a priori* perspective." Glory to science and hard proof but in its proper place. Each discipline must be judged by its own protocol.

Some critics of ESP study, whether scientists like C.E.M. Hansel or magicians like James ("The Amazing") Randi have concluded that all ESP evidence is the result either of sloppy experimentation, lack of rigidly strict scientific method or fraud.

The Committee for the Scientific Advancement of the Claims of the Paranormal

This organization is known under the abbreviation "CSI-COP." It is unfortunate that its title would not allow for the abbreviation "PSI-COP," for this organization has set itself up as a kind of policeman to oversee PSI study. Founded in 1976, the Committee lists some distinguished Fellows, such as Isaac Asimov, Carl Sagan, B.F. Skinner, *Time* senior editor Leon Jaroff, Martin Gardner, formerly of *Scientific American,* and the magicians James Randi and Milbourne Christopher. It is headed by Dr. Paul Kurz, teacher of philosophy at the University of Buffalo and editor of *The Humanist.* The Committee evolved into a kind of debunking group in the manner of debaters. The weaker experiments in the parapsychological field were attacked and the rest of the field then was tarnished by association. This kind of approach brought serious dissension into the ranks of the Committee and one of the members, Marcello Truzzi, a professor of sociology at Eastern Michigan University, broke away and founded a much more open journal, *Zetetic Scholar.* In 1981 he set up the Center for Scientific Anomalies Research (CSAR). It will "promote open and fair-minded inquiry that will be *constructively skeptical.*" The function of such a group could be of much value. Parapsychologists would at least be made more careful in descriptions of their work. However, some of the works from the CSICOP Committee members bunch together as objects of their attacks astrology, Tarot card beliefs, U.F.O. experts as well as cultists, and parapsychological personalities like Uri Geller as well as some parapsychological investigation.[11] Recently the academic straightforwardness of the Committee has been seriously questioned in a well-documented article by Dennis Rawlins, himself a skeptic on the paranormal.[12] This is not to say that some of the criticisms of this group should not be heeded by parapsychologists. But the Committee has sponsored work which seems to arise from a kind of *a priori* dogmatism, written in a debunking style. And finally, if an experiment in every way cannot be shown to have reached the highest standards of scientific method (a demand which is not made for many other disciplines), and if one can conclude that a given position has not been rigidly scientifically proved, then the implied presumption is that no account should be taken of the evidence, no matter how solid or widespread. One feels in this sort of writing that the author is out to win points rather than to pursue the real. Where sound points are made, we will refer to various authors from the group throughout the present work.

Critical study must respect the protocol for the investigation of the various aspects of reality. It cannot set up *a priori* rules which demand that we observe only certain aspects of reality. The critical sciences are divided up into various perspectives to facilitate our investigation of reality, not to tell us what we must find.

On the other hand, some of the better critics of parapsychology have performed a valuable and even necessary function. Some parapsychologists, like some of the discoverers of new therapeutic drugs, tend to overvalue their findings. Like all of us, they are prone to wishful thinking. Critics, like C.E.M. Hansel, for example, have shown carelessness in some of the experiments, insufficient controls to rule out fraud, and even the possibility of fraud in some cases. Hansel has made use of some careful computerized studies of Soal's figures in the work with Shackleton, for example, to suggest that fraud may have been present. He thinks that Soal may have doctored some of the figures in the Shackleton study, and before he died Soal was unable to locate his original documents! Yet this position is not conclusive and, as John Palmer points out, it is unfortunate that Soal is no longer alive and able to defend himself. Similarly, David Marks and Richard Kamman in *The Psychology of the Psychic* have shown that Uri Geller has almost certainly cheated at times and that his associates have admitted to knowing this. Marks himself overheard Geller tell his associates, "Keep that guy away from me. He'll pick up my signals." But often enough it is the parapsychologists themselves who have detected the fraud when it is present. The doctoring of the figures by Walter Levy,

Jr. in an experiment at the Laboratory in Durham was originally disclosed by parapsychologists themselves.

Some Other Qualities of Telepathy and Clairvoyance

(1) Some experiments have been run which are called "the sheep-goats effect." Sheep are those who believe in ESP, goats are those who do not. Gertrude Schmeidler of CCNY has postulated as a result of her experiments that belief in ESP increases the chances of success. The evidence for this conclusion, while very strong, is not as conclusive as that for the *existence* of telepathy and clairvoyance. (In these experiments I have not seen the following question handled: which comes first, ability at ESP which engenders the belief in it or belief which facilitates the emergence of ESP ability?) (2) Consistent negative scoring which is below chance probability ("psi-missing") is also a form of telepathic or clairvoyant ESP. As the one tested does not know whether he or she is right or wrong on any given call until the experiment is completed, consistently missing the correct card or number can reach a certain statistical point at which it demonstrates a paranormal factor. This seems to indicate an unconscious avoidance of the target. The theory is that ESP takes place when the guards set up by evolutionary development against constant bombardment by paranormal phenomena are let down, as in relaxed states or in the hypnogogic moments just before falling asleep. Telepathy or clairvoyance can be such disconcerting forces that one can unconsciously keep up guards against them. (3) Telepathy and clairvoyance do not seem to be influenced by lead blocks or electrical currents such as found in "Faraday cages" which screen out known electro-magnetic currents. These paranormal powers continue to operate. (4) Whether telepathy and clairvoyance are uninfluenced by distance and whether these abilities are inherited are still debated questions. Many parapsychologists venture a tentative affirmative answer to both questions. (5) Some tests suggest that the anxious, inhibited person (at least at the moment of the test) is less likely to produce ESP phenomena. The expansive, more spontaneously

imaginative and extrovert type seems to produce more significant scores. Relaxed and alpha states (states where brain waves are slowed down to 8–13 cycles per second) facilitate ESP scoring. On the other hand, waves of anger or hostility also have produced ESP phenomena. The common denominator seems to be an altered state of consciousness (ASC). (6) Sensory isolation which also produces an ASC has been shown to improve scoring. One form of this isolating process is called "the Ganzfeld Effect." In this experiment half of a ping-pong ball is placed over each eye and other sensory stimuli are blocked out. Strong evidence for the effectiveness of the Ganzfeld effect has been discovered. There is also some evidence suggestive of the probability that hypnosis may be a catalyst for ESP scoring.

Theories about the Nature of Clairvoyance and Telepathy

The theories and models presented to explain the nature of telepathy and clairvoyance have proliferated to such an extent that it is impossible to list all of them here. A few of the main theories are: (a) A purely *spiritual* power transcending matter-energy of any kind. The most probable existence of animal psi (Anpsi) and the fact that we do not fully comprehend the limits of matter-energy should make one cautious about this first theory. (b) A power of "discarnate" *spirits* using human subjects as kinds of mediums. Some spiritualists have maintained this position. But there is no evidence of spirit operation in card and dice experiments in university laboratories. The total context of these experiments suggests that such a position is unacceptable, apart from some exceptions to be handled later. (c) *An unknown physical energy operating through space.* This physical energy may consist of "psi-fields" which surround all bodies and which cause similar energies to interact. (d) *An unknown form of energy which does not cross space but which reaches inward to the essential psychic center of a person.* At this center a transpersonal mode is reached where all humans and perhaps all reality are united. This is similar to the Collective Unconscious of Carl Jung. We will explain this idea in more detail in Chapter III on paranormal healing.

Theories "c" and "d" are the most consistent with the data. Theory "d" has become increasingly more prominent, however, as the data from the whole of parapsychology are collected. It seems to cover paranormal events not sufficiently explained by theory "c." This point will be discussed in various parts of the following chapters.

Some Religious Implications

Thus far this study has been heavily parapsychological. The religious reader may sense a budding impatience to get on with the "real subject," the religious implications in parapsychology. As our study continues, more and more will we begin to see the religious and theological implications of parapsychology. However, at the beginning we must lay the groundwork for what will follow. In any dialogue with another discipline, this is a prerequisite for theology. While theology hitches its wagon to a star, here it must also humbly hitch its star to a wagon.

The perceptive reader will have already noticed implications for religion in what has preceded. For example, the telepathic feats of some saints and holy people, like St. John Vianney, the Curé d'Ars, and Padre Pio, seem to be human abilities. Both Padre Pio and the Curé d'Ars were able, according to excellent witnesses, to read the minds of their penitents and other people. This power does not seem to require any *unique and different intervention* by God. It seems to operate according to God's normal providence over the world. (For the meaning of "unique and different intervention" see Chapter III.) When St. Francis Xavier paused during a sermon which he was delivering on the island of Tarnate in the Indonesian islands to tell the congregation that some of their relatives were in danger as their ship was now sinking far out at sea, this again seems to have been the result of a special human ability of St. Francis and not a miracle produced *directly* by God.

Furthermore, some of the implications of parapsychology for theology seem applicable to Jesus also. I say this as a Catholic theologian who accepts the unique God-manhood of Jesus. Jesus certainly had some remarkable powers of telepathy and clairvoyance. In St. John's Gospel, Nathaniel asked Jesus how he came to know him. "Jesus replied, 'I saw you under the fig tree before Phillip spoke to you' " (Jn 1:48). The findings of parapsychology support the position that many of the paranormal powers attributed to Jesus by the evangelists are not simply the results of later redactional insertions by the evangelists to heighten his significance and to increase the faith of later followers. Rather, these paranormal powers, which are so widely mentioned throughout the Gospels that it seems impossible to separate them from the fabric of the Gospel itself, can be taken as generally factual. Individual incidents we will treat in later chapters. The implications of the human quality of these powers for the belief in the divinity of Jesus will be treated in Chapter III on healing and in Chapter X on apparitions.

It merits noting here that the Christian Church and its theologians have long held that there were strange *natural* powers possessed by some people which were not the results of direct divine intervention. While we call them "paranormal," the Church Scholastics called them "preternatural." Preternatural meant not "supernatural" and not natural in the ordinary sense. No one has ever been canonized because of telepathic or clairvoyant powers. As St. Gregory put it, "The test of sanctity is not to perform miracles but to love everyone as oneself, to have true thoughts of God." The possession of paranormal power does *not necessarily* imply sanctity. Many Eastern religions too, through the voices of their gurus and spiritual masters, have expressed caution about such phenomena. Both East and West have often seen the possession of such powers as an occasion of human pride. But we must not draw too black and white a picture. Lately, critical studies of such phenomena in Eastern religions have pointed out that, while such powers were considered dangerous in that they might lead to pride in one's achievement, or they might call a halt to the spiritual journey at the superficial level of ego and block advancement into the higher levels of consciousness, still, of themselves, they might be indications of advancement beyond the first rungs of day to day ego-living and superficial perspectives.

Chapter II

Psychokinesis, Poltergeist Manifestations and Demonic Possession

Psychokinesis

Psychokinesis (PK) is the direct influence of the mind or intention of an agent on matter in a manner which is beyond any known medium or cause. In most cultures there has been a long anecdotal tradition about psychokinetic feats. The histories of religion, both Eastern and Western, also contain large bodies of evidence concerning strange reactions of matter in the presence of saints and gurus.

With regard to Christianity, Herbert Thurston, S.J. (1856–1939), in his marvelous scholarly work, *The Physical Phenomena of Mysticism,* has documented many cases of saints and sinners in whose presence PK phenomena have occurred. There is good evidence that a number of saints, such as St. John Bosco (1815–1888), have been able to multiply food. Others have been able to levitate as, for example, St. Joseph of Cupertino (1603–1663) and St. Teresa of Avila (1515–1582). Some mystics, like St. Francis of Assisi (1181–1226), Gemma Galgani (1878–1903), Theresa Neumann (1898–1962), and Padre Pio (1887–1968), have had the stigmata appear on their hands and feet. Some whom the Church has regarded as pseudo-mystics have also had the stigmata appear on their bodies, such as the sixteenth century Spanish nuns, Magdalena de la Cruz and Maria de la Visitacion.[1] St. John Vianney, the Curé d'Ars (1786–1859), was plagued for many years by what he believed to be attacks by the devil. Some of these involved manifestations similar to PK phenomena, as his biographer, Lancelot Sheppard, points out.[2] The Curé d'Ars said his bed was shifted around on its casters during the night "by the devil." Loud raps were heard from the furniture and from the floor as if a wild horse were stamping on them.

What do these phenomena have to do with religion, or with God, or the devil? We do not claim to be able to solve all these problems. Many mysteries remain. However, by a methodical investigation of psychokinetic phenomena, much light can be thrown on the nature of some of these manifestations.

In order to make the subsequent historical and experimental investigations more germane to the religious reader's interest, I wish to anticipate some of the more important conclusions drawn from these data by many theoreticians. 1. Psychokinesis is a rare but actual human power. 2. Poltergeist (from the German *polter*—noisy, *geist*—spirit) manifestations are frequently unconscious activities of a living agent, though at times some transhuman agency may be involved. 3. Demonic possession is a rare but possibly genuine phenomenon. 4. Many "possession" cases are not genuine possession but the result of unconscious PK manifestations by a living agent. 5. In genuine possession cases, the agency of possession may not be the devil or an angelic demon but a "discarnate" spirit. (The term "discarnate spirit" is frequently used to designate a human being who continues on after death in a state which is not "bodily" in exactly the same sense as our present state of embodiment.)

A Brief Historical Retrospect

The Church has been most careful in its official pronouncements as to attributing phenomena such as the ones previously mentioned about saints to the *direct* intervention of God. This caution goes back to St. Thomas Aquinas in the thirteenth century, to some of the earlier Church Fathers, and even to the New Testament, as in Paul and the Book of Acts. Benedict XIV (then Cardinal Prospero Lambertini, 1675–1758) who revised the rules for the canonization of saints from 1734 to 1738 knew about the existence of what we call "paranormal" powers.[3] At times he called them "preternatural" powers. This term is based on the Scholastics' distinction of three kinds of phenomena: (1) supernatural, (2) natural and (3) preternatural. Preternatural events were not produced by the *direct* power of God (supernatural). These extraordinary events were seen as brought about either by human power or by the agency of the devil.

Miracles

Supernatural events, either interior movements of grace and inspiration or exterior marvels, were those brought about by the *direct and unique* intervention of God. (Remember, however, that the whole of life involved "the supernatural" in the sense that it was impregnated with the steady offer of the divine presence of man.) Miracles could be interior miracles of grace ("moral miracles") or marvelous external happenings ("physical miracles"). I will center on physical or external miracles. Such a miracle was defined by the Scholastics of the late Middle Ages as an event which went beyond the powers of created nature and was a sign of an intervention by God. "Going beyond the powers of created nature" came to be stressed as the central aspect of a miracle. St. Thomas in many places takes a similar view, but he also has statements which are almost identical with St. Augustine's famous statement, "God does not act contrary to nature but only contrary to the order of nature known to us." Prospero Lambertini warned that when something new happens in the world, it should not necessarily be attributed directly to God. With astounding insight and perception for his time, Lambertini listed many criteria for deciding whether an event in a saint's life was a miracle. We will discuss these more at length under "paranormal healing." But one of the phenomena which he listed as a genuine miracle was the "multiplication of natural objects," a topic which enters into our discussion in this chapter.

With the introduction of the term "the laws of nature," a miracle began to be defined as an event which broke the laws of nature. This idea persisted among Catholic theologians until about the beginning of the twentieth century. Gradually the

realization dawned that "a law of nature," at least on the microscopic level, was a conclusion drawn from statistics about
events. "Laws" are statistical concepts. They are the best present
working hypotheses. Eventually they may need to be revised in
view of new discoveries. With the omission of the controversial
"laws of nature" concept, a miracle is now seen as "a wondrous
sign in a religious context which draws attention by its very
nature to a religious truth."

However, there are different types of "wondrous" events. It
is true that for the believer all of life is a wonder. But in the
dialogue with other disciplines (in what was called "apologetics"
and today is known as "fundamental theology") the question
still arises, "But how can one know when there is a definite,
unique and different intervention of God in the natural processes? For the believer all of life is a sign, but how can we know
when there is a unique and special sign from God?"

In 1966, Louis Monden, S.J., a Belgian Jesuit, published one
of the most authoritative studies on miracles, *Signs and Wonders.*
Monden used the word "prodigy" to describe a miracle. He
distinguished two types of prodigies, a *minor* prodigy and a *major*
prodigy. Minor prodigies were wondrous events in a religious
context which also occurred at times in a secular context. Examples of minor prodigies would be certain kinds of paranormal
healing, sudden answers to prayer which could also have a
natural coincidental explanation, visions, levitations, stigmata,
and in general the manifestation of parapsychological powers.[4]
In minor prodigies it is difficult to discern whether these events
are *directly* related to God's immediate action or whether they are
the results of natural coincidence or of natural human powers
(though admittedly God through the power of evolution would
still be the ground of all these powers). Theologians suggest
cumulative criteria or a kind of pattern of evidence which enables one to make a judgment about God's special causality.
Some of these criteria are: the immediate chronological connection of a minor prodigy to prayer, its uniformly beneficial effects
(it never does spiritual harm), the nature of an effect as pointing
to a spiritual meaning (such as matter in the service of a higher
purpose), and the manner in which such an event occurs (for

example, a healing which is of an *organic* disease, which is complete and perduring). Even then, it may be difficult to distinguish a minor prodigy from certain parapsychological phenomena. But often enough one may reach a private conviction about the overwhelming probability of God's special intervention in a given event. Remember, however, that as Monden puts it, "the miraculous never becomes a formal motive of faith." A prodigy which one experiences in one's own life is not the formal base for belief in Christian revelation, though it may be corroboratory. Parapsychological manifestations in certain patterned contexts might, for a certain person, be a sign of God's special intervention.

However, Monden believes that there are certain events which are particularly relevant for theology's dialogue with other sciences. These he calls "major prodigies." A major prodigy is an event in a religious context, the like of which is never found in a purely secular context. Examples of such prodigies would be: cosmic manifestations like the sudden stilling of a storm, multiplications of matter, such as food or fuel, instantaneous or extremely rapid healing of properly diagnosed organic functions, and raising of the dead or resurrection from the dead.[5] If an empty barn, subsequent to prayer to God for food, were found filled with grain, if one could exclude all other causes, this might well be a sign of God's direct causality. Even though "laws" are only statistical on the microscopic level, one can have reasonable certitude on the level of everyday events about God's intervention in such cases. Our subsequent parapsychological investigations may demand some qualifications in Monden's fine presentation. We will return to this point after considering the evidence.

However, for the moment my main point is that the Church has evolved in its thinking on miracles, and for many hundreds of years it has shown a certain sophistication in dealing with what we today call paranormal phenomena. For example, no saint was ever canonized solely because he or she levitated, or because a halo was seen around him or her, or simply because one bore the stigmata. No saint was ever canonized because he or she predicted the future or because he or she practiced a kind of telepathy, as with the Curé d'Ars. The Church in its canonization procedures has always insisted on heroic charity as the chief criterion for sanctity, although "prodigies" are seen as having corroborative value. Canonization rules, it is true, require a certain number of "miracles" as witnesses to the saint's heroic life. But these are never the point of central focus. On the other hand, some of the experiments and critical study which follow will no doubt call for some revisions in Church thinking in the area of "major prodigies," and in its treatment of miracles in general.

Spiritualism

Outside the mainstream of Christianity, both in the secular world and among esoteric groups, there also has been a long tradition of paranormal events which belie past explanations. As an example, let us consider the origins of spiritualism which seem to be connected with psychokinetic phenomena. In 1847 John Fox, his wife and his two daughters, Maggie, fourteen, and Kate, twelve, moved into the town of Hydesville, New York. In 1848 the family began to hear strange noises, like rappings, in the walls. Mischievously, the girls began to communicate with the raps. They would hold up two fingers and ask how many fingers were there. Two raps would come forth. Mrs. Fox addressed questions to the sounds and replies were rapped back which stated that they came from a spirit, a male, who had been murdered in the house and whose remains were buried under the dwelling. No body was ever found in the cellar, but David Fox, the girls' older married brother, claimed to have found a few bones, teeth and a few wisps of hair. Not very well documented reports include the sound of a death struggle, the gurgling of a throat, and the sound of the dragging of a heavy body across the floor night after night; also *The Boston Journal* published reports fifty-six years later of the finding of a skeleton in an area behind a rough wall about a yard from the true wall of the cellar.[6]

Strange phenomena continued to follow the girls. Under the

leadership of their older married sister, Leah, they made public appearances in Albany, Rochester, New York City, and even London and Russia. Many journalists and scholars were extremely critical despite the enthusiastic crowds which the girls' appearances drew. Two camps formed. The critical camp claimed that the noises were made by the girls clicking their knees in some double-jointed way or else by other tricks. The critical explanations which were given at the time do not satisfy us today. For example, occasionally noises were heard even when the girls were not in the house, or when one of the girls was in a room asleep. Many devotees of the girls paid no attention to the critics. Rather they believed the message which had been tapped out from the walls which said, "Dear friends, you must proclaim this truth to the world. This is the dawning of a new era. . . ." Gradually there arose the movement which today we call Spiritualism. (Spiritualism had existed earlier but not recognizably as a movement.) This spread rapidly especially in England. The origin of the British Society of Psychical Research, mentioned in the previous chapter, was occasioned by reactions to the movement in England.

These two camps still exist today. The first is manifest in many modern sociological studies of Spiritualism and of the Fox sisters' role. For example, Nelson's *Spiritualism and Society* considers that the entire episode is an example of fraud, ingenious fraud. The view of the second group appears in Spiritualist writings which maintain that a spirit manifested itself during these episodes. However, the views of neither group seem adequate to many parapsychologists today. The most rigidly scientific of these believe that what was happening was an example of psychokinetic phenomena. The girls themselves were unaware of what we would call unconscious PK. An excellent case that PK was involved can be made from what follows in this chapter. A case for concomitant fraud might also be made, especially because of the subsequent career of the girls. Maggie Fox, always under great pressure, gradually became an alcoholic and seemed a pathetic figure. During this time, on stage she publicly asserted that the phenomena had been fraudulently produced. She said that many of the clicks had been made by the moving of her big toe. But before she died in 1893, Maggie recanted her confession and once again resumed "rapping" and even séance work. Lastly, some recent work warns us against too easily dismissing the presence of some kind of spirit manifestation in the episode. In my tentative opinion, a full explanation may require elements from all three positions.

PK: Controlled Experiments and Gifted Subjects

The most famous of the original PK experiments were performed by Joseph Rhine in the 1930's and 1940's. Rhine began working with dice throwing. First the experimentee would throw dice by hand; later on he used a cup; finally a machine was used for throwing the dice. The experimentee would attempt to influence the number which would turn up on the dice or else he would try to influence the place where the dice would land. By 1941, with a number of gifted subjects who had thrown 651,216 times, Rhine attained the odds of ten to the 115th power to one against chance. These results were published in 1943. During these tests he gradually improved his control. For example, he substituted machines for throwing instead of throwing by hand; dice pits which are grooved into the face of the dice were changed so that the weight on the faces would be equal. Lastly, he photographed the results of the experiments to prevent experimenter error. The statistics he used were verified.[7]

Helmut Schmidt, who was a physicist at Boeing and is now running a parapsychologic institute in San Antonio, built a machine which used strontium 90, a radioactive element whose decay sends off sub-atomic units. These decaying particles act, apparently, in a completely chance or random way. The decay sent forth by strontium 90 sets off lights because of a kind of Geiger counter in the machine. The experimentee tries to influence the lights (that is, he or she stops the light going in a circle from bulb to bulb. He or she stops, then, either the decay or the lights). A total of 15,000 trials were run and the results were well above chance probability. Out of the group he worked with Schmidt selected three gifted subjects. With these, 36,066 trials were made. The results against chance here were two billion to one.

Experiments with Gifted Subjects

Uri Geller was the most famous personality involved in PK phenomena during the 1960's and 1970's. However David Marks and Richard Kamman in *The Psychology of the Psychic* have clearly shown not only that Geller was a magician in Israel, but that he almost certainly cheated at times in PK displays. This was admitted to the authors by two of Geller's own close associates. In one episode, as we mentioned, Geller was overheard by Marks telling his associates, "Keep that guy away from me. He'll pick up my signals." Geller was tested at the Stanford Research Institute by Puthoff and Targ (1977). In these experiments Geller scored well above chance probability. However the experiments have been trenchantly criticized by many people including James ("The Amazing") Randi.[8] But these criticisms underline how Geller *might* have cheated. They have not shown clearly that he cheated in these experiments. People like Randi insist that a magician should be included on the board which evaluates these experiments. However W. E. Cox, a magician, was involved in observing Geller in a key bending episode in which he detected no fraud. I also have before me a photo of a sturdy hotel key which belonged to Alan Vaughan, a respected author in the field of psychic research.[9] Without touching the key which Vaughan held in his hand, Uri Geller bent it merely by touching Vaughan's hands to produce the effect. Despite the conviction of myself and others that Geller probably has genuine paranormal abilities, he has been discredited of late and has not been accepted by most parapsychological investigators.

Matthew Manning has repeatedly been tested in Canada and other countries and not only has he shown the ability to bend nails but his presence seems to make objects move, for example chairs and other objects. No fraud that I am aware of has ever been detected in Manning's work.[10]

Gertrude Schmeidler of CCNY has run controlled experiments with Ingo Swan in which he paranormally raised a thermistor, a heat recording instrument, a small but significant degree.[11]

R. D. Mattuck of Copenhagen has worked with a seventeen year old psychic, "Lena Ilsted D." She has raised the mercury in the clinical thermometer from 36°C to 40°C while holding between the thumb and the forefinger the end of the thermometer opposite the mercury.[12]

Professor John B. Hasted, head of physics at London University's Birbeck College, has conducted dozens of metal bending experiments with a sixteen year old schoolboy, Steven North.[13] Hasted's conclusion: "I am satisfied that the results we have obtained with Steven are genuinely due to a power which we do not understand." Dr. Elizabeth Rauscher, a research physicist at the University of California, has come to the same conclusions about Steven North.

According to J. G. Pratt, Nina Kulagina (USSR) has repeatedly shown the ability to move objects at a distance.[14]

Benson Herbert, a respected psychic investigator, has come to the same conclusion with regard to Nina Kulagina. She has been shown to be able to move the hands of a compass at a distance of two to three feet and she also seems capable of exuding a type of heat energy which causes a very unpleasant scorching sensation on a person's arm.[15]

Karlis Osis and Donna McCormick, of the American Society for Psychical Research, have demonstrated kinetic, paranormal effects during an investigation of out-of-the-body experiences (OBE) with Alex Tanous, a psychic from Maine.[16] Tanous affected strain gauge sensors in another room during an alleged OBE.

It has been clearly demonstrated by J. Eisenbud, J. G. Pratt, and Ian Stevenson that Ted Serios, who, it is claimed, can imprint impressions on film paranormally, is using a genuine PK mechanism. The authors have shown a type of distortion in the photograph itself which seems to rule out all possibility of fraud.[17] It has been shown, but perhaps under less carefully guarded conditions, that the Japanese youth Masuaki Kigota is able to produce similar paranormal effects on unexposed film.[18] There is also abundant anecdotal evidence which has been reported in various newspapers that numbers of children in the United States, Great Britain, Japan and China seem to produce such paranormal effects. However, until careful studies of these cases are published, we cannot use them as solid evidence for the subject under investigation.

The reader should notice that in these PK experiments it is not a question of the validity of statistics. Metal, for example, is either bent or not. It seems to me and to many psychic and psychological investigators that the evidence for PK is at least as strong as, if not more so, than that for telepathy and clairvoyance.

Theories To Explain Psychokinesis

A bewildering array of theories has been proposed to explain PK. Tentatively, I have chosen four of the most plausible theories to help clarify our later discussion.

1. *Physical energy emanating from the person.* This would seem to be the most logical explanation of PK. However, people have only enough electromagnetic energy to light up a weak bulb. Therefore, unless there is some unknown physical energy, this explanation does not seem to be the most useful.

2. *A kind of spiritual energy.* It is not clear that animals manifest any PK ability. This might seem to be positive evidence that PK is a spiritual power. However, this is the point at which materialists become either enraged or terrified. It may always be unclear whether the energy through which PK operates is spiritual energy of some unknown, as yet unmeasured, physical energy.

3. *Hyper-space.* PK action at a distance operates without any intermediary medium because of hyper-space, or a fifth dimension, or world #2. All objects are equally distant from this hyper-space. Therefore action operates not so much at a distance but through this hyper-space which is equally present to all things. However esoteric this explanation may seem, still it represents the best theory to help one understand cases of teleportation. Teleportation is a term used to designate the paranormal movement of objects over great distances. Sometimes these objects disappear in one place and appear in another. At one time derided, teleportation is now supported by a great deal of anecdotal and even laboratory evidence. This theory explains the medium but not the nature of PK itself.

4. *Spirits.* Some people still maintain that spirits are behind

PK phenomena. But, for example, at Duke with the PK dice experiments (a) nothing religious is happening; (b) why is success achieved only part of the time if spirits are operating? (c) why does PK decrease with distance if spirits are present and acting? However, this does not mean that we rule out the activity of spirits in all PK phenomena. As we will see shortly, some poltergeist phenomena are so mysterious that the spirit explanations may well be the most plausible solution.

Poltergeist Manifestations

One of the better known poltergeist episodes is that which was investigated by W. G. Roll.[19] On January 14, 1967, the police received a call from the owner of wholesale novelty item business, Tropication Arts, in Miami. The owner, Alvin Laubheim, said that there seemed to be a ghost in his warehouse. Police arrived and found there Laubheim and Julio Vasquez, a nineteen year old refugee, who worked as a shipping clerk. Items seemed to be jumping off the shelves. W. G. Roll, an eminent parapsychologist, was invited to come and investigate the case. Roll too noticed objects falling from the shelves. Often mugs moved from behind other mugs, up above them, over them and onto the floor. This was true of backscratchers, ash trays and mugs. Roll noticed that the movements usually occurred in the vicinity of Julio. One day Roll noted that Julio was angry at his boss and he seemed happy at the breakage. At least on one occasion, something happened when Julio was away. Parapsychologists call this phenomenon "linger effect." Roll made a chart of the position of Julio and the direction of the objects. He plotted out a type of vortex in which objects closer to the center moved a shorter distance and with more force, and those on the outer edges moved a longer distance and with less force. Roll believed that he discovered a kind of law in the movement of poltergeist objects. However, this phenomenon has not been duplicated in most other cases. Roll had a psychologist at Duke, Dr. Randall Harper, give Julio psychological tests. Julio, it was found, had a very rich fantasy life associated with turbulent emotions. He had many aggressive feelings and impulses which were disturbing and unacceptable to him. He had been brought up in a family with high moral standards but he also was deeply repressed and had great feelings of unworthiness and guilt. He had a tendency to disassociate his feelings with regard to aggression. He was not a happy person. There was a lack of strongly pleasant experiences in his life. About ten days before these events, Julio had been asked by his stepmother to move out of the house. He was having nightmares of killing and he was experiencing suicidal feelings. Interestingly, Julio showed no evidence of ESP in card tests. The phenomena I have mentioned represent a typical pattern in poltergeist cases. Someone is present who is an agent. When the agent is absent rarely does anything happen. Usually the person is about the age of puberty or somewhat beyond, but rarely beyond the teens. The psychological tests usually show some type of repressed hostility and very frequently a very disturbed family environment.

Another famous poltergeist case is that of Annemarie Schaberl from the town of Rosenheim in Bavaria.[20] In the fall of 1967, a number of inexplicable events began to happen around her. She worked in a lawyer's office. Lights dimmed in her presence, telephones rang, and a huge bill for telephone usage was run up. Engineers were called but nothing out of the ordinary was found. Pictures fell from the wall or rotated at extreme angles; heavy furniture moved without being touched. This was all photographed. While an investigator was watching, a heavy storage cabinet weighing 400 pounds moved almost a foot from the wall. When Annemarie lost her job, the disturbances ceased. Dr. Hans Bender, a respected German parapsychologist, found that Annemarie suffered from intense frustration and pent-up hostility. Other cases have been investigated in Germany and in the United States, and the researchers have come to conclusions similar to those above.

However, it is not at all clear to me that hostility is an ever recurring element in poltergeist manifestations. Many of the poltergeist phenomena in the lives of the saints show no depressed hostility at all. Secondly, an experimental manifestation of poltergeist phenomena conducted by A. R. G. Owens in Toronto reveals the same fact.[21] A group of eight people met regularly and in their minds they invented a fictitious character named Philip who lived in a castle hundreds of years ago. They fabricated the entire story. They then attempted to make Philip manifest himself. Nothing happened until the group began to relax and to tell jokes in a humorous atmosphere. Then they heard certain raps and they directed their questions to the raps. They asked for details of Philip's life. Answers came back which verified everything that was in their own minds. A chair began to move in the room and even acted almost as if it were a small dog moving toward the door to meet a newcomer. The results of this type of investigation are awesome in reminding us of the power of the unconscious. Here we are involved with a group of people, each of whom alone might not be highly psychic, yet when they gathered together they were able to cause the audible manifestations and movements of a poltergeist. (However no apparition appeared.) This case makes it clear that repressed hostility is not the sole emotional cause of poltergeist manifestations.

However, as this case is a dramatic exemplification of the fact that a living agent or agents can cause poltergeist manifestations, we might feel tempted to conclude that not only poltergeist cases but also "possession" cases which resemble them in many ways are also simply the PK manifestations of living agents. But this would be too rapid a step to take in view of some possession evidence.

Possession

The investigations we have just described certainly have rendered outdated some studies of possession which, until recently, have been considered very solid. Two examples of studies which are of high quality but which are now in need of updating are those of Juan Cortes, S.J. (with Florence Gatti), *The Case Against Possessions and Exorcisms* (1975), and Henry Ansgar Kelly, *The Devil, Demonology and Witchcraft* (1968). Fr. Cortes, like many psychoanalytically oriented investigators, believes that all possession cases are simply examples of psychiatrically unbalanced people. But he had insufficient knowledge of the findings of parapsychology. The same is true of Kelly's work. This is not to imply, however, that in most cases psychiatric explanations may not be the chief factor, and in some cases the only factor. "Possession" may be "a cry for attention," "a ritualized tantrum."[22] "Possession" may be an escapist enjoyment of the pleasure of not being responsible for one's own actions. "The devil made me do it." It may be the result of a transcendent urge to be somebody else. It may be the result of the exorcism ceremony itself. That is, it may be a kind of "doctrinal compliance" by which one fits one's emotional unbalance into the safety of a Church ritual.

In fact, the Church itself and its theologians today are most cautious about attributing the cause of unusual phenomena to Satan. Fr. William Van Roo of the Gregorian University in Rome believes that the main character in the film "The Exorcist," which is based on a true story, was simply ill and not possessed.[23] Fr. Joseph de Tonquedec, S.J., for a long time an exorcist in the diocese of Paris, once told me that in his many years, and in thousands of cases, he found only one or two people whom he believed to be truly possessed. These judgments are probably based in part on the sound principle proposed by Christian spiritual masters that a supernatural explanation of the facts may be accepted only when every natural explanation is improbable.[24] Unless this principle is adhered to, what is really an illness may be encouraged by the exorcism ritual itself. As Henry Ansgar Kelly put it, " . . . diabolical possession is caused by belief in diabolical possession." At the American Psychological Association's meeting in 1977, similar conclusions about possession were presented.[25]

However, if we broaden the psychiatric categories to include ESP factors such as PK, may we conclude that all alleged possession cases are merely cases of psychiatric deviation enhanced by unconscious ESP powers?

An Extra-Human Agency?

D. Scott Rogo, a parapsychologist who has made a special study of possession phenomena, distinguishes two types of cases, a conventional poltergeist experience ("Type I poltergeist"), and possession poltergeist experience ("Type II polter-geist").[26] There are features in the Type II poltergeist experience which seem to suggest some agency which is both dependent on the psyche of the "possessed" and at the same time in some way *independent*.

Signs of this independence I see as the following: (1) The ability to understand and show fluent skill in an unknown and unlearned language. Speaking in an unknown language is called "xenoglossy." Speaking a few phrases is known as "recitative xenoglossy." Speaking such a language skillfully is called "re-sponsive xenoglossy." According to a careful study done by Dr. Ian Stevenson of the University of Virginia, responsive xeno-glossy cannot be attained simply by telepathy or clairvoyance.[27] One can tap from another's mind words from a foreign language (recitative xenoglossy), or take from that mind some piece of knowledge or some picture. But one cannot by this tapping procedure learn a skill which involves so many learned muscle responses. One cannot tap another's mind and achieve the skill of riding a bicycle or of speaking fluently in an unknown language. This skill seems to involve some agent beyond our space-time continuum. The Church's ritual for exorcism in-cludes the ability to speak an unknown language as one of the criteria for discerning when there is real possession. (However, some of the other criteria in the *Rituale Romanum* cannot be said to clearly indicate possession, for example, precognitive and telepathic abilities, and a display of super-human strength.) (2) The feeling of horror on the part of the possessed about what is happening to him or her. Hysteria cases, it seems, often show indifference to the events which center about them. (3) Trans-ferred possession and simultaneous cure of the possessed. In some cases a possessed person is cured at the same time that the possession phenomena take hold of another person, such as a doctor or an exorcist. At times this happens with a number of exorcists in the same case. One could understand a type of "contagious hysteria" which could be caught as it were, but it is difficult to see how this theory could sufficiently explain (a) the sudden appearance of paranormal powers in another person or in a number of persons, together with (b) the disappearance of the possession phenomena in the originally possessed. (4) Some secondary criteria which possibly might have other explanations are: cases where the exorcism is successful in which the possessing spirit is believed to be a deceased human and is seemingly convinced to go on to other tasks in continuing to evolve in the afterlife; a horrid stench and a feeling of clammy cold; blasphemy and malicious actions where humans are hurt, burned or killed; vomiting gallons of strange matter such as pins; malicious happenings which are frequent when no one is present but whose after-effects can be seen; independent voices coming from a distance while the victim's lips remain unmoving; sensational levitations, violent contortions and swelling of the body.

Parapsychological study has made it much more difficult in any given case to make dogmatic pronouncements about the reality of a possession. At the same time, I believe one should hesitate to say that all possession cases are exclusively cases of pathological hysteria combined with paranormal powers in the "possessed."

Satan: A Spirit, or an Independent Part of the Self?

D. Scott Rogo, in his fine study *The Poltergeist Experience,* carefully developed the theory that possession cases are examples of the operation of an agency which is part of the victim's own psyche, but which has attained a kind of independence of its own, and is thus the cause of the strange phenomena. "Some split-off portion of the agent's mind" controls the activity. Rogo uses as evidence experiences like those of Alexandra David-Neel in Tibet who tried to make an apparition of a monk appear and was amazed when the figure did appear. It took "six months of hard struggle" to rid herself of this creature phantom, and it was also seen by one other person.[28] Likewise, he uses data from OBE study in which part of a person's personality separates as if into a kind of "ecsomatic" state. According to this theory, possession phenomena are caused by a quasi-independent agency but which is ultimately traceable to the person's own psyche, its dark side. I regard this explanation as in many ways appealing, but I find that it does not explain some of the phenomena mentioned previously, especially the responsive xenoglossy cases.

Are we at the point, then, where we could conclude that the rare but genuine possession cases are cases of possession by the devil? This is not the place to discuss whether Satan is an individual, an objective reality beyond man, or whether he is a symbol of the mysterious ubiquitous power of evil in the world. Pope Paul VI and Pope John Paul II have stressed that belief in Satan is a traditional part of the Catholic faith. However some reputable theologians, admitting that their position was non-traditional, have claimed that, while they did not deny Satan's existence, affirmation of it is not a central part of Christian faith. To say that "the devil" is a symbol which represents the irrational power of evil in the world would not put one outside the Christian faith.[29] However, our question is not whether Satan exists as an individual reality, but whether possession cases necessarily involve possession by Satan, understood according to traditional Christian teaching.

I believe the answer to this question is "no." Many cases of possession suggest that the possessing reality is a deceased person who remains "earthbound." This "person" seems to be in a confused or bewildered or malicious state, and his or her energy is turned toward the earth. The evidence for this is certainly not overwhelming, and D. Scott Rogo's position is at least probable, but it does possess a certain solidity. The careful investigator, Dr. Ian Stevenson, has uncovered cases where this is the most plausible explanation.[30] Other investigators have come to the same conclusion. Finally, the evidence for "benign possession" which we will discuss in Chapter XI is further support for possession by a deceased person. (The fact that exorcisms have involved conversations through the possessed which are intelligible and coherent on the assumption of possession by a deceased person, and that often such an assumption seems to be related to the success of the exorcism in which the possessing being is convinced to go on to its tasks, cannot be taken as decisive evidence for my present position. It might be claimed that the exorcism was successful precisely because the exorcist came down to the belief level of the "possessed.")

It has been noted by Fr. Cortes that Satan is never credited with actual possession in the New Testament. Rather the possessed is said to have "a demon" or "an unclean spirit." While Satan is part of New Testament belief, still possession is by "a dumb demoniac" or "demons." In one case, a man whom Matthew in 17:15 calls an "epileptic," Mark in 9:17 calls "a dumb spirit" and Luke in 9:39 calls "a spirit." In the New Testament, what are commonly accepted illnesses (e.g., leprosy) are never attributed to demons. Illnesses without a perceptible cause (e.g., brain disorders) are often attributed to demons. Jesus himself is not said to have cast out Satan. Rather the charge is made that "he casts out *demons* by Beelzebul, the prince of demons" (Lk 11:15). In modern cases where there seems to be genuine possession by an independent reality, possession by a deceased human being often seems more probable than possession by an angelic demon.[31]

Summary

Before treating some final topics in this chapter, let me summarize the points which we have made. (1) Psychokinesis is a rare but actual human power. (2) Poltergeist manifestations are frequently unconscious activities of a living agent, though at times some transhuman agency may be involved. (3) Demonic possession is a very rare but probably a genuine human phenomenon. (4) Many possession cases are not genuine possession but the result of unconscious PK manifestations by a living agent. (5) In genuine possession cases, the agency of possession may not generally be the devil or an angelic demon, but perhaps a quasi-independent fragment of the human personality, and in very rare cases a "discarnate" spirit.

Jesus

A more important question arising from the existence of PK phenomena as we have described them is their relationship to Jesus' life and miraculous works. For example, in Luke 5:1–11

Jesus oversees a miraculous catch of fish. In Matthew 8:18 Jesus stills the storm at sea. In Matthew 14:22 Jesus walks on the waters. In Matthew 21:18 Jesus curses a fig tree and it withers up. In Mark 6:30 Jesus multiplies loaves and fishes.

The miraculous catch of fish of itself could be a psychokinetic action, but one which is incorporated by Jesus into a higher significance as a sign of the mission to bring men into God's loving power, the Kingdom. The stilling of the storm, seen by the evangelists and probably by Jesus himself as a sign of Yahweh's power over nature, of itself and isolated from its context, is not unparalleled in other people's lives. For example, Rolling Thunder, the American Indian Spiritual leader, seems to have the power to start and stop rain in small areas.[32] Walking on the water reminds us of levitation. This we find in other people's lives, for example St. Joseph Cupertino, and in the secular world, for example D. D. Home (1833–1886).[33] With Jesus it may have represented an anticipation of resurrected life. The multiplication of the loaves and fishes is one of Fr. Monden's major prodigies which he said are not found in secular contexts. This claim should be used with greater caution. It is true that with saints like John Bosco multiplication of matter occurred in a religious context of prayer and belief. The feats of materialization of matter by Sai Baba, the Indian guru, have now been fairly well authenticated by researchers from the American Society of Psychical Research.[34] Ash, fruit, and rings have been materialized, without trickery as far as can be discerned. Now that attention has been called to this phenomenon, a large body of modern anecdotal evidence from a *secular* context is gradually taking shape. (See the Appendix for Chapter IV.)

If these processes, rare as they are, occurred in other people's lives and we can attribute them, directly at least, to a human power, then according to the law of parsimony we should be able to do the same with many of the miracles of Jesus. (I am not speaking here of his resurrection.) The law of parsimony, you will recall, says that we should not attribute to a supernatural agency that which can be explained by a natural human power.

Some might think that here we are encroaching upon belief in the unique divinity of Jesus, but this is not so. The apostles and evangelists themselves knew quite well that in the Book of Kings Elijah and Elisha were said to have multiplied oil and bread and to have brought a dead person back to life. Both types of action they attributed to God's agency. Thus, even these major miracles of multiplying matter and of raising the dead did not immediately produce belief in Jesus' unique divinity as Son of God in a qualitatively higher sense. The apostles did not automatically believe in Jesus' unique divinity or call him Son of God because he performed miracles, even great ones. What really sealed this belief was Jesus' resurrection and the experience of the Spirit on Pentecost. Previous to that, what made this belief begin to bud was not simply the miracles but the total context within which Jesus' miracles were performed. For example, in Acts 16:17 Paul and Barnabas cured a man who could not walk from his birth. The crowds said that the gods had come down upon them in the likeness of men. But Paul and Barnabas tore their clothes and said, "We are also mortals, human beings like you." We never have this type of disclaimer from Jesus. For example, when he stilled the storm at sea in Mark 4:35, the people marveled and said, "What sort of man is this that even the winds and sea obey him?" Jesus did not reply, just as he did not reply in many other cases. The belief in the transcendent numinosity of Jesus arose not so much out of what he claimed as out of *what he did not disclaim.* And this was the context in which, over and over, Jesus' works were performed: an implicit, tacit claim and an explicit insertion of his works into the "sign language" of the Father's power and Kingdom.

This type of implicit claiming-action, for a Jewish audience, would be the equivalent of blasphemy. It seems to me that Jesus as a human being was blessed and gifted with incredible paranormal and psychokinetic powers.[35] These powers he used at will. Others had such powers occasionally and in a limited way. Jesus seemed to be master over these powers, though occasionally, as Scripture says, it was limited by a lack of faith.

We will return again to this question of Jesus' divinity in the context of paranormal healing in Chapter IV and in Chapter IX on apparitions and the resurrection.

Summary

In view of modern parapsychological investigation, it would not be the most advanced thinking to hold, as the higher critics once did, that Jesus may have performed some minor psychosomatic healing cures, but that the alleged display of powers over cosmic forces and over matter were without doubt the results of later legends and accretions. On the other hand, we should be careful in following the opinion that the storm miracle and the miracle of the multiplication of the loaves and fishes were major prodigies the like of which are never found in a secular context. Lastly, the wondrous acts of Jesus must never be isolated from their context. Jesus never did so isolate them. They were seen as part of the irruption of the Kingdom of God, through men, into this world, and they find their goal and significance only in the culminating point, Jesus' own resurrection. As will be seen from our later development, I have no desire to reduce the miraculous entirely to the paranormal. As Canon Michael Perry has put it, "The paranormal and the miraculous are not identical phenomena, though they overlap; to remove either from the pages of the Bible would be to emasculate it intolerably."[36]

Chapter III

A Theoretical Interlude: The Collective Unconscious and a Psychic Universe

Let us now change our perspective and move in a more theoretical direction. In this chapter, I will present a brief sketch of the thought of two major figures, Carl Gustav Jung and Pierre Teilhard de Chardin, and I will add one insight from Karl Rahner. My purpose is not to set up an *a priori* Procrustean bed into which we will force the evidence. Rather, the aim is to offer tentative pointers, relevant to the dialogue between parapsychology and theology, which will enable us to find some inchoative coherence in the data.

Carl Gustav Jung

Jung (1875–1961) is best known for his theory of the collective unconscious.[1] Jung's psychological topography centers around the conscious and the unconscious. He calls the totality in the individual "the psyche." The rational and central focus of consciousness he terms "the ego." The unconscious he also calls "the objective psyche." This unconscious is both individual and collective. The individual or personal unconscious contains repressed feelings and wishes and countless forgotten experiences. We can see its operation in dreams, for example. The collective unconscious is a deeper stratum of the uncon-

45

scious than the personal. It is the unknown material from which our consciouness emerges.

The goal of Jung's system was to reach totality or "individuation." Individuation is the result of a lived dialogue between the conscious and the unconscious. This dialogue involves both harmony and friction. As a result of this "coincidence of opposites," an individual would be forged into an indestructible whole where sensation, feeling, intuition and thinking would constantly interact.

Jung often presented his ideas in the form of a spiritual journey into man's deepest center. To make an authentic journey, one must understand the unconscious and its operations. The energy which dynamizes both the conscious and the unconscious he called "libido." Libido connotes all forms of psychic energy. It is set in motion chiefly by symbols or archetypes. All human beings have archetypes in the unconscious. At this point we must be careful to distinguish between archetypal power and archetypal images. The archetypal power is an innate patterning power which tends to form motifs. Archetypal images are not innate. The concrete, specific images which form into archetypal images are gathered from culture. Many psychologists accuse Jung of claiming that we are born with fixed images in our unconscious. He left himself open to this interpretation because of his early expressions. However, for Jung the archetype is primarily an innate patterning power and not a specific image. Jung's doctrine of archetypes arose from his empirical study of myths, legends, fairy tales, dreams, the art of schizophrenics and religious doctrines. Similarities seemed to exist which transcended mutual influences.

As one journeys into the unconscious, one first meets the archetype of the persona. Men and women wear a persona or a mask which hides their authentic self. The persona is the result of the compromise one makes between the demands of society and the desires of the self. To some degree a mask is necessary in order to live. But it is largely to be discarded if individuation or wholeness is to be achieved because it blocks not only selfish but also healthy movements of the unconscious. If one is totally unconscious of the existence of the persona, the result is "possession" by it, or "inflation" as Jung liked to call it.[2]

We can see how "demonic possession" may, at times, be seen in these terms. Such possession is the total grasp by a persona or a secondary personality of the one possessed, although this process does not seem to explain all possession cases. In Chapter X we will see how mediums who allegedly contact spirits in another world very frequently communicate by means of what is called "a control," a kind of otherworldly master of ceremonies. Most parapsychologists consider this control to be the unconscious persona of the medium.

Jung next speaks of the shadow.[3] The shadow is also an archetypal figure. It is what we consider to be the inferior side of ourselves, the side that wants to do all the things that society or one's moral standards will not allow. This shadow may be genuinely evil or it may represent a very positive creative element. Everyone has a shadow. It exists in both the personal and the collective unconscious. The integration of the shadow into the psyche not only presupposes knowledge of its existence but also requires the solutions of the moral and emotional problems connected with it.

The shadow in the individual unconscious, if it remains unconscious, tends to be projected unto others. "Why don't you like me?" often means "I don't like you." But the shadow also exists in the collective unconscious. Jung takes Satan as a projection of the collective unconscious. But he insisted that he spoke only of our subjective images and not about their foundation or non-foundation in objective reality, though he creates the impression that Satan is merely such a projection.

Moving deeper into the unconscious, one can become conscious of the anima and the animus.[4] The anima and the animus are the archetypal counterparts of our primary sexual characteristics. (If Jung were alive today, I think he would say that in everyone there is a psychic sexual mix. Occasionally males may have more of a female or anima orientation and a female may have more of a male or animus orientation. This would be true apart from the presence of homosexuality.) The source of the anima or the animus is the age-old archetypal experience of man with woman or woman with man. It is also formed by parents or authority figures, usually of the opposite sex.

Obviously we are unable to enter the rich details of Jung's

thought in this study. Suffice it to point out how often the "control" in medium work is of the opposite sex from the medium. This suggests that we are dealing, at the very least, with deeply unconscious and archetypal material.

As one moves to the center of the psyche, one meets other archetypal figures, such as the earth mother, the old wise man, the eternal child and the trickster, as well as mandala symbols, symbols of psychological wholeness. These latter are usually accompanied by strong feelings of harmony and integration. Joseph Campbell, who has been influenced by Jung, claims that the most universal archetypal dynamic is that of the journey.[5] This he calls "the monomyth," in which the hero (ego) leaves the earth mother (home), receives counsel from the wise old man (father or a surrogate), and faces some great evil challenge, such as the dragon. The hero is either wounded or killed. If wounded, he returns as the wounded healer with his life-giving message. If killed, he returns in a new birth.

At the deepest center of the psyche, we meet the archetype of the self.[6] This is a deep power within us which generates all the other archetypal images. It is not an inner visual *image* but an inner self-experience. I think it is best characterized as one's ideal self, the hero self. This is not the "neurotic should" self but the self which results from authentic dialogue between the conscious and the unconscious.

The God Image is practically identical with the archetype of the self. Again, the God Image is not simply an image. It may include images. But it is the base or ground of our numinous experiences. The closeness of the archetype of the self to the God Image is evident when we realize that we often fill in the outlines of God or the numinous with our own "hero" or ideal characteristics. Thus Jung called it "the inner empirical deity."

Our archetype of the self is evoked and brought to self-realization when we are faced by great historical figures such as Christ. (Jung included Buddha here also.) Thus the Christ Image is also closely attached to the archetype of the self. There are obvious Christian theological objections to this point of Jung but it is not our purpose to discuss them at this moment. However there is obvious validity in Jung's point that the archetype of the self comes to self-realization only in the face of great figures who lived out archetypal lives such as that of Jesus.

Let us recall that Jung claimed to speak only as a psychologist discussing phenomena of the psyche. He often said that he did not intend to encroach upon the domain of faith or theology. He said he spoke of "the Imprint" while theologians spoke of "the Imprinter."[7] Jung did not respect in all his statements the limits he had set upon himself.[8] However, Jung did not claim that "God" was nothing more than the contents of the collective unconscious, or human consciousness in general. That he did not so identify God in his own private thought is evident from many statements which he made. "We find numberless images of God, but we cannot produce the original. There is no doubt in my mind that there is an original behind our images, but it is inaccessible."[9] Or again, "Nevertheless, we have good reason to suppose that behind this veil there exists the uncomprehended absolute object which affects us and influences us."[10]

Because we do seem to share a collective unconscious, we may well affect each other and have knowledge of each other in ways which are not conscious.[11] Some parapsychologists believe that the brain is not so much a *receiver* as a *filter*. It preserves us from constant bombardment by unconscious stimuli. This filtering function, however, lets down at certain moments, as in sleep and meditation. These are ESP moments. Telepathy and clairvoyance may work, not so much by going outward as a radio beam, but by going inward into our unconscious, the collective unconscious.

Pierre Teilhard de Chardin

Let us now turn our attention to Teilhard de Chardin (1881–1955). Our chief points of interest will be his notions of the universe as a domain of psychic consciousness, the "within" of the spirit, and the objective reality of God in this psychic universe.

Teilhard held that as evolution progressed, matter became more complex.[12] On the *micro* level, matter moved from atoms, to molecules, to cells, then to pluricellular creatures, from the most primitive of these up to man. On the *macro* level of the heavens, matter moved from energy perhaps originating with the Big Bang to atoms, to clouds of atoms, to stars, and from the stars were formed the humble planets, where the necessary requirements for human life existed.

He did not mean only that matter became organized into larger units, though this is usually also involved. He was speaking about the complexity of the organization of matter, as in the human brain. Teilhard saw evolution as in some sense designed for man. At least, evolution only after "great struggle" gave birth to humankind. To characterize this process Teilhard coined the phrase "complexity consciousness." That is, as matter becomes more complex, it becomes more conscious. This is easily seen with regard to man. But did Teilhard mean that realities inferior to man and animals are "conscious"?

The "Within." Teilhard believed that nothing suddenly appeared higher up on the ladder of evolution that did not exist in some pre-form in earlier evolution. If "consciousness" appeared with man, something like it must have existed earlier. But it would be so tenuous and minimal that we might not detect it. He began calling this reality "the within."[13] For him, all non-artificial reality had a "within" as well as a "without." The "without" was what science studied. He did not imply that science does not penetrate deeply within matter, but that it was strictly quantitative. The within could be concluded to by reason as it pondered the results of science. It was reached by what he called a "hyperphysics," a blend of science and philosophy.

This "within" might be defined as the interior organizing principle of an organism. It is the inner bonding power or principle of unification which makes a thing what it is. It is not itself precisely a physical energy but it is what gives energy its pattern. If we think of a cell, for example, the "within" is not the membrane, nor is it the code in the nucleus. The within is what determines the code.

Everything, therefore, has its signature, as it were. In an atom, it is the rhythm of the field around the nucleus. The within is the organizer of this rhythm. Is the within conscious?

Even the lowest fragment of matter has some inwardly organized action. Whatever is centered and acts has a within. In matter on the lowest level, as we know today, there is organization, action and probably some indeterminacy, somewhat loosely akin to what we call freedom. Heisenberg called this "indeterminacy." Therefore, even in the smallest particles, there is a within, a reflection of consciousness which is found higher up in man. Teilhard, therefore, stretching the word and using it metaphorically to an extent, says that "psychism" is in all reality and all through the universe.

The Within and Science. Teilhard said that science by its nature must analyze, that is, break up into parts.[14] But the within will not be found in the parts. Nothing in reality exists in broken-up parts. Think of a television set, for example. There is some organizing reality (a within) in everything. Science by its own limitations misses the whole of a reality. This becomes most evident when some scientists say that man is a vial of chemicals worth so many dollars.

The Within in Things Reflects the Great Within or Omega. Teilhard believed that there had to be a deeper reason for this apparently purposeful organizing power all through things and all through the universe. Because, as he saw it, the universe was "centering," there had to be some power to account for this organizing phenomenon. Notice that Teilhard did not see a sharp dichotomy between matter and spirit as many have in the past. They are not the same, to be sure. But matter and spirit are, as it were, on a continuum. He wrote, ". . . a natural connection is drawn between the two worlds of physics and psychology, hitherto irreconcilable. Matter and consciousness are bound together: not in the sense that consciousness becomes directly measurable, but in the sense that it becomes organically and physically rooted in the same cosmic process with which physics is concerned."[15] At the lowest end is congealed matter. As matter rises higher and higher in its evolution, it becomes more complex and more perfect in its action. There are *jumps* between stages.[16] Finally there is spirit. Karl Rahner said that matter is congealed spirit and Teilhard said that spirit is the outcome of energized matter.

Animated by his thinking and by his religious faith, Teilhard believed that this process had to be organized by some power beyond matter. He called it "Omega" or God.

Design or Chance? Teilhard saw the universe as being organized or lured by Omega. Omega, from this aspect of luring the world forward, he called "the Final Gatherer."[17] Out of evolution the Final Gatherer has lured love, the highest production yet. The power behind the universe must be both Spirit and Loving, since it is the ground of these qualities. What he presents, admittedly in a much more complicated and scientific way, sounds very much like the older argument from design. But modern man has problems with this approach to God. Teilhard himself was aware of the problem, and his answer to it is intimated throughout his writings.[18]

Let us look at this problem. Many thinkers say that what looks like design is really the result of many chance collisions of things, operating according to the laws of natural selection. Whatever is not lucky dies off. The results are really from chance but they look like design. For example, a Siberian tiger seems to be beautifully designed. But suppose that when the climate of Siberia was warm there were three types of Siberian tigers. When the climate changed, tiger number one had too short a coat to withstand the cold and tiger number two had not enough speed to survive when other animals became scarce. Thus, type number three, the beautiful Siberian tiger, is very well suited to the region, but it is by chance. At least, so the objection runs.

To handle this problem, the approach from the Ultimate Gatherer is not enough. There must be added to it the idea of a Prime Mover. (Teilhard combined both approaches by speaking of "the Prime Mover Ahead.")[19] One must push further and further into the past. At each stage, one will find some organized beings and chance happenings, random mutations, climate changes, etc. One is finally forced back to the very beginning, however the world as we know it began. At that point, it seems that there already was structure and countless laws (order), laws of gravity, of light, of magnetic attraction, of speed, and of the interaction within orbits of atoms when they began to exist.

In such a picture, how can one explain such and so many

ordered realities. As Michael Novak, following Lonergan, has put it, "Without an intelligent source, the intelligibility of the real is a mere accident and hence unintelligible."[20] Here we are at the central option in the intellectual life. Teilhard believed that the only reality which he could see that could account for such structuring was Mind, or Omega. We might say that just as your mind and my mind organize reality in thinking and perceive reality only through its being ordered (we could not fathom pure chaos), so there must be "behind" the universe something akin to Mind, Consciousness. No doubt Teilhard's religious faith played a central role in coming to this decision. But what is not pointed out when this is remarked upon is the fact that faith is not blind feeling. Faith too involves intelligence.

For Teilhard, then, the whole universe is, as it were, alive. Even matter isn't "dead." This is what is often called Teilhard's "panentheism" (all in God). He once said, "The world is God's body." He did not mean this literally as if he were a pantheist, but he took it in an extended sense. The world as mind is very close to what many psychic investigators have held as a result of their study of paranormal phenomena.

Before we leave this point, let me mention that Teilhard also held that chance in a certain sense also existed in the universe. There are "chance" happenings together with design.[21] He liked to call this "directed chance." Chance was designed into evolution. He spoke of "a constant direction" together with "a billionfold trial and error." The universe "gropes," he said. Groping implies a constant goal but a diversity of short-run directions. "Chance" happenings represent something loosely analogous to freedom on the human level. Creatures grope toward goals. Sometimes they meet dead ends and die out. But without groping, there would be no advance in evolution, unless God directed it like someone who winds up a toy. One of Teilhard's great principles was, "God makes things make themselves." We will recur to this principle in our next chapter on paranormal healing.

Evil. But there are not only the effects of lure and direction in the world. There is also evil. Teilhard held that God is both good and omnipotent, and yet he cannot prevent evil. By this he meant that if God set up a world in which (1) there was to be evolving matter, and (2) there was to be free will, then he could not also prevent in this world moral evil or physical pain and death. God cannot in our kind of world have matter plus change (evolution) and not have friction. God cannot have a law of gravity which works only in a helpful way. Secondly, God cannot give man freedom, leave him really free, and then prevent all evil, as in the concentration camps.

Teilhard saw the universe as having two forces in it. One force was luring the world toward unity. All creating is a kind of unifying. All love is unifying. He called this lure by many names: "the evolutionary drive," "Spirit," "Omega," "Love," "Eros." The second drive was mysterious. It was counter-evolutionary, that is, it moved backward against the flow of evolution. It broke up. It caused disunity on the human level. It brought entropy on the physical level. It is mysterious. Maybe, as St. Thomas said, it is a desire on the part of humans to return to their origins in nothingness. For Teilhard, sin is not so much a fall. It is a refusal to ascend. The only moral duty, he said, is to grow. The only moral imperative is to unite, to unify, to create, to love.

Christ played a central role on Teilhard's thought, a role which I am unable to do justice to in this brief sketch. Jesus' purpose on earth was not to die but to bring man to unity with God. "Christ is he who structurally in himself, and for all of us, overcomes the resistance to unification offered by the multiple resistance to the rise of Spirit inherent in matter."[22] Teilhard called God Omega, and Omega and the Cosmic Christ are often identified. Teilhard wrote, "The God for whom our century is waiting must be: (1) as vast and mysterious as the Cosmos; (2) as immediate and all embracing as Life; (3) as linked (in some way) to our effort as mankind. . . . A God who made the World less mysterious, or smaller, or less important to us, than our heart and reason show it to be, that God will never more be He to whom the earth kneels."[23] "Now, a Christ who extended to only a part of the universe, a Christ who did not in some way assume the world in Himself, would seem to me a Christ smaller than the Real. . . . The God of our faith would seem to me less grand, less dominant, than the universe of our experience."[24]

Death and After. Teilhard spoke often of the future of our race on this planet. He spoke less often of the fate of individuals after death. But he has some powerful reasons, apart from his faith, why he believes human beings go on beyond death.[25] Spirit, he said, cannot dissolve. Spirit, unlike matter, contains the power of *self-reflection,* something which is beyond the power of matter. Self-reflection includes the power to research, to criticize, to discuss, to be attracted by the appeal of the future, to love, to know, to know one is knowing. All this transcends the power of matter. Teilhard held that spiritual energy was by its nature irreversible or evolution would be frustrated. "In all sincerity it seems more difficult to dissolve a soul than to smash an atom."[26] Spirit is beyond space and time. Second, without "immortality," he saw no solution to the problem of evil. Evil is not balanced off for people in this life. Without immortality, life is absurd, and then the problem is this. More and more, evolution rests in the hands of finite creatures. If they see that life is absurd because of the problem of evil and that there is no transtemporal future, human beings may decide that the evolutionary endeavor is not worth prolonging. Man will not lift a finger, he said, if he really believes that what he achieves, especially in his own growth, will not endure. Third, Teilhard asks where the desire for immortality comes from. As humans are the products of evolution, so too are their desires for immortality. If the desire arises from evolution, then evolution would be frustrating its own inspiration if the desire has no goal and leads merely to extinction. Also, there is a colossal wastage if the highest reality as yet brought forth by evolution, "centers of consciousness," is outlived by the material works which humans produce.

Lastly, he says that if one believes in Omega, immortality is the corollary of this belief. Man is the first being that we know in the universe to search for the Infinite. During his life, he is always restless to move to greater truth, love and beauty. Humans have a taste for the Infinite. And evolution, which itself generates beings who can love, must be animated by a loving Omega. To extend Teilhard's thought here, we might say that if there is no immortality, then it is not so much a relationship of love but one in which we are used for a while as a means to some unknown further end unconnected with us. No believer could hold this.

I have lingered on these points because they are related to many of the topics which we will consider shortly when we discuss parapsychological efforts to discern signs about post-mortem destiny.

Toward the Future of the Race. Many who agree with Teilhard thus far have reservations about his optimism for the future, an optimism not necessarily based on his Christian faith. Others see his vision as genuinely inspiring and part of the modern "consciousness explosion" (see Chapter XIII).

Just as Christianity sees all human destiny as ultimately related to Omega or God, Teilhard saw even the earthly destiny of human beings as a convergence upon a central point in the future.[27] This would result in an emergence of a kind of "hyper-consciousness" in the future. Though he admits that this movement could be frustrated by humans unless they see a Personal Face ahead and act on that vision, Teilhard believed that humanity, though at present only "in embryo," will evolve into a state of single consciousness. This will be caused by (a) the increase of social unification, the social compression of peoples wherein "attraction will one day be born of enforced nearness"; (b) the growth of technology which is shrinking the globe; (c) heightened vision coming from more time to reflect—and nothing can stop a sound idea; (d) perhaps the development of telepathy. Toward the end of his life, Teilhard thought that telepathy might play a role in giving humans empathy with one another. There is a sort of hyper-humanity at the heart of things, he felt. While he admitted that the counter-evolutionary forces could succeed, they would not. However, Christianity does not guarantee his conviction.

Karl Rahner and God

Before concluding this chapter, I wish to make one further point, a theological point about God as presented by Karl Rahner. As this will be one of the central considerations in the following chapter on paranormal healing, it is worth mentioning here. Rahner says that religious people in the past tended to see God as a factor in the universe almost like an object surpassing them but facing them. "God was thought of in the world as an element of it, and not as that which supported it or as the unfathomable depths beyond it. . . ." Rahner says that for modern man "this kind of God does not exist, that he is not to be found within the world, that he has no heaven above the clouds, that he does not work miracles in order to remove any disturbances in the machinery of the world." God is no longer to be thought of as "one item within our calculations." God is the Ground of the movement of the world itself. God is the presupposition of everything in the world. He is not a "God of the gaps" brought in to compensate for our lack of knowledge in certain areas. No, God is the unfathomable Holy Mystery who is always present, always unfathomable.[28]

In this chapter, we have presented ideas which will give us perspective and balance, it is hoped, in many of the questions which we will now proceed to discuss. We have seen evidence for Jung's collective unconscious, Teilhard's ideas on a psychic universe and his approach to God as a reality existing before man with his collective unconscious emerged, his ideas about immortality, and finally Rahner's concept of God. Let us now move on to the consideration of paranormal healing.

Chapter IV

Paranormal Healing

Christianity has been associated with paranormal healing from the beginning. Jesus and his disciples practiced paranormal healing as a sign of the presence of the Kingdom of God. The recent upsurge of paranormal healing groups in the Church, therefore, should not be seen as some fringe phenomena or fad. It is not "below the dignity" of Christian faith to be interested in practicing physical healing as well as spiritual healing. However, in view of the new popularity of the phenomenon, and in the interests of truth, which alone is helpful to Christianity in the long run, theology should probe as deeply as possible into the nature of this healing.

Three Prevalent Explanations of Paranormal Healing

Secular and religious commentators present varying approaches to paranormal healing. Three prevalent explanations stand out: (1) Paranormal healing is caused either by a coincidental "spontaneous remission" or by psychosomatic processes which bring about self-healing. (2) Paranormal healing is the result of a miraculous and *direct* intervention by God. (3) Paranormal healing is the transfer of some sort of "energy" from the healer to the healed, and probably it is a form of a human PK power.

(1) *Coincidental Spontaneous Remission or Psychosomatic.* An example of this position is found in *Healing, A Doctor in Search of a Miracle* by William Nolen, M.D., a surgeon, author and novel-

ist.[1] Nolen says that all paranormal healing is caused by the body healing itself. Positive subjective states help a person's organism. However, many unusual healing phenomena are simply cases of coincidental spontaneous remission. Nolen estimates that this occurs in from one in ten thousand cases to one in a hundred thousand. With the thousands of sick seen by psychic healers, it is not unreasonable to expect a chance meeting between a healer and a case where spontaneous remission is in process. We also know the power of suggestion and of hypnosis on the body. Nolen believes that most cures are the result of the powers of suggestion. However, many psychic healers are unconscious fakes. They are wishful thinkers and, making no follow up, they are unaware that diseases, whose symptoms are momentarily alleviated, return again and often the patient dies. Nolen studied Kathryn Kuhlman as well as other healers. To study Kuhlman, he even became an usher at one of her events. He found no genuine organic healing in his follow-ups of those who were "healed." He considers Kathryn Kuhlman, who died in 1976, a good-intentioned wishful thinker. Psychic healers, he said, may help but many of them cause cruel deception. Some of them are pure fakes who are chiefly out for money. Nolen also studied "psychic surgery" in the Philippines. ("Psychic surgery" as practiced by people like Tony Agpaoa in the Philippines is a process in which the healer claims to remove a tumor by psychic power, with or without opening the patient by psychic means.) Nolen's judgment is that psychic surgery is simply a fake. Nolen performed a genuine service with his book, which was the result of a great deal of investigative effort. However, as one takes time to consider his claims, Nolen's work begins to appear very one-sided. Evidence which does not fit these claims, for some reason, makes no appearance in this book. Some of this evidence with regard to Kathryn Kuhlman was gathered together by H. Richard Casdorph, M.D. and published in 1976, two years after Nolen's work, in *The Miracles.*[2] The book shows "before and after" x-rays of some patients healed by Kathryn Kuhlman. There is an instantaneous healing of a crippling rheumatoid arthritis. Spontaneous remission, says Casdorph, is always gradual. There are also photos of an instant cure of chronic osteoporosis, cure of a brain tumor in which the symptoms cleared up instantly while the cure itself was gradual, a carcinoma of the kidney with metastasis which disappeared in a similar fashion. Kathryn Kuhlman may have been irritatingly overdramatic and a wishful thinker, but *all* of her claims to paranormal healing may not be simply dismissed. Similar evidence is available from other studies which we will present under #3 below. Thus, one may conclude that the orthodox attack on paranormal healing movements may have two effects: first, a sobering and braking effect on the too-easy claims made by many psychic healers, a kind of case study of wishful thinking in the concrete; but, second, an overkill which produces cynicism in many people who know that all the evidence is not being considered, and an ironic display of wishful thinking by those out to undermine wishful thinking. (Nolen's treatment of psychic surgery, which involves discussion of rare and esoteric processes, is handled in an appendix at the end of this chapter.)

(2) *A Miraculous and Direct Action by God.* Many charismatic healers claim that they are nothing but channels for God's power. But when investigation is undertaken in a probing scientific and theological manner, it is quickly seen that some qualifications must be made. An example, illustrative of this point, is that of Francis McNutt. In 1974, Fr. McNutt, who was at that time a Dominican priest, published his book, *Healing,* in which he approached the position that most paranormal physical healing is directly caused by God.[3] In his later work, *The Power To Heal,* published in 1977, he identified different sources of healing.[4] These included natural forces which might be released or speeded up by prayer, suggestion and love, as well as the creative act of God. A solid theological principle which we mentioned previously supported such a change: the direct intervention of the supernatural should not be postulated when a natural explanation suffices. Or to put it more religiously, a *direct* and *unique* action by God must not be postulated when the *ordinary action of God* through nature and evolution suffices. (Notice I have avoided the word "intervention" as applied to God. If God is present everywhere, as St. Thomas said, either by his presence or by his power, then God cannot be said to "intervene" into that to which he is already present by his power. More correctly, we are speaking about an action by God which

is different from that of his normal providence, rather than about an intervention.)

Many Fundamentalist writers would not agree that natural forces rather than God may be the cause of much paranormal healing. They feel that to speak in this manner is to push God out of the world. I believe that there is a misunderstanding here between two parties who are speaking in two different languages or using two different models. To clarify my meaning here, it is necessary to take a brief look at the history of the question. A few of the points have already been touched upon in Chapter II, but it will not hurt to repeat these in the interest of clarity.

In the New Testament and among the Church Fathers, like St. Augustine, a miracle was a *sign* in a religious context to call attention to God's action. There was no mention of breaking a law of nature. As Augustine had said, "God does not act contrary to nature, but only to the order of nature known to us." Or again, "Man himself is a greater wonder than any wonder done through his instrumentality." The chief influences on the New Testament writers were Hebrew and Hellenic. The chief influence on the Church Fathers about whom I am speaking was Platonic, or neo-Platonic. Hebrew theology and Augustinian-neo-Platonic thought emphasized *participation,* both of the world and of man in God's world, and it made little distinction in wondrous events between what came from God directly and what came directly from man.

Beginning in the Middle Ages, the rediscovery of Aristotle brought a change of perspective. Aristotle was used to replace Plato as the philosophical background for the theological schools which followed St. Thomas.[5] The budding of modern science in the late Middle Ages received a strong impetus from Aristotle in his attempt to understand natures in themselves apart from God. So, too, theology began to stress what was in man's autonomy, though ultimately derived from God, and what was God's gift or supernatural. Schools still existed which remained largely Augustinian—for example, the Franciscan school with St. Bonaventure as an outstanding example.

By the late nineteenth and early twentieth centuries, St. Thomas had become the official theologian championed by the

Catholic Church in training its seminarians. The result has been that while books on spirituality and piety generally took almost instinctively to the neo-Platonic-Augustinian model, scientific theology generally followed the model or paradigm used by the Aristotelian-Thomistic school.[6] The first movement, which was interested in religious experience, emphasized God's activity in all things. All of life participates in the divine presence which impregnates it—"the world is charged with the grandeur of God." As Augustine had said, for a believer in Christ, all of life is a miracle; it is just that we have become used to it. The second approach, interested in scientific theology and modeled to a large degree on contemporary science, stressed the autonomy of nature's action (grounded on God, of course), and made a stark distinction between the natural and the supernatural.

Both models have their advantages and deficiencies. But this bifurcation brings disastrous results when groups of Christians face each other and, speaking in different models or "language games," begin to trade charges because of unconscious misunderstanding. A few years ago, in the auditorium of a church in a small town in Connecticut, I was told by a few members of CUFF (Christians United For the Faith) that I was "in league with the devil" because I held that man himself had some human healing powers. I was using the Aristotelian-Thomistic model but they were listening with Platonic-Augustinian ears. However, I am convinced that there was no essential disagreement in our positions.

In the light of this digression, I think it will be more clear that if I assert that one cannot claim all paranormal healing is the result of the miraculous and *direct* action of God, I am speaking in the model or language game of the Aristotelian-Thomistic tradition. I am not denying that God's power is ultimately the ground of man's healing power. But I am claiming that human beings have these powers as their own to develop, or, as Teilhard de Chardin put it, "God makes things make themselves." The evidence for this position was offered in the second chapter on psychokinesis where it was shown that PK is a human power. No other power seems as suited to paranormal healing as PK.

(3) *A Transfer of PK Energy from the Healer to the Healed.* In

recent years we have witnessed an ever increasing number of controlled experiments in paranormal healing. Probably the most famous of these experiments were those performed with the healer, "Colonel" Estebany, a former Hungarian army officer living in Canada. The original experiments were conducted by Dr. Bernard Grad, a biochemist from McGill University in Montreal. Grad experimented with mice and barley seeds, and thus conducted healing experiments where interpersonal relations were not involved.[7] Grad writes, "In the first experiments, skin wounds were made on the backs of mice, some of which were subsequently treated by Mr. E. [Estebany] simply by having the mice in suitable containers placed between his hands for two fifteen-minute periods daily, five and a half days per week, until the wounds were healed twenty days after they were made. Control mice were placed in similar containers and either were left untreated or were treated in the identical manner of Mr. E., but by persons making no claim to a healing gift. The results showed that the rate of wound healing was significantly faster in the group treated by Mr. E. than in the other two groups."[8] Similarly Grad experimented with barley seeds. Estebany and controls, who did not claim to be healers, held in their hands for thirty minutes vessels with solutions with which the plants were later watered. Grad used both open and sealed beakers in different experiments. Significant growth in the barley seeds followed for the plants watered by the solution held by Estebany. The results were not due to suggestion (even if plants were open to this, were only the plants watered by Estebany's solution suggestible?). Neither was it due to sweat or breath. These experiments imply that some "force" or "energy" is involved. Grad believes that healers who claim that the healing is not done by themselves but by some Higher Power evoke a positive emotion in themselves by their faith. A positive emotional state in the healer is conducive to healing. Unconditional positive regard, empathy, and genuineness are all conducive to paranormal PK healing. When the healed is a human person, trust seems vitally important.

Sr. Justa Smith, a biochemist from Rosary Hill College, Buffalo, also worked with Estebany.[9] Justa Smith says that disease is a failure of adaptation to the environment. Medicine changes the environment, but there is also something within the body which helps the adaptive healing process. This "something" within is not understood but it acts like an innate intelligence. (The reader might notice that this concept is much like Teilhard de Chardin's "within.") Cells are catalyzed by enzyme reactions. Enzyme failure is the cause of disease. "The intricate workings of our body's cells are largely controlled by enzymes. In essence enzymes are the brains of the cells, instructing them on how they must behave to maintain healthy organs."[10] Working with Colonel Estebany, she had the enzyme, trypsin, placed in a vial. Estebany placed his hands around the vial for an hour. He may have prayed but he also slept. Four vials were used: (1) the one held by Estebany, (2) one put in a magnetic field, (3) one placed in ultra violet light to damage the enzymes and then held by Estebany, and (4) the control. The enzymes in the vials held by the healer showed increased activity to the effect of a magnetic field of 13,000 gauss (the natural magnetic field of the earth is less than one). The damaged enzymes also showed a similar increase.

Estebany's hands, therefore, seem to activate a "psi-field." Sr. Smith says that we need a new word for this power. She dislikes "energy" as it is not energy in any known sense. Interestingly, it seems to have some of the characteristics of a magnetic field. Once again, enzymes do not seem capable of anything resembling faith, and this experiment, too, shows that some power actually crosses from the healer to the enzyme.

Olga Worrall is one of the most successful and most tested healers in the United States. An interesting feature is that she is not only a healer but has also been shown to have PK power. In 1974, Dr. Robert Miller, an industrialist research chemist, and Dr. Philip B. Reinhardt, head of the Physics Department at Agnes Scott College near Atlanta, conducted an experiment with a cloud chamber to determine whether some measureable energy was given off by the healer's hands.[11] A cloud chamber is a bowl-like instrument with glass on the top. When charged alpha or beta rays pass through the chamber, they ionize the air and produce a visible trail of positive or negative ions. Olga placed her hands at the sides of the chamber without touching it, and visualized energy flowing from her hands as she does when she heals. An energy-wave pattern was observed in the chamber. But more spectacularly, when she was about six hundred miles away in Baltimore, the experiment was successfully conducted twice. This time the effects were published in photographic form. Other experiments have been made with Olga Worrall. For example, Elizabeth Rauscher and Beverly Rubik at the University of California at Berkeley and Lucio Gatto of the Human Dimensions Institute at Canandaigua, N.Y. reported that she was able to influence the growth and/or motility of bacteria.

Hoyt Edge of Rollins College, Florida, in an attempt to replicate Justa Smith's work, reported that a local psychic "was able to exert a moderately significant effect on the activity of the digestive enzyme, trypsin."[12] Unlike Smith's subject, however, Edge's subject generally deactivated the trypsin when apparently trying to activate it. Dean Kraft, a young psychic healer, was tested in 1977 at the Science Unlimited Research Foundation in San Antonio by Dr. John Kmetz, and previously at the Lawrence Livermore Laboratories in California.[13] In both tests he was able to cause cancer cells to detach and float from the surface on which they were growing. Dean Kraft does not claim any specific religious motivation except love. It has not been my intention here to give an exhaustive list of paranormal healing experiments. However, sufficient experimental evidence has now been presented to enable us to conclude that paranormal physical healing is often the result of a human power, most probably a psychokinetic one.

Why have I been at pains to demonstrate that all healing is neither exclusively psychosomatic nor due to the direct action of God? There are two reasons for this emphasis. All healing is not due to subjective emotions like faith and trust *in the healed,* though these are extremely important. Certainly barley seeds do not have faith, and neither, it seems, do mice! (We do know that holding and "gentling" animals can facilitate healing, but controls in the experiments have ruled this out as a factor in the healing.) Further, it may be that, just as certain personality types, such as obsessive-compulsives, are unable to have "peak experiences" as Maslow claimed, so also certain personality types, through no fault of their own, may not be able to create certain emotions which facilitate faith healing. One must be careful, especially in spiritual books, about assigning a culpable "lack of faith or trust" as the sole cause of the absence of healing. Undue guilt feelings are created in religious people by this approach. Second, if all paranormal physical healing were caused directly by God, then perhaps we could prepare ourselves for this gift, but we could in no way achieve it on our own. But if this physical healing power is also a human power, then we can endeavor to learn how to develop it, if this is possible. This would have incalculable social consequences. Such, in fact, is what is happening.

Dr. Dolores Krieger of NYU has trained many nurses in touch therapy. In controlled experiments this technique has been shown to change hemoglobin content in the blood.[14] It has been introduced into many hospitals in the United States. Still, while there is some evidence that PK is involved, it is not totally clear that this is PK-psychic healing and not faith healing.

Faith Healing and Psychic Healing (PK)

Renée Haynes, of the British Society for Psychical Research, distinguishes three types of healing: faith healing, psychic healing, and miraculous healing. "The author views faith healing and psychic healing as different though overlapping forms of paranormal healing. In faith healing, conscious and unconscious trust in the healer's power is mediated through the mind and psyche of the patient to stimulate bodily processes. Psychic (or psychokinetic) healing appears to be based on a transfer from healer to patient of some form of energy not yet understood that provides a direct physiological stimulus. Faith healers often use suggestion which may stimulate the body's immunological system to work harder and can heal psychosomatic illnesses. The energy involved in psychic healing resembles that involved in psychokinesis; laboratory research shows its effects are comparable to the effects of magnetic fields."[15]

Thus faith healing might be linked with ESP, psychic healing with PK. But what of miraculous healing? Miraculous healing she sees as linked with meaningful coincidences. "The concept of miraculous healing is only meaningful if one assumes that ultimate reality is more than a philosophical idea or a scientific abstraction or a source of overwhelming transcendental experience; that it is, in fact, alive, purposeful and active."[16] In a moment I will speak at some length on the subject of healing which seems to be caused by the direct action of God. But first, let us look at some of the wondrous miracles in the life of Jesus.

Jesus

The Gospels are so filled with the healing miracles of Jesus that one cannot discount them without discounting the historicity of Jesus himself. Jesus heals *instantaneously* Peter's mother-in-law (Mt 8:14; Mk 1:29; Lk 4:38; hereafter I will mention only one Gospel), and a leper (Mk 1:40). He healed the centurion's servant *at a distance* (Mt 8:5); he healed the paralytic as a sign that he could *forgive sin* (Mk 2:1). *Large groups* of sick people are healed at eventide (Mt 8:16). The power is *transferred* to his disciples (Mt 10:1). A man with a withered hand is healed to show that the Sabbath is made for man (Mk 3:1). Jesus *feels power leaving him* when he is touched by the woman with the flow of blood and she is healed (Mk 5:24). Faith is connected with healing as with the blind Bartimaeus (Mk 10:46). He has power over death as in the case of the son of the widow of Naim (only in Lk 7:11), and of Jairus' daughter, dead in the house, who Jesus says is "sleeping" (Mk 5:35), and of Lazarus (only in Jn 11:1).

The characteristics of Jesus' healing are rather startling. He acts as *complete master* of the power. He does not experiment to see if he can achieve a healing. He is always described as taking the power for granted. However, faith is generally required by Jesus, but probably not always—the centurion's servant did not even know what was taking place at a distance from where he lay. Jesus heals by touch, by word, both close and at a distance. His power reached out over apparent death. Power leaves him in a way that he can feel. This power, however, is always considered secondary to stirring up *faith* and *love* and *dedication* to the Kingdom.

What are we to say of these powers in view of our present

evidence? Might these be human powers? If so, as other men besides Jesus had paranormal healing powers, does this imply that Jesus was not God-man in some unique way?

The Quality of Jesus' Healing Powers. First, we must remember that the word "human" in this question does not exclude God. Using the framework we drew from Teilhard, we can say God is the "Within" of all things and all action. However, the real point of the question is the implication that Jesus may not have been divine in such a unique way that we can call him God-man. This question should be approached by reflecting on the fact that the early Christians did *not* affirm Jesus as uniquely divine simply because of the paranormal powers exercised during his lifetime. Other people of his time, such as Apollonius of Tyana, performed marvels, as did the apostles themselves. Also, the early Christians knew from the Scriptures that some prophets from the Old Testament had such powers. Occasionally, they had the powers of telepathy, clairvoyance, psychokinesis, precognition, and healing. Elijah and Elisha had the apparent ability to multiply matter and raise the dead (1 Kgs 17:7–24; 2 Kgs 4:8–44). And the final conclusive piece of evidence on this point is that the apostles did not see Jesus clearly as divine Son of God until after the resurrection, despite the paranormal powers shown during his lifetime.[17]

Miracles were only one element in the constellation of factors which contributed to the belief in Jesus as the Logos or Word (John's Gospel), or as the image of the invisible God (Paul). However, the *quality* of Jesus' miraculous power was an important factor. Jesus produced paranormal effects with ease (Matthew, in 13:58, said that Jesus *did* no mighty works in Nazareth because of their unbelief, while Mark, in 6:5, says Jesus *could* do no mighty work there because of their unbelief). Jesus acted as if he was master of these powers. Others have power at times, for specific cases, or only for some effects. Even though Jesus downplayed the continual seeking after paranormal signs as not sufficiently spiritual, still he left the impression of one who acted as master of the paranormal. This, however, might be but what befits the perfect man.

Jesus' Words and Actions. Jesus' words also entered into the construction of belief in him as a uniquely numinous being. In the parables he spoke as the unique agent of the power of God on earth. In the "Son of Man" sayings, which seem to be genuine sayings of Jesus, he claims that he will be God's agent of judgment, and that this judgment in the case of his contemporaries will be related to their reactions to him. Often, he *spoke and acted* as someone with his own divine authority. For example, in the Sermon on the Mount, he altered the precepts of Moses, thus claiming superiority to Moses who was considered by the Jews as God's lawgiver and spokesman (Matthew, ch. 5, "Of old it was said to you . . . but I say to . . ."). Jesus even claimed and acted out the claim to have "authority on earth" to forgive sin, an incredible claim for a Jewish audience. When people reacted with numinous awe, as we have said previously, he never disclaimed any implication. Jesus spoke of God as "Abba," an Aramaic term used in intimate family relationships, a mode of addressing God "otherwise completely unattested in Jewish prayers."[18] Jesus' frequent use of "Amen, Amen" in contrast to the prophets who said, "Thus says Yahweh," indicates "that he lays claim to an authority which does not need any outside justification."[19]

The Resurrection. Jesus' resurrection was essential to belief in his unique divinity. (We will see more on this under "apparitions.") When joined with the factors we have just described, the resurrection certainly was the chief force in the generation of belief in Jesus as unique Son of God.

Yet the Scriptures never quote Jesus as explicitly saying, "I am God." In fact, in Mark 10:17, Jesus says to a young man who runs up to him, "Why call me good. None is good but God" (i.e., Yahweh). Mark, who concentrates on Jesus' *acts,* depicts him as the great enigma who *acted as* God and with the power of God. Matthew, who concentrates also on Jesus' *words,* saw him as one who *spoke like God.* The early Christians had to struggle in trying to explain who he was. After all, the Jews believed in Yahweh, and there was only one God. Who then was this Jesus? One solution they adopted was to take two titles from the Old Testament, *El* or God, and *Adonai* or Lord. The first they attributed to Yahweh (who now, as Jesus had taught them, became Father), and the second they attributed to Jesus (who now became Lord and Son). Over the centuries, while living with theoretical problems, they accepted Jesus' unique divinity. At the Council of Chalcedon in 451, a consensus was reached. Using terms from Hellenic speculation, they said Jesus had two natures, divine and human, but only one divine person at his center united these two natures ("hypostatic union"). Today, theologians point out that there is only one "intellect" and one "will" in the three "persons" in the Trinity. Thus, "person" does not mean what modern psychology means by person. Many theologians today say that there are three simultaneous modes of existence in God: one as totally beyond time (Father), one as uniquely involved in a particular time (Son), and one as immanent in all men (Spirit). But there is only one God, one "will," one "intellect," transcending time.[20]

The reader may wonder at the length of the preceding treatment. Parapsychological discussion of miracles certainly raises many questions as well as offering much light for our understanding of Jesus. But when we ask the question as to how such a fact in parapsychology affects the belief that "Jesus is God," the very neat packaging of the question implies a tight and boxed-in idea of "God" which is very misleading. My very inadequate treatment of the question here—and we will return to it again—aims at keeping us aware of the mysteriousness of God as well as the mysteriousness of Jesus himself.

It has been necessary to present at some length, and even then very inadequately, some idea of the genesis of belief in Jesus as God-man. But only in this way are we able to see that if we hold in the light of recent parapsychological research that the healing miracles might have been the result of a human power, or that the miracles of raising the dead, while the direct action of God may be operating through man, do not immediately imply that the one performing them is divine. This does not imply that the traditional claims for Jesus are therefore invalid. Jesus' resurrection and his own implicit claims are of paramount importance.

Belief in the unique status of Jesus (and we do not fully comprehend the mystery of who he is except that he is the unique act of God in our regard) was not based principally on the healing miracles. The respected exegete, G.W.H. Lampe, writes, "Miracles might commend Christ but Christ was first needed to commend the miracles. It was not enough to ask men to believe in Christ's divinity because of the miracles; they had to be asked to believe the miracle stories because they first accepted his divinity."[21] I believe that too stark a dichotomy is drawn here between Jesus' person and the miracles. Yet, I think the main thrust of the statement is true. However, it has been said that in times past the miracles helped people believe in the divinity of Jesus but that today it is these very wondrous acts that cause doubt and are a hindrance. But in view of parapsychological study, this need not be so.

Nature Miracles? Many liberal scholars today are willing to accept that Jesus may have performed some healing miracles, i.e., psychosomatic or faith healing miracles, but they are reluctant to think that the Gospels present genuine history in those passages which describe Jesus' control over the winds, or those which describe him multiplying matter.

Even the careful moderate Roman Catholic scholar, Fr. Walter Kasper, seems to accept this approach. He insists that Jesus performed many wondrous acts, for the miracle tradition in the Gospels would be totally inexplicable without many miracles. Yet, he writes, "Jesus performed extraordinary actions, which amazed his contemporaries. These included curing various diseases and symptoms which at the time were thought to be signs of possession. On the other hand, the probability is that we need not take the so-called 'nature miracles' as historical."[22] Among these he seems to include the stilling of the storm, the transfiguration, Jesus' walking on the lake, the feeding of the four (or five) thousand and the miraculous draught of fishes. His position on the narratives about raising the dead is not clear. Hans Küng, generally a courageous and honest theologian, takes the same position, but he includes the three incidents of Jesus' raising the dead in the same category.[23]

However, it seems to me that knowledge of parapsychology might change the presentation here very drastically. One does not have to be a Fundamentalist to make this suggestion. I personally believe in many of the tenets of form criticism and redaction criticism. I hold with many scholars that some events were written back into Jesus' life after the resurrection when they now believed he *could* have done much he had not done

during his earthly life because of his self-emptying or *kenosis.*
This kenotic theology is based on St. Paul's idea in Philippians
2:6, "His state was divine, yet he did not cling to his equality
with God but emptied himself to assume the condition of a
slave, and became as men are, and being as all men are, he was
humble yet, even to accepting death, death on a cross."[24] Some
great acts seem to have been written back into his life as
statements of who he really was in a hidden way. One such
miracle might be the one where Peter is told to go and catch a
fish, and take from its mouth a shekel and pay the temple tax (in
Mt 17:24, only).

However, if judged in the light of parapsychological evidence, some of the positions of recent critical scriptural thought
seem to be carried to an extreme; they are too colored by
contemporary bias as well as by ignorance of the paranormal.
Are the descriptions of the transfiguration, of the multiplying of
the loaves and fishes, and of the stilling of the storm necessarily
non-historical? Are they necessarily examples of this "writing-
back"? I think not. It seems to me that parapsychology has its
own modest contribution to make to the investigation of Scripture. Exegetes would be well advised to become acquainted with
its investigations.[25] Let us now move to another question.

Direct Actions by God Causing Paranormal Effects. In seeing paranormal healing as at times the result of a human PK power, I do
not mean to imply that God never acts in a unique way to bring
about wondrous healings. There are some overwhelming and
instantaneous healings which may be beyond the human power
of PK. I would see the narratives of Jesus' raising the dead as
well as those of Elijah and Elisha, if they really raised the dead,
to be such actions. However, let us not concentrate on such
ancient events. There may be *unique* actions of God in our daily
lives which are not necessarily the result of any human psychokinetic power. This question involves a very important theological issue.

Christianity has always opposed Deism. Deism held that
God, as it were, wound up the world-machine and then left it to
its own processes. God was its source but not its companion.
The Deistic God is a "cold outsider" as George Tyrrell put it.
Modern Christian theologians, of course, would not hold this.

But some seem to hold that, while God is not indifferent to the world—he is always its silent companion—still his action on the world is in the moral area of inspiration and grace. In the physical area, he does not act on the world in a way different from that of his general providence. The model of Teilhard de Chardin, on its surface, seems to lean in this direction. In some places Teilhard speaks as if Christ came forth from God naturally when the world of Egypt, Greece and Israel had been prepared for him.[26] It is as if God is like the sun which is always shining and never changes. The sun's rays do not get through simply because a cloud covers the earth, or because a side of the earth has revolved away from the sun. (This model was dear to the medieval school of Alexander Hales, a Franciscan.) However, like all images, this model is defective and not totally adequate. It implies that God's action is the same everywhere and always. It is only human persons who act differently.

But the question must be asked, "Does God never do anything in particular in any other sense than that in which he does everything in general?"[27] This is an extremely important question. I believe it is at the cleaving point between those who consider God as "personal" and those who claim he is "impersonal." Many "atheists," like Albert Einstein and Abraham Maslow, do not deny a power in the universe which is the ground of intelligence and love. This power they call "impersonal" because they believe that it never "intervenes" in human affairs—"an interventionist God."

Does God, then, ever act differently, or is his shining relatively unchanging like the sun? Popular piety may immediately reject this implication about God never changing. Still, many spiritual people see a certain truth here. For instance, St. Thomas once said that we pray not to change God but to change ourselves. Gerard Manley Hopkins wrote:

> 'But tell me, child, your choice; What shall I buy
> You?'—'Father, what you buy me I like best.'[28]

Fred L. Fisher in *Prayer in the New Testament* says, "God will do nothing for us that we can do ourselves. . . . God will not change nature for us but if we love Him, He will make all, good and evil, for our good. . . . God will not change nature for us in the sense of instead of us. He does not work on us by miracle but by grace."[29] "God makes things make themselves," as Teilhard said.

These insights are certainly illuminations resulting from an advanced and sound spirituality. However, are they universally true, unvarying and the last word? In principle, I believe, in the long run, Christianity must say no to this question. The reason is that Christianity rests on the incarnation of the God-man in some qualitatively unique way and on the unique resurrection of Jesus. It seems impossible, without presenting a completely revised Christianity, to say that these wondrous events represent no different action of God than that found in his universal providential action with all men. If Jesus is seen simply as the greatest, or one of the greatest, prophets, one might assert this. When the earth was prepared, God's unvarying action "got through." But if one adheres to what seems to be essential to incarnation and resurrection, I think one must make room for God's acting in unique and different ways. And if God so acted in incarnation and resurrection, we immediately see that God may so act at other times. We are not thinking here of a "God of the gaps," that is, finding God only where science cannot, for the moment, explain a given event. I am saying that God's action in Jesus may be repeated, in the sense of his going beyond his normal providence, with others. But if these were the only times when we could say God acts, then we would be speaking of a God of the gaps. But God is found both in the gaps and in the non-gaps, or in the ordinary.[30] Teilhard said that God visibilized himself in Jesus so that we could know that the universe ahead had a face and a heart. Is this not possible, too, in the lives of others today? Resurrection from the dead is, in the opinion of most Christian theologians, a "major prodigy" as we have defined it. But are there not events today which are signs that God is involved in human life, at least occasionally, not as in his general providential manner, but in a more unique way?

No Christian is obliged to believe this. The great theologian, Karl Barth, believed that God acted once and only once in this unique way, in his act in Jesus. But is there not a reasonable basis for believing that what is "the direct intervention of God" has happened many times since then?

This general position seems most reasonable. But when we endeavor to apply it to any given concrete case, some objection will usually arise which prevents us from saying that we are certain that this is a special action of God beyond any possible doubt. But are there cases where the conviction seems to stand up sturdily against all reasonable doubt? Let us consider a case from Lourdes as an example.

John Traynor, 40, a British marine, is wounded in the head during October 1914 at Antwerp. Although unconscious for five weeks, after surgery he is able to leave the hospital and rejoin his outfit in 1915. In February he suffers a superficial wound in the right knee in Egypt. In May he is wounded by three machine gun bullets at the Dardanelles. Two pass through the chest; the third hits the arm at the height of the inside end of the biceps. At Alexandria an unsuccessful attempt is made at resewing the severed nerve. Shipped home, another unsuccessful attempt is made to reconnect the nerve. Traynor has an epileptiform attack. After a third unsuccessful attempt to mend the nerve, amputation is recommended. Traynor refuses and is retired on one hundred percent disability.

Epileptic attacks become more frequent, and amputation is again recommended after another attempt to connect the nerve. In 1920 a disc of bone (trepanation) is cut out from the skull; afterward there ensues partial paralysis, vertigo, and epileptic convulsions which make him fall out of bed. At the end of 1920 he loses control of sphincters of bladder and anus; his arm is completely paralyzed and the muscles are atrophied.

Despite numerous attacks on the way, he arrives at Lourdes on June 22, 1923. He is examined and the doctors find a trepanation opening of approximately 8″ by 2″ through which the brain pulsations are visible. The patient must be protected by a metal disc.

At the second bathing in the pool, there is abundant bleeding through the mouth followed by an epileptic attack. The attacks stop, but at the ninth bathing there are violent convulsions of the legs. Carried to the procession of the Blessed Sacrament, his arm shakes with the same kind of convulsions. He walks a bit but collapses. Examination that day reveals recovered usage of the legs with nervous reflexes reestablished. His feet hurt and he walks with much difficulty. He is given morphine for pain all over his body. At 5:30 A.M. he jumps out of bed and runs barefoot to the grotto. He is examined the next day. He has recovered full use of the right arm. The trepanation opening has been considerably reduced. After removal of the disc, the hole will disappear completely in a week. Back in England, Traynor takes up work as a seller of coal. He lifts two hundred pound bags. The trepanation hole leaves only a sign at a bony depression on the cranium and there is a slight atrophy of the hand. Often he goes to Lourdes as a stretcher bearer. He dies of a hernia in 1943. This is not one of the Lourdes cases in which the cure is complete and instantaneous.[31] But it is not simply a cure of a functional disease, and it is indeed dramatic.

One would think that here we have a sign of a rare and different kind of action by God. The water at Lourdes has been examined and found to be in no way chemically different from other water. H. Richard Neff in his excellent little book, *Psychic Phenomena and Religion,* believes that there is a healing force in the water, mediated through a spiritual being or through the prayers of the faithful.[32] Notice, however, that some people are healed while not in contact with the water but while participating in "exposition of the Blessed Sacrament."

Is it possible that a healing force is generated in the environment by the prayers of the faithful? This is the opinion held by the respected parapsychological writer, D. Scott Rogo. He believes that just as the small groups in Canada and in England were able to generate by unconscious power a psychokinetic force, so too in large and fervent groups such a power can be unleashed.[33] Jerome Frank mentions an interesting point which seems to give backing to this hypothesis. Except for the original cures, "Lourdes has failed to heal those who live in its vicinity. This suggests that the emotional excitement connected with this preparatory period and journey to the shrine may be essential for healing to occur."[34] Similarly Ronald Finucane in *Miracles and Pilgrims* has made an extensive study of healing shrines in medieval England in which he found that "shrines rose and fell in public estimation as curative centres; the tumult came and went leaving behind it strings of wax or metal figures to dangle above the (saint's) tomb, mute evidence that people once seized upon the reputed saint as a new source of healing, a new therapy."[35] Is the fact that healing shrines lose their healing power connected with a certain habit of familiarity one acquires from frequenting a certain place? This is possible. But Lourdes has continued with its healing power since 1858. And there also remains the stream once discovered by Bernadette who, in response to a vision, scratched away some sand and drank from it as she was told. On the other hand, if God is working there in a unique fashion, the Mysterious Presence still works through secondary causes. No amputated limbs suddenly reappeared. Ordinary processes seem incredibly speeded up.

For those who believe that God still works in a unique way even today, most examples will not remove all reasonable doubt that some psychokinetic agency may be at work. The conclusion will usually be based on a person's existential decision connected with his or her vision of the meaning of life and of the relationship of God to the world based on personal experience.

Let us look at one other dramatic example of an apparent "intervention" by God or by some agency from the beyond. In a work which deserves a great deal of attention, *The Incorruptibles,* Joan Carroll Cruz has made a study of many saints whose bodies remained incorrupt, either for many years or until this day.[36] These cases are not of bodies embalmed as in Egypt or left in very dry places and preserved in a leathery fashion. Some, as was the case with St. Francis Xavier, were placed in quick lime; others were found floating in water. Yet they remained incorrupt. Some retained perfect flexibility, even with blood flow! These cases are well documented by the witnesses, including doctors, who assembled at the disinterment. Perhaps the most amazing example is that of St. Charbel Makhlouf, a holy and ascetic Lebanese monk of the Maronite rite, who lived from 1828 to 1898. "In all probability he would have been forgotten had not a certain phenomenon occurred at his grave in the form of an extraordinary light, which surrounded the tomb for forty-five nights following the interment." Permission was obtained to exhume the body. "When the common grave was opened in the presence of the Superiors of the Order, the monks of the monastery and many villagers, the body was found in perfect condition, even though, as a result of the frequent rains which inundated the cemetery several times since the burial, the body was found floating on mud in the flooded grave. . . . A strange phenomenon accompanied this exhumation, one that has continued to occur to the present day. From parts of the body there exuded a liquid described as perspiration and blood." The blood-stained clothing on the relic was changed twice a week. In July 1927 the body was placed in a new coffin of wood covered with zinc. On February 23, 1950, pilgrims noticed a liquid seeping from a corner of the tomb. The tomb was opened and "the body was found completely free of any trace of corruption and was perfectly flexible and lifelike." The sweat and liquid continued to exude from the body and the garments were found stained with blood. Part of the chasuble had rotted and a zinc tube which contained some official documents was covered with corrosion.

Over a two year period twelve hundred records of miracles were recorded. In one important case, accepted by the Sacred Congregation, a Mr. Alessandro Obeid "was blinded when the retina of his eye was torn when it was struck by the branch of a tree. His sight was miraculously restored at the tomb, and he was privileged to see his heavenly benefactor in a vision." In another case, a Miss Mountaha Daher, a Lebanese, was cured of "a hunchback deformity, a chicken-breast and misshapen shoulders," all testified to by her doctor. Charbel's body is still exuding fluid and remains soft and flexible. It appears like that of a person who has just recently died.

What is one to make of cases such as this, well witnessed to and documented? What of the incorruptibles in general, a unique phenomenon according to the author and found only in the Catholic Church? I have no hidden apologetic purpose in this question. I am speaking of a phenomenon. For a scientific verdict, we may have to wait many years. And then science, if it must, can only say that this cannot as yet be explained.

Science is interested in strict proof according to its own paradigms. But human beings are interested in the real, whether reached by strict science or by some other means. Is it reasonable to believe that either God, or the saint from the beyond, is operating here in a manner beyond the normal, even beyond the paranormal, beyond human PK power? Christian faith places no burden on us in this matter; one can believe or not that the special action of God or of the saint is in operation. But it is because of cases like this that I would hesitate to explain all "miraculous" happenings today as only special cases of human PK agency.

Summary. "Paranormal" healing may be the result of coincidental spontaneous remission or of psychosomatic processes. Yet it cannot be reduced to this. In some cases, there is a transfer of some form of PK energy from the healer to the healed. The fact that many of Jesus' cures might be conceived of in this fashion in no way detracts from the traditional belief in Jesus' numinosity, his God-manship, his ontological status as being both man and Son of God in a unique sense. On the other hand, all paranormal healing cannot, it seems, be reduced to the prior two explanations. In some cases, even apart from Jesus' resurrection and incarnation, there appears to be probability that God acts even today in physical nature in a way which is different from his normal providence.

Some Final Thoughts

Two prerequisites for faith healing are of capital importance: (a) caring, empathy and at-one-ness with the one to be healed, and (b) an altered state of consciousness from which one moves into the alpha state. Furthermore, negative attitudes on the part of either the healer or the one to be healed seem to block the healing process as, for example, with people who believe that God wants them to suffer. The same may be true of healing through PK power. This is a power which may possibly be developed and improved through training.

Many theories abound as to how paranormal healing works. Let us look at the model we have chosen to structure our approach, that of Teilhard de Chardin. Teilhard's explanation of the "within" in all reality is a useful concept for explaining paranormal healing. The "within" is in all non-artificial reality. It is the reflection of the Great Within, the Hyperpersonal Within, or Omega. Absolute Consciousness or the Great Within touches man through its imprint on man which is man's "within." The powers of the within seem to be able to cross the boundary between persons, and the within of the healer may assist the within of the one to be healed to regulate his or her organism. As Sally Hammond puts it, "Healing seems to come about where there is self-attunement to the Source of all healing power and energy. It seems to be a matter of raising one's vibrations to a state that enables one to receive the energy that is available to all. It is our task to discover the laws that govern this."[37]

However, this does not mean that there is a special act of God in paranormal healing. It might be truer to say that we "intervene" in God. Even sanctity itself does not guarantee healing power. In fact, we seem to be stumbling by accident, as it were, into the discovery of these powers: "God makes things make themselves." There seems to be some paranormal dimension, the laws of contact with which we have not yet discovered. It seems that one is entering into some deeper attunement with Absolute Consciousness which is not identical with genuine spirituality but which may overlap with it. Explicit belief in any one religion or even in God is not required. But caring is a central prerequisite. As I see it, paranormal healing keeps mystery alive for those who cannot see their way to God, and it keeps "mysticism" alive for those who cannot taste God in the ordinary. But, more importantly, it is a sign that the Kingdom of God is everywhere. The Kingdom of God is "at hand."

For hundreds of years the healing *movement* gradually died out in Christianity. It came to be considered unbecoming for mature faith. However, the movement continued under the sponsorship of Spiritism and Christian Science, among other groups.[38] The reassimilation of this movement belongs to the Church's mission in proclaiming the Kingdom of God which is found in the most natural as well as in the uniquely divine.

Appendices

I. *Evidence for Materialization*

- In 1913 Baron von Schrenck-Notzing published a detailed study of ectoplasmic materialization.[39] The book is a careful study which contains 225 photographs. A strong case is made for ectoplasmic materialization. Ectoplasm is an amorphous substance with vestiges of a membrane of cell-like tissue and bacterial forms and fat, looking like vegetable fat, and sometimes like cotton, which was exuded. There is something strange in the last group of photos which look like cutouts of photos which appeared in newspapers, but they are distorted. This caused a major problem at the time.

- Charles Richet, Ph.D., a French parapsychologist, summarized his own experiments in a book, published in 1923 in English as *Thirty Years of Psychical Research.* He concluded that, though he did not take the materializations as signs of contact with the dead, he was convinced they were genuine materializations.

- Franek Kluski, a Polish psychic, was tested between 1901 and 1920 by Geley, by Dr. Joseph Venzano, an Italian parapsychologist, and by the Polish Society of Psychical Research. Kluski produced not only ectoplasmic materializations but materializations of "phantoms" fully independent of himself, and these were photographed. Conclusions were that the materializations were genuine and not faked. Note: the Continental parapsychologists were mainly biologists and worked often with ectoplasmic phenomena. The American and British parapsychologists were mainly psychologists or philosophers. They did little such work. Generally they looked with scorn on such phenomena. (But Sir William Crookes, a Nobel prize laureate in physics, did study such phenomena. In English-language literature, he is often charged with fraud and naiveté, but there are signs that this was due to British and American ignorance of such phenomena.)[40]

- In 1958, Keith Rhinehart, a psychic from Seattle, was tested under controlled conditions by parapsychologists in Japan. He was locked in a specially constructed chair where the slightest move would be recorded. Among other feats, he produced a milky-white ectoplasm which contained some human cells. This was photographed.[41]

- In recent years, Uri Geller is alleged to have caused materialization and dematerialization. "Apports," objects appearing from other places, are said to manifest themselves, or objects disappear.[42] Many witnesses have attested to the phenomena. However, with Uri's penchant for showmanship and occasional deception, the weight of this evidence is reduced.

- Matthew Manning has often been tested in Canada, especially by Dr. A.R.G. Owens. No evidence has been uncovered of any attempt on his part to deceive. Both PK phenomena and materialization-dematerialization phenomena have been produced.

- In 1977, Karlis Osis and Erlendur Haraldsson published their full study of Sai Baba in India.[43] Despite close and long inspection, although no strict laboratory controls were feasible, the phenomena seem connected with no magic or trickery. The number of objects materialized could not have possibly been hidden on his person.

Conclusion: this phenomenon definitely deserves more intense research. However, past studies do not seem to have been sufficiently controlled to allow a solid judgment in this area.

II. *Psychic Surgery*

Psychic surgery is a process in which it is claimed that a patient is opened by psychic means, diseased matter removed, the wound closed, and the patient healed. At times even a knife may be used, but there is no infection. Is this totally unbelievable?

The evidence is overwhelming that Arigo, a Brazilian psychic healer, actually removed material, such as a tumor from an arm, with an old knife, following which there never was any infection.[44] He also correctly diagnosed individuals waiting on a long line to see him, and this he did with incredible speed.

Medicines he prescribed worked, though how often is uncertain. Arigo offers an incredible phenomenon for study. Unfortunately, he died in a car crash in 1971. Perhaps some laser-like effect was connected with his PK power. Laser energy also sterilizes.

Psychic surgery has been studied more often in the Philippines. William Nolen rated it a fake, as has been mentioned. However, a mass of evidence has now been accumulated which makes it impossible to pass such a simple judgment. Much psychic surgery seems to consist of tricks and suggestion. Some seems to involve suggestion with PK power. And some seems to involve only PK power, with real healing following.

Nolen's work has been seriously challenged as to its facts and honesty by Alfred Stelter, Ph.D. in psychology.[45] Stelter, George W. Meek, and Sigrun Seutemann, M.D. have presented overwhelming evidence that something paranormal is taking place.[46] Dr. Seutemann has watched more than three thousand operations, and she basically agrees with Stelter that we are dealing with "completely new parapsychological phenomena, quite unfamiliar to Western scientists." In a study like the present one, I am unable to discuss details. But take, for example, the reports of Dr. Hiroshi Motoyama and Dr. Lyall Watson about Jose Blanco, a Philippine psychic healer.[47] Merely by pointing at the midriff, Blanco was able to make cuts on x-ray photographic paper and on the skin.

George Meek has summed up the present state of the evidence as he sees it.[48]

1. The physical body is not opened in ninety-five percent of the cases.
2. The liquid and tissue which appear in the "operations" are, in some cases, a genuine apport of materialization phenomena; in other cases, they are produced by deception and sleight-of-hand. (Some apports have been photographed by materializing, seen frame by frame, in the photos.)
3. The resulting psychological impact is often beneficial to the patient. Besides suggestion, there is often involved an energy emanating from the healer which stimulates and reactivates cells. With cotton and body-like tissue

materializing or dematerializing, the result is at times remarkable healing. At other times, after a long trip from the United States, a person finds simply the "cruel deception" mentioned by Nolen.

4. Some bodies are pierced by a psychokinetic power. More research is needed to make further conclusions about genuine operations.

5. A specific, traditional form of faith is not required in the healer, but usually they have a strong belief system in a higher power.

I would think that science would be fascinated by the possibilities in such a kind of study. Instead, what is usually displayed is an *a priori* denial. And according to Stanley Krippner, scientists who do investigate the phenomena are afraid to publish their studies for fear of damage to their reputations.[49] However, at present I do not believe that we have enough solid evidence to venture a judgment in this area. We all know of a kind of ingenious, and at times unconscious, pious fraud which operates in the area of paranormal healing, and it seems especially appropriate to conclude this appendix on psychic surgery on a strongly cautionary note.

Chapter V

Precognition and Prophecy

Precognition is knowledge of the future through no known process of the mind or senses. If precognition is a fact, the religious and philosophical implications are vast and it is obvious that the evidence must be carefully assessed. The philosopher, the religious believer, and the agnostic or atheist will all be touched by influences coming from the depths of our being where our views of the meaning of life are germinated. We should aim to sift the evidence while remaining aware of this influence.

The reality of precognition would involve the capability of existing in some form in a dimension which is not limited by the boundaries of space-time as we know them. The finality of death, which occurs in this known space-time dimension, would become questionable if part of us is independent of the time-space dimension. For this situation to emerge, it would not be necessary for each human being to experience precognitive episodes. If only a few people throughout history had this experience, this fact would tell us something of the capacities of human nature in general.

Precognition in its true sense involves the knowledge of an event before its causes. Speculatively and philosophically, this seems impossible. Accordingly, we must decide whether the formal criterion for judgment about the real is the purely critical and speculative, the purely empirical, or, as I would hold, the combination of both the empirical and the speculative.

I am speaking of "genuine" precognition. The word "genuine" suggests that there are events which resemble precognition but which may be explained in some other fashion. The following rules, proposed by Alan Vaughan, make it clear what these other explanations might be and how they may be ruled out.[1]

1. The prediction must be told or recorded before fulfillment.
2. It must include enough details so that chance fulfillment is unlikely.
3. It must restrict itself to fairly narrow limits of time, or else it must contain details which fix the occasion of fulfillment, e.g., on visiting a certain place.
4. It must be of such a nature that inference from wider knowledge could not reasonably explain it.
5. It must be clear that suggestions or unconscious knowledge could not have brought it about.
6. The information must not have been in the possession of any other person.
7. It must be possible to exclude telepathy and clairvoyance of a present event or PK as reasonable explanations.

Anecdotal Evidence

Anecdotal evidence for precognition is frequently inconclusive. To illustrate this point, let us look at a few of the more famous cases. Abraham Lincoln had a dream, shortly before he was killed, in which he walked through the White House amidst sounds of mourning. He arrived in the East Room and found there a corpse on a catafalque wrapped in funeral vestments. There were soldiers stationed around the catafalque, and he asked them who was dead. They answered, "The President; he was killed by an assassin."[2]

Though this might have been a precognitive dream, it cannot be taken as clear evidence of such. Public officials of high rank are often in such danger and the rituals of their funerals are well known. It might have been a dream caused by an unconscious or subliminal suggestion.

One of the most famous modern psychics connected with precognition is Jeane Dixon. In 1952 Jeane Dixon had a vision in

St. Matthew's Cathedral in Washington. The White House suddenly appeared before her. "Almost immediately the numbers '1960' formed above it, and, as she watched, a dark cloud spread from the numbers and 'dripped down like chocolate frosting on a cake' over the White House and a man standing in front of it. The man, she recalls, was young, tall, and blue-eyed, with a shock of thick brown hair. An inner voice told her that he was a Democrat, and that the President elected in 1960 would meet with violent death while in office."[3] Four years later in 1956 the prediction was repeated in *Parade* magazine: "As for the 1960 election, Mrs. Dixon thinks it will be dominated by labor and won by a Democrat. But he will be assassinated or die in office though not necessarily in his first term."[4]

However, (a) famous political figures are high risks, (b) the chances of a president being a Democrat are better than one in two, and (c) a cycle exists in which, since 1840, every twenty years a president was killed or died in office, though not necessarily in his first term.[5] The prediction as described thus far, therefore, could not be taken as solid evidence for genuine precognition.

But Mrs. Dixon gave indications to others that she had seen two black hands reach up and remove the plaque from the Vice-President's office, the hands of death. Then she saw an unknown man with a two-syllable name. The second letter was definitely an "s," and the first looked like an "o" or a "q." This, of course, seems to refer to Oswald. With the addition of these details, the anecdotal evidence assumes greater weight.

Jeane Dixon apparently has made some remarkably accurate predictions. However, she has also made an enormous amount of predictions which have been totally wrong.[6] Jeane Dixon distinguishes between "prophecy" and "revelation." Prophecies are subject to error and depend on reading the minds of men. Revelation is infallible and the will of God.[7] Unfortunately, this difference seemingly is not made at the time of the prediction. Jeane Dixon seems to have some precognitive power, but it is not clear as to when it is present and when there will be an error in the prediction.

Eileen Garrett (1893–1970) was a highly successful medium who often cooperated with scientists in testing her gifts. In 1926 while walking in London's Hyde Park she saw a great silver airship moving westward into the sunset.[8] Again in 1928 she saw an airship which now wobbled, gave off smoke and disappeared. In 1929 she again saw the ship over London. This time it was burning and gave off clouds of smoke. A year before, in 1928, in a mediumistic sitting, she received a warning to an Ernest Johnson that his ship would crash. A year later, it was announced that England would build two dirigibles, the R-100 and the R-101. Ernest Johnson was to be the navigator of the R-101. Eileen tried to warn that it would crash. In 1930, the R-101 on her maiden voyage to Egypt and India crashed near Beauvais, France with the loss of forty-six lives. This is solid anecdotal evidence. However, consider the following anecdotes.

On May 25, 1979, America suffered its worst air catastrophe at O'Hare Airport in Chicago in which 271 people lost their lives. Less than three months before, a Denver psychic, Mrs. Lou Wright, predicted on Denver radio station KIMN that an American Airlines DC-10 would crash at O'Hare in Chicago, and well over two hundred passengers would be killed. These details were accurate. She did not give the exact date but said that it would be within a few months.[9] On January 29, 1979 a twenty year old Jersey youth, Ted Karmilovich Jr., had a prediction notarized and placed in a sealed envelope. He predicted that "there will be a tragic jetliner crash on October 31 of this year. Mexico City will be the site of this tragic accident which will be due to a foul-up in runway lighting conditions. I sense that 77 people may be killed and that either the number 2065 or 2605 will be associated with the accident."[10] The details were accurate, and the flight number was 2605.

Four times on TV and radio, from December 31, 1976 to February 6, 1977, Miami psychic Micki Dahne predicted that within a few months the worst crash ever would occur. According to the cumulative predictions, two planes would crash in the Canary Islands, at least one of the planes would be a 747, one plane would not be American, and the crash would happen on March 25 or 26. The crash, accurately predicted, occurred on March 27.[11]

Shawn Robbins, who also predicted the previous crash, made a notarized prediction that in one of the worst crashes in this country, over a hundred people would be killed (at least 113 died).[12] It would happen at New York's Kennedy Airport and an Eastern Airlines plane would be involved (Eastern flight 66 crashed at JFK on June 24, 1975). She said it would happen in June or July, in the midst of a violent thunderstorm. The last detail was also correct. In these cases, at times vivid visions of events were seen; at other times numbers came to view in visions.

The source of these anecdotes is *National Enquirer.* In view of much that is printed in *National Enquirer,* the accuracy of these anecdotes is certainly open to question. However, without anecdotal tradition, scientific study of precognition would never have been initiated. Louisa Rhine, the wife of Joseph Rhine, believes that the anecdotal tradition is very important for gaining insights into ESP, including precognition. Her books, *Hidden Channels of the Mind* and *The Invisible Picture,* are impressive gatherings of such data.

Controlled Experiments

At Duke Joseph Rhine decided to test whether ESP operated outside of time as well as space. A precognition experiment was conducted in 1933 in which guesses were made before the cards were shuffled. In 4,500 runs of 25 Zener cards which were at first hand-shuffled but later machine-shuffled, Rhine found results which were three million to one against chance.[13] In 1938 Rhine published the results of tests with 49 subjects in which the odds against chance were more than one hundred thousand to one.[14] Great efforts were made to ensure that precognition was really the power operating and not PK, i.e., that the guesses through PK were not influencing the choices to be made. While theoretically PK might be in operation, because of the complicated safeguards which were taken, such as basing the shuffling on numbers drawn from market reports or local temperature records which were published after the guesses were made, PK as an explanation of precognition seems to have been practically ruled out.[15]

In a report published in 1966, Jarl Fahler, a Finnish parapsychologist, and Karlis Osis of the American Society for Psychical Research had subjects under hypnosis try to predict "in what order the numbers one through ten would be randomly listed on a sheet the next day." Each subject was also asked to indicate "whenever he or she felt *certain* a specific prediction would be correct."[16] The next day, an assistant who had not been present at the predictions listed the numbers in a random order and later compared them to the predictions. Where the subjects had felt certain about their predictions, the odds were 50 million to one over chance, one of the highest ever reported.

Helmut Schmidt, a physicist, who followed Rhine at Durham after working at Boeing, invented a machine, as previously mentioned, which was set off by the decay of radioactive strontium 90, one of the most random elements in the universe. In a precognition experiment, 11 students in 10,000 guesses obtained odds of 1000 to 1 over chance. Three star pupils attained odds of one billion to one against chance.[17] Theoretically PK is not ruled out here.

At Maimonides Dream Laboratory in Brooklyn, a British sensitive, Malcolm Bessent, was tested in 1969–1970 by Montague Ullman and Stanley Krippner. After sleeping and dreaming, during which time his brain waves were monitored, he told of his dreams. The next day, and in one experiment a few weeks later, an assistant chose art prints from a pool. In two tests in which judges tried to match dreams with pictures, Bessent scored five thousand to one and one thousand to one against chance.[18]

The famous precognitive experiments by S.G. Soal in England cannot now be safely considered as evidence for precognition. C.E.M. Hansel and others have presented evidence that figures may have been altered in these tests.[19]

Louisa Rhine in her Book, *Psi—What Is It?* summed up her conclusions about precognition. She wrote, "Today the evidence for it is too strong for reasonable doubt."[20] She claimed that precognition is rejected only because people say it is impossible philosophically. J. Gaither Pratt, the prominent parapsychologist, wrote in 1975, "My personal opinion is that the laboratory results we now have from a large number of experiments, combined with the more striking and well studied spontaneous cases, provide strong but not fully compelling evidence of precognition."[21] Even the slackness of scientific controls in Rhine's early work seems to be cancelled out as a factor by what is called "the decline effect." The decline effect is a gradual decline in successful scoring over a long period of time. Such a patterned decline cannot be accounted for by pure chance. It seems connected to such factors as monotony and fatigue, as mentioned in Chapter I.

But what of the alternative explanations to precognition? Let us look at four of them.

PK as a Cause of the Predicted Event. Precognition so defies our normal philosophical assumptions about cause and effect that a few investigators have suggested that a person uses PK to fulfill a prediction. A great deal of malice would be implied here, especially in predictions of plane or car crashes. However, the weakness of the theory is found in the fact that people have predicted volcanic eruptions and earthquakes, the temperature on a future given date, and events to come after their own lifetimes. We have little evidence that a subject by using PK may cause an assistant to pick a certain card. But that natural phenomena such as volcanos and temperature over a fairly wide range are subject to PK processes seems contrary to the evidence which we do possess. PK certainly does not stand as a reasonable explanation for many correct paranormal predictions.

The Subliminal Computer Theory. As presented by Herbert Greenhouse, this theory postulates that at very deep levels of the psyche there is a kind of computer that *clairvoyantly* scans the "etheric pool."[22] This is a dimension where many minds come together and where the totality of knowledge is stored. The mind then makes rapid calculations and extrapolates an event that will later take place. Finally the "playwright mind" takes over and dramatizes the extrapolation. This theory actually denies the existence of precognition, but it relies heavily on a postulated kind of remarkable telepathy and clairvoyance.

There is no question that many apparent precognitive events may be explained by a kind of subliminal knowledge. For example, before retiring I subliminally and inadvertently notice that one of the tires on my car is very low. I dream of crashing and, in fact, this happens the next day due to the flattening tire. However, the theory fails as a universal explanation of precognition. It cannot satisfactorily explain the laboratory experiments. Certainly they cannot be explained by extrapolated telepathy and clairvoyance. Second, the anecdotal tradition provides many examples of events, like plane crashes, which are so far in the future and so varied in causes that present knowledge, even paranormally obtained, cannot explain the precognition.

Déjà vu. Déjà vu itself is not an explanation. In fact, one explanation of déjà vu is that it is the result of forgotten precognitive dreams.

The Backward Flow of Time in Physics. To handle this question in depth, one would have to be both a professional scientist and a professional philosopher. Here, I wish merely to sketch a few salient points. British psychologist John Beloff has presented a defense of "backward causation."[23] Backward causation, at least, cannot be dismissed on logical grounds alone, and some experimenters are taking it seriously. Beloff says that although we cannot alter the past in the sense of making something to have happened which did not in fact happen, it does not follow that what did happen might never have happened or might have happened differently but for certain later events. There is a distinction between altering the past and influencing the past.

This resembles an approach used by many theologians like St. Thomas when they have attempted to explain the effects of prayer, even of prayer after something has happened. However, in the theologian's world, there is a variable which is not included in the scientist's world—God. I might mention here a clue to solving the dilemma raised by many in the face of precognition: if the future is known, then we are not free, for it is determined. Knowledge of the future does not determine the future. It is the agents whose effects are seen who determine the future.

However, if backward causation is not an *a priori* illogical concept, is there evidence for its existence in reality? Physicists speak of what they called "advanced potentials" in quantum mechanics. Each point in space contains some information about the whole of space. Perhaps this is true also of time where each point in time contains some information about time future and time past. If an electric current is cut off, two precursor waves go ahead of the cutoff event. One goes at the speed of light, but the other is slowed down. Thus one can get information from the first precursor wave, even if the event does not occur because it is deflected. Similarly waves may precede events and give precognitive information.

The discussion of this point is beyond the scope of this book and my abilities. However, as the parapsychologist K. Ramakrishna Rao points out, quantum theories of psi assume "that the underlying unpredictability at the quantum level may be extended to nonquantum situations. It should be remembered that while quantum theory explains certain anomalies at the subatomic level, as far as the world of our experience is concerned its implications are hardly different from those of classical physics. So any extension of quantum principles to explain the phenomena at the level of our experience is no less inconsistent with quantum theory than it is with classical physics."[24] The existence of a precursor wave arriving a tiny fraction of a second ahead of an event's impact seems unable to explain knowledge of an event hours, days or months ahead of its occurrence. Research in this area will certainly be of interest for precognition studies, but as of present these theories do not seem sufficient to explain most precognitive events.

Spirits or God as the Cause of Precognition

It is not my intention to deny that spirits, living outside of our time, or God himself might be the cause of precognitive knowledge. However, the direct action of God or spirits should not be postulated unless there is some sign of their presence. We have no sign that God or spirits "intervene" in card tests in university laboratories, or in dice throwing procedures, or in dream tests. Furthermore, if they did, why are the predictions not correct one hundred percent of the time? The special action of spirits or God cannot be postulated as a general rule to explain precognition.

Models Used for Precognition

We cannot explain the exact nature of precognition, for it remains mysterious. However, certain models have been offered which may aid us in approaching the subject in an orderly fashion. Some of the models which I believe are the most coherent are the following.

Synchronicity. C.G. Jung presented his theory of synchronicity as a kind of "a-causal orderedness which lies behind phenomena." This "a-causal" (i.e., not causal in our known physical sense) "orderedness" is a type of ordering power which has two loci of operation, one in the psyche and one in the external world. While an admirer of many of Jung's broad positions, I find that this model is not of great assistance, though it may contain a truth. In a sense, it offers a new word for precognition without advancing our investigation very far.

The Theory of Two Kinds of Time. The physicist Raynor Johnson presents a theory which has been held by many philosophers and theologians. There are two times, time 1 and time 2. Time 2 is really the Eternal Now. If time 2 is seen as a dot in the middle of a circle and time 1 is seen as any point on the circle, all points in time 1 are equally distant from time 2. (Notice that time 2 could be a different kind of time or it could be the Eternal Now, the vision of God as it were.) Part of man exists in this dimension of time 2. When under hypnosis or in the alpha state, man receives glimpses from the part of him which is in time 2. This is precognition. There are many variations of this theory. It makes a great deal of sense but it needs certain qualifications.

Take, for example, the anecdotal case in which a woman places her child in a crib under a chandelier before she retires.[25] While sleeping, she dreams that there is a violent storm and the child is crushed by the chandelier as it falls from the ceiling. She rises and moves the child. The clock on the child's dresser says 4:35, and there is a full moon. Then she returns to sleep. She is awakened by a loud crash. During a storm the chandelier has been loosened and has fallen. The child would have been killed had it been left there. The clock reads 4:35 and there is a storm raging. In another anecdotal case, a woman dreams she has brought her little girl on a picnic by the side of a lake. She turns and sees it. But she is too late. The child drowns. Later, this same scene unfolds, except that she now turns in time to see the child and is able to rescue it before it drowns. Because of such cases, the following theory was developed.

The Theory of Three Times. J.B. Priestley developed the theory of three times.[26] Time 1 is present chronological time. Time 3 is the real future. Time 2 is an intermediate time, a kind of pliant time which is like putty. It grants certain glimpses of the future already shaped but somewhat pliant. Its actualization can be achieved by any actions we may take.

This theory was developed to handle cases like the ones I have mentioned. However, I believe a simpler explanation exists which allows us to dispense with the unnecessarily complicated "pliant time." What is it, if it is not to be real? Let us say that there are but two times, time 1 and time 2. We know that in ESP in general, and in religious matters like those involved in Divine revelation or inspiration, man often embroiders with his own imagination either the genuine ESP message or the divine message. In religious communications this principle was strongly held by two masters, St. John of the Cross and St. Ignatius of Loyola.[27] In an analogous fashion, a person may have a precognitive experience while awake or dreaming. The vision may come, as so often happens, in a fragmented fashion or in a symbol. The person having the experience, which is genuinely precognitive, may add details from his or her own imagination to fill in the picture in order to obtain a gestalt, or a complete picture. These details are embroidering which comes from one's imagination rather than elements from some strange dimension of pliant time. The details added would depend on the type of personality one possesses, e.g., optimistic or pessimistic. This theory at least may be tested. I prefer it as the best explanation of precognition while adhering to the theory of two kinds of time.

The two-time theory seems to be the best model to use in approaching precognition. Priestley says that in time 2 we do not go beyond the grave. The brain ceases to supply us with information and we move out of history. Our home, he says, is in time 3 (or time 2 in my presentation). Many philosophers, apart from studies of precognition, hold such a position. For example, the late philosopher Peter Koestenbaum in *The New Image of the Person* based his theory of man on the reality of two selves, an empirical self and a transcendental self. Jung postulated an ego and a deeper self, the individual self and a Collective Self. Mystics from all ages, East and West, have held a similar position.

If these ideas have substance, and they seem to correlate a vast amount of data, then we would have to say that there is only an egg-shell thickness between us and some mysterious world. "Radial man" begins to emerge. Michael Foucault suggests that "man as we know him was invented in the late 18th century and we are approaching a time when he will disappear and a new understanding of ourselves will emerge."[28] The model of man as a certain quantity of chemicals in a vial with a definite cash value now seems like a joke. Part of man seems to exist in a dimension beyond the limits of space-time as we have known them. We are thus forced into the domains of philosophical and religious questions. If there is genuine precognition, and if the alternative explanations are deficient, this seems to be a logical move and not an *ad hoc* position brought in for religious purposes.

Precognition and Prophecy

Let us now turn our attention to the religious notion of prophecy and to the Bible. I believe that the existence of precognition as a human phenomenon may help us to solve some long-standing and perplexing problems with regard to prophecy in the Bible. However, before we begin to discuss biblical prophecy, it will be necessary to say a few words about the notions of biblical inspiration and revelation.

In the United States Fundamentalism has surfaced in a most visible and influential phenomenon in recent years. I have no intention of launching an emotional attack on Fundamentalism. Fundamentalists share many beliefs with other Christians as part of their central vision. Moderate theologians differ with Fundamentalists without rejecting their central belief in Jesus as the revelation of God. In order to secure their beliefs, however,

Fundamentalists adopt a position toward the Bible which most theologians, including Catholic theologians, do not adopt. They see the Bible as the direct word of God which is so received that the human contribution is negligible. Some have held that the Bible is the direct word-for-word dictation of divine revelation to men. Some hold rather that it is the direct transfer of ideas from God to mankind, though the words may be the result of human selection. This concept of the Bible does not give evidence of standing up to modern critical study of the Bible, even in its moderate form. It should be noted that one's idea of revelation is not merely an academic question. Conservative notions of revelation have influenced Ayatollah Khomeini's policy in Iran, the actions of groups of conservative Jews in Israel, the role of women in religion, ideas of the Moral Majority in the United States, and probably even some decisions of Ronald Reagan. I propose the model below as a paradigm for God's way of acting with human beings.

Yahweh or God→Prophet or Jesus, or New Testament Author

{A. *experience or message from "the Nameless one"*
{B. *additions from one's own personal culture and world-view*

1. All prophecy and revelation involve A and B above. Fundamentalists, in the main, reject this view and hold only A above. Non-Fundamentalist theologians hold that B is required in order to explain what seem to be changes in aspects of revelation. For example, the picture of God evolves from a vindictive God in some parts of the Old Testament, a God who even orders the Israelites to slay whole towns, men, women and children, to the image of God pictured in Jesus' parable of the prodigal son. The biblical picture evolves from one in which either nothing or only a shadowy existence awaits man after death, to belief in the immortality of the soul, to belief in ultimate resurrection. The Old Testament originally sees retribution for sin as occurring on this earth. Retribution affects a whole nation directly in such a way that, when a nation suffers, it can be said that it is the result of its own sins. Or when a child suffers it can be said to be the result of the father's sins ("I have never seen a virtuous man deserted or his descendants forced to

beg their bread"—Ps 37:25). However, Ezekiel rather sees each one suffering only for his or her own sins, thus rejecting the proverb, "The fathers have eaten sour grapes, and the children's teeth are set on edge" (18:2). Job calls this opinion into question and struggles with God (i.e., the notion of revelation) over this point. Finally Jesus denies that it is a general rule that physical suffering is the direct result of personal sin. "Or those eighteen upon whom the tower in Siloam fell and killed them, do you think that they were worse offenders than all the others who dwelt in Jerusalem? I tell you, no" (Lk 13:4). "Your Father who is in heaven . . . makes his sun rise on the evil and on the good, and sends rain on the just and the unjust" (Mt 5:46). Many other such examples might be pointed out.[29]

To most theologians, this evolution is seen not as the direct result of God's revelation. Does God change his message? Rather the evolution is the result of man's growth in the understanding of God. Man colors the revelation with ideas or prejudices drawn from the culture in which he lives.[30] During a period when a sense of vengeance is strong, humans color their reception of God's communication with ideas already existing in their own minds. As I have said before, this is a principle which the spiritual masters of all ages have used in discerning mystical illuminations, visions and inspirations. It is the function of the living Church to discern what is from God and what is from man alone. This process does not cease with the Old Testament. It continues into the New Testament and, in fact, down to our own day.

As far as I can see, Fundamentalists totally reject this idea. Rather, they say that God gradually changed his revelation to accommodate the level of the minds and hearts of the people he was dealing with. He "accommodates" to their weaknesses and "condescends" to their ignorance. The position one chooses here will have decisive influence on one's theory of biblical prophecy.

2. *Revelation* consists in the experience or message from the "Holy Mystery" as Rahner calls God, as in "A" above. However, intertwined with this, there are usually elements which have their source in human limitation and cultural differences, as in "B" above. It is for this reason that most Catholic theologians

today make a distinction between divine *revelation* and prophetic
or biblical *inspiration*. Inspiration is the result of the movement
produced by God to *speak* about God (prophetic inspiration) or to
write down a record of God's dealings with mankind (biblical
inspiration). These latter will almost inevitably contain elements
which are humanly and culturally derived. It is not an easy
matter to discern what is essential to the divine experience and
what is human cultural accretion. The whole Bible as well as
prophetic speech is seen as inspired, an inspired record but one
which may also include strictly human elements. However, the
entire Bible is not seen as a collection of "revealed" statements.
The Bible witnesses to revelation and embodies revelation. But
the entire Bible is not revelation strictly so called, unless we
mean by this a record of the way revelation has evolved. Some
inspired parts of that record we do not accept as the revelation
of God, e.g., that evil is always punished in this world, or that
God at times wants vengeance, or that we do not know whether
man lives after death, as Qoheleth implies.

Fundamentalists, on the other hand, maintain that everything in the Bible is revealed. For them, inspiration and revelation are identical. It is for this reason that many Fundamentalists
reject form criticism. Form criticism maintains that parts of the
New Testament, for example, existed as fragments, and that
differing fragments about the same event could exist which
reflected not only historical facts but also the differing interests
of the varying New Testament communities.[31] They also generally reject redaction criticism. According to redaction criticism
the New Testament authors, for example, were not simply recording messages which they received directly from God, but
were also editors or "redactors" of the already traditional fragments. These forms or fragments they arranged like beads on a
rosary in the order they thought important and aesthetically
pleasing. This method, while not distorting essential historical
facts, makes exact chronological dating extremely difficult; and
the coloring of events and statements makes finding the exact
historical words of Jesus most difficult in many cases, though we
can recover the essential thrust of his message. For example,
Jesus could not have said to the Jews what Mark, writing for
Romans, has Jesus say, "A wife may not divorce her husband."

This statement would have been unintelligible to the Jews, as a Jewish woman had no right to divorce her husband, though the husband had such a right.[32]

With these preliminary remarks, we can now return to the question of biblical prophecy and its possible relation to precognition. There is no doubt that some of the Old Testament prophecies foreshadowed in a remarkable way the life of Jesus. Recall, for example, the image of the suffering servant in Isaiah 52:13. However, to say this is not to accept the point for point fulfillment held by many Fundamentalist scholars. I think modern scholarly opinion might be roughly summed up in the words of John McKenzie, "Does the Old Testament point to Christ? We cannot accept the idea that the Old Testament is a collection of clues which point to him: but it points to the ultimate fulfillment of the power and will of God for good. It hopes for something to which Jesus is the answer."[33] The suffering servant section in Isaiah might involve more than this. Yet the prophecies in the Old Testament about the future messianic kingdom are not the most clear sections to choose for an application of the notion of precognition.

It is true that there are many examples of precognition in the Old Testament which were fulfilled in a remarkable manner.[34] To choose two very specific ones, Jeremiah confronts the prophet Hananiah and predicts his death within a year (28:16). And so it happened. Ezekiel in Babylon had precognition of the death of his wife in Jerusalem (24:18). Many prophets correctly predicted the fall of the northern kingdom of Israel, and Jeremiah and Ezekiel correctly predicted the fall of Judah.

However, many of the prophet's predictions were never literally fulfilled. As Dr. Boyce Bennett, Jr., states, "For instance, in the 8th century B.C. Isaiah predicts the destruction and fall of Jerusalem, but when the Assyrians invade a few years later, Jerusalem is *not* taken after all. . . . Furthermore in the 6th century B.C. Ezekiel prophesied that Tyre would fall to Nebuchadnezzar, and although Nebuchadnezzar besieged Tyre for thirteen years, it did *not* fall to him. Ezekiel prophesied that Egypt would fall to Nebuchadnezzar but that never happened."

Scholars often approach difficulties like these by claiming: (a) a prophet's real role was to speak forth God's message and to challenge people to right living rather than to predict—the prophet was a forthteller rather than a foreteller; (b) prophetic messages are often symbolical and quite enigmatic; (c) in prophetic prediction, there is often a "foreshortening" or telescoping of perspective. Like a man who sees three mountains from another mountain top, the prophet cannot tell how far apart they are and judges them much closer together than they really are. These are sound exegetical principles of interpretation, and I have no intention of denying their validity for various prophecies.

But they do not touch the heart of our problem. Some prophecies were not fulfilled. And even though it is quite true and of paramount importance that the prophet was *predominantly* one who spoke forth for *Yahweh* and not a predictor, still prophets *did predict*. It is also a fact that the faithful in the Old Testament were upset when these predictions did not come true.[35] They did not always seem to take them symbolically in some wide sense.

The Old Testament was actually plagued by the problem of false prophets. (Ezekiel 13:8: "Therefore thus says the Lord God: 'Because you have uttered delusions and seen lies, therefore behold I am against you,' says the Lord God.") The only norms they had for distinguishing true prophets from false prophets were, first, did the prophet believe in Yahweh, and second, did the prophecy come true? (Dt 18:31).

There is a difficult problem here upon which parapsychology may shed some light. Let us use the general paradigm I have presented above with regard to revelation and apply it to prophecy. Perhaps in Old Testament prophecy there were two strands, (a) a message from Yahweh, and (b) human, fallible precognition. The prophets themselves would have been unaware of this distinction. In the meditative state in which they received God's burning communication about serving him, they were also open to precognitive experiences.[36] These they joined with the prophetic message from God, thus uniting a divine experience with a startling but at times fallible precognitive power. We would thus account for the burning experience of the divine, plus correct predictions, as well as predictions which were not fulfilled.

The New Testament

Jesus himself made some striking predictions about the future. He predicted that Peter would deny him three times before the cock crowed (Mark 14:30 says "twice"). He predicted the destruction of Jerusalem. This is true, even if we hold with many scriptural scholars that some of the more exact details were inserted *post eventum* (after the event). Jesus is said in the New Testament to have predicted his resurrection. This is an open question. Many balanced scholars, such as Raymond Brown, believe that Jesus did predict some final triumph of God through him, but that the more concrete and specific details of his resurrection predictions were added afterward by the evangelists.[37] The chief reason he holds this is not because he does not believe in prophecy as prediction. Rather the reason he gives is that, if such exact predictions were given, it would be totally surprising that, after the death of Jesus, the disciples seemed to expect no such thing. They were in despair. Had they simply forgotten such marvelous predictions? The solution seems to be that Jesus did indeed predict some triumph, but that after the event the evangelists made these details more specific in the light of the resurrection itself. Here we are certainly in the area of probability only. Yet this approach makes much sense. Jesus did have precognitive power as we have said, but on the resurrection it was limited to a general conviction about the triumph of the Father in him.

Jesus also predicted the "coming of the Son of Man" in the Kingdom. In Matthew 16:28 he says, "Truly, I say to you, there are some standing here who will not taste death before they see the Son of Man coming in his Kingdom." Scholarly opinion today is that the "Kingdom" is a many-leveled symbol.[38] It involved something already present (as shown in Jesus' parables), events still to come (the resurrection, the destruction of the temple), and some final event under whose shadow all history unfolds (the final triumph of God).

Jesus may have been like the man standing on the mountain top who was unable to judge the distance between the other peaks he saw. He seems to have shared the opinion of his time that the final coming was imminent, at least within the lifetime of those listening to him.[39] The imminent coming of the Son of Man was not a false prediction. He did come in the world-shaking event of the resurrection. However, the expectations that the final coming and the other events would roughly coincide were not fulfilled.

However, all these predictions are so intertwined by the Gospel writers that scholars conclude that they themselves probably did not understand them, and thus we may never be able to arrive at Jesus' exact predictions. Discussions of Jesus' exact precognitive powers in this area, therefore, are unproductive.

Still, Jesus himself shared in some of the presuppositions of his time. Even his unique relationship with his Father did not erase the human elements in his unique experience of his divine center. If this is true of Jesus, it would be much more true of the prophets of the Old Testament. As Gabriel Moran has put it, "Jesus' presence to the Logos did not provide any objective communicable knowledge," that is, knowledge of the events of history.[40]

I am proposing that Jesus had precognitive power which may have been a human power. The Old Testament prophets had human precognitive powers. This at times was mingled with the experience of the divine which they underwent. The result was a burning divine experience which for thousands of years has spoken to the hearts of men, together with human predictions, some of which were fulfilled and some not. The picture is a coherent one, and I believe this is an insight which emerges from the study of parapsychological evidence.

Modern Predictions Connected with the Bible

As we approach the year 2000, an avalanche of predictions is descending upon us about some great but disastrous events which are about to come. These events, it is claimed, were explicitly foretold in the Bible. Hal Lindsey, whose books such as *The Late Great Planet Earth, There's a New World Coming,* and *Armageddon* have been read by millions, is convinced of this. Lindsey bases his convictions on the Book of Revelation or the

Apocalypse. The Book of Revelation, he believes, predicts Armageddon shortly. The Apocalypse in 20:7 refers to Ezekiel 38 and 39 where it is predicted that Gog (the lands near the Black Sea) will invade Israel but will be defeated by Israel in a massacre. In chapter 20 Satan has been said to have been cast into a huge pit for one thousand years. "Then when the thousand years are over, Satan will be released from his prison, and will set out to deceive the nations in the four corners of the earth, Gog and Magog, and to lead them to battle. . . . They encircled the army of the saints defending the beloved city. But fire came down from the sky and consumed them." As Lindsey interprets the Book of Revelation, Russia will invade Israel, the West will become involved, and China will enter, but the West will finally win. Then will come the final judgment.

As many people today are reading these prophecies, it seems worthwhile to say a few words on this question. First, remember that in the revelatory experience of Jesus there is no timetable of these events. It is not clear that the signs which he does mention refer to the destruction of Jerusalem only or to the final end also. In fact, Luke in Acts 1:7 presents Jesus as saying to them, "It is not for you to know the times or seasons which the Father has fixed by his own authority."

Second, down through the ages the Book of Revelation has been interpreted countless times as referring to a given day and year, whether the year be 1000, 1524, 1665, 1736, 1843, or 1945.[41] The knowledge of history makes one rather wary of such predictions, although the cry of wolf may not always be false.

Third, Revelation or the Apocalypse begins, "The revelation of Jesus Christ which God gave him to show to his servants what must soon take place." "Soon" Lindsey interprets as "suddenly." The book ends, "Surely, I am coming soon." Literally, at least, these words do not prepare us for an event two thousand years later.

Lastly, most biblical scholars see the Book of Revelation as a book which falls within the literary genre of "apocalyptic." Some of the characteristics of apocalyptic are: (1) it is written during a time of persecution; (2) it contains a code encased in a number of symbols; (3) there is a stylistic use of surrealistic, cosmic visions offering a message about end-time, culminating in a great battle between God and anti-God; (4) the purpose is to inculcate the conviction that all stands under the transcendent power of God. Many of these "visions" refer to events which have already happened but which are placed in the future. Thus, apocalyptic is not primarily prophecy in the sense of prediction, and I did not consider it previously under predictive prophecy.

To understand the *literal* sense of a book of the Bible, one must consider not only the text, but the context, that is, its literary genre. Thus, John's Apocalypse refers primarily to the time of the Roman emperor Domitian, circa 90–96 A.D. The beast with the blasphemous name may be the Roman emperors who bore the name "Augustus" or divine. The number 666, which is the number of the beast, probably refers to Nero. The numerical value of the Hebrew letters of *Neron Caesar* adds up to 666. Domitian would be Nero come back to life. The seven heads of the beast would refer to the seven hills of Rome. Thus, the Apocalypse predominantly refers to events contemporary with the early Christian persecutions. It is a book of trust and hope offered to a people in great suffering. Daniel, to which it refers, similarly is related to the contemporary persecutions by Antiochus IV Epiphanes who desecrated the Jerusalem temple about 167 B.C.

But is there not in the Apocalypse a prediction about some final triumph of God, and might it not refer to our own day? It is true that apocalyptic writings placed the visions about the outcome of contemporary events within the framework of some final victory of God. Lindsey takes the signs mentioned by Jesus, which may have referred to events preceding the destruction of Jerusalem, and finds these signs fulfilled today. This he sees as an indication that the end is at hand. But from the Book of Revelation it is impossible to make any predictions about times or dates of God's final triumph in history. Lindsey's conclusions are based on many weak and false presuppositions.

Not a Religious Prophecy But Precognition?

However, we have a spate of predictions circulating today which predict some great cataclysm to come within the last two decades of the twentieth century. Edgar Cayce said there would be a shifting of the poles, countries would slide into the sea, and Atlantis would arise. These earth changes would occur between 1958 and 1998 or 2001.[42] Jeane Dixon said that in the mid-1980's a comet would strike the earth and there would be a great tidal wave. Cheiro (Count Louis Hamon) made some remarkable predictions about world events in 1931. These included predictions of the Spanish Civil War, World War II and a civil war in Ireland between the North and the South. Finally he predicted Armageddon in which Russia would in some way be involved. In 1790 an anonymous Polish monk predicted a universal world war beginning in 1938, peace in 1986, and in 1998 a terrible comet which would strike the earth and cause great disruption. There would be an earthquake in which many countries would vanish, and finally in the year 2000 the Lord will come to judge the living and the dead.[43] Finally, Nostradamus predicted that "in the year 1999 and seven months, from the skies shall come an alarmingly powerful king . . . and Mars will reign at will."[44]

What are we to make of this convergence of predictions? My only definite conclusion is that, whatever happens in the future, one cannot assert that there is an explicit prediction of these events in the Book of Revelation. Apart from reference to the Bible, we move into another shaky area. Are most of these authors returning to one source, Nostradamus, and adding details of their own? It seems unlikely that Edgar Cayce, at any rate, is using Nostradamus. His predictions, made in a trance, often contradict his conscious knowledge, and he seems to need no one to lean upon. Is it possible that what we are involved with here is not some revelation from God, but perhaps a kind of convergence of human precognition, working deep in the unconscious of mankind, which, in a kind of "synchronicity," is catching something from time 2, a time warp, as it were, which leaks occasionally into time 1? I am not proposing this possibility as my conclusion. We simply don't know. In view of some world events which were predicted accurately long ago, it might be a mistake to wave away all these predictions as total nonsense. However, while predictions are at times incredibly on the mark, they are much more often totally wrong.

We have no rule to use in distinguishing between what is

false and what is true in precognitive study. There was a convergence of doomsday predictions toward the end of the eighth and ninth centuries which were totally erroneous. But is today's convergence different, preceded as it has been by some accurate (as well as false) predictions about the forerunners of this event? We do not know the significance of this convergence. Many scholars maintain that Jesus himself did not foresee his ultimate triumph in any clear detail, and that he might have been surprised by the resurrection. If there is any truth to the present confluence of predictions about a great coming event, I suspect that even the predictors will be surprised by the real events. God's ways are not our ways, said Isaiah.

Some Conclusions

Some form of precognition has been made almost certain by laboratory tests and by spontaneous cases. But God need not be thought of as intervening in a special way in precognition. Does God intervene in card tests? Precognition seems to be a human power (ultimately resting on God's presence in the universe). Apart from a small core of genuine precognition, most predictions come from some human emotion like wishful thinking, yearning or fear. Precognition is not a useful basis for *practical,* day-to-day living. Even the predictor does not know infallibly when he will be right and when he will be wrong.

But the fact that precognition seems to be a reality is of great importance in a larger sense. Precognition, and reflection on its meaning, frees us from the imprisoning box in which secular man has lived since the Enlightenment. What we see is not all there is. Time itself is incredibly mysterious. Materialism, at least in the old form in which we have known it, cannot handle precognition. Part of us, it seems, is outside of time, or is capable of assimilating another kind of time. We now have empirical evidence to support this ancient conviction.

Let me conclude with a final word on the connection between precognition and a special theological movement today. I speak of process theology. What can we make of process theology's claim that God in his consequent nature does not know the future? Process theology says that there are two aspects in God, his primordial nature and his consequent nature. The primordial nature is "unconscious," outside of time and eternal. The consequent nature is our silent companion. God in his consequent nature arises with us each day to share our joys and sufferings. The events in our lives are novelties to him as well as to us.

Admittedly, my swift sketch is an inadequate presentation of a very subtle theology, and one which I find very attractive. However, process theology must face the question arising from this chapter. If man knows the future at times, how can God, even in his consequent nature, not know the future? Perhaps there are logical answers to this question, but it is a question which process theology must address to maintain its coherence.

My main point in this chapter has been that the study of paranormal cognition offers clues which might help us solve the prickly problem of biblical prophecy in its predictive aspects. On the more general level, precognitive study suggests that there are dimensions in human beings which either dwell within or are open to levels of reality which are beyond our ordinary space-time continuum. This inference certainly has profound theological ramifications.

Chapter VI

Retrocognition

Retrocognition is the knowledge of the past through no known means. Retrocognition has not been studied with the depth or sophistication found in precognition studies. In this chapter I will present some examples of this phenomenon together with the various theories offered to explain it. Most of the evidence is of the anecdotal variety, although some controlled study has been made by experts.

Alleged Retrocognition Cases

Our bookstores are filled with the books of Jane Roberts— *The Seth Material, Seth Speaks,* etc. Jane Roberts enters a trance. She changes her facial expression and begins to speak in the role of an ancient male figure of wisdom, Seth. Seth is a long-winded pedant who makes you listen because of his occasional diamond. He seems to be Gnostic in some sense. Personally, I believe Seth is an excellent example of the Jungian archetype, the wise old man, and the persona. Jane Roberts *writes* her material, and these books are rather good examples of "automatic writing" which we will discuss under "mediumship." However, we are not given data which would enable us to make a judgment as to whether Seth was a real person in the past. Jane Roberts' books cannot be used as examples of retrocognition. They might, however, be useful instruments for studying the unconscious, as Seth seems to me to be Jane Roberts' "deeper Self."

Edgar Cayce (1877–1945) was both a healer and a predictor. He also gave some details about Essene life which later were found to be generally correct with the discovery of the Dead Sea Scrolls.[1] Cayce presented excellent pictures of Old Testament and New Testament life, but he had read the Bible. We have no means of verifying his claim that Jesus went to India and Egypt or that Jesus was educated by Essenes. His prophecies about great land-sea changes in the world between 1968 and 1998 have not yet been verified, although some ruins have been discovered which could match his predictions that Atlantis would begin to rise in the Bahamas. Stephan Schwarz in *The Secret Vaults of Time* has given some indications of Cayce's accuracy as evidenced in recent archeological digging. However, there are also many discrepancies, and only further excavation can settle the question. Thus, Cayce also cannot at present be considered as an example of genuine retrocognition.

The Patience Worth Case

In 1913 a St. Louis housewife, Mrs. Pearl Curran, through a ouija board received the message, "Many moons ago I lived. Patience Worth is my name."[2] Patience Worth had the character of an astringent, caustic wit with an "unusual creative power and unparalleled spontaneity of production." She spoke in a strange composite of languages which resembled early English. Ninety percent of the words were Anglo-Saxon and ten percent were old French. She claimed to have lived in the first half of the seventeenth century in England. All objects mentioned came from that period. Her speech had no modern idiom. She spoke of the "me-o-me" as the essence of man. The soul was called the "inman." At great speed she delivered poems and proverbs, and even dictated many books at once. A number of novels showed detailed familiarity with the customs, clothing and topography of Palestine. *The Sorry Tale* was said by *The New York Times* to have given an excellent picture of the Roman world when the Empire was at its height. A recognized historian, Professor Usher of Washington University, wrote of *The Sorry Tale*, "They seem to be, inside as well as outside, men and women of the years when Christ was on earth."[3] Scholars agreed that a lifetime of reading would be required for such verisimilitude.

This might have been a case of genuine retrocognition. Yet, even though Patience Worth emerged as a personality from a previous time, many psychologists believe that she represented the unconscious of Pearl Curran. Mrs. Curran once wrote a novel while not under the influence of Patience Worth, in which the main character developed a secondary personality and said, "Well, I just didn't want to be me. I was sick of myself."[4] The language of the Patience Worth scripts has never been identified as any known language. Furthermore, the case does not offer sufficient evidence of paranormal knowledge of the past to rank it as an example of genuine retrocognition. However, if it is not a case of retrocognition, it is a striking example of the power of the unconscious mind.

Patience Worth's phraseology remains in the mind. Asked whether God set aside his laws at the prayer of his creatures, she replied, "Yea, and hark, much word o' prayer be but words, and he doth list not unto the word. Nay, he knoweth e'en the mite whose wings-whirr be all o' its voice."[5]

Because it may be an excellent example of the creativity of the unconscious, I quote a passage which was tossed off rapidly and which reminds us of Teilhard de Chardin. Asked about "relativity," she replied: "What be the harmony in this thing? It be but the law of harmony, which wert the first law. . . . Look ye' upon it—this honey of God which holdeth one atom unto another and keepeth the universes spinning each in its own orbit, and outstrippeth man's imagination—this magic, which hath planted in each man, that which is kindred with God, which maketh man to itch at conquest, to fret at the fetters of flesh—aye, and maketh his spirit to leap free of its fetters, for it is unfettered, limited only by man's own limitations, his egotry—which undoeth his humility—this thing a man hath called a mouthing word, aye, and hath forgot that God writ that simple law in the first urge of the first atom, and left the magic of his being as the honey which hangeth all things together."[6] When asked whether women should express themselves or stay home and work for the race, a poem came forth which might have special relevance today:

When labor is done (the wench-taskies),
What bit it that a thirsted soul sup;
That it sing; that it expand,
That it give forth?

The tide hath gone
(And I may say, with a thank)
It hath gone when a wench be bound in a kirtle,
Ribboned and shoon by law.

Behold! Womankind shall lead,
Yea, with a sweet intuition,
Shall pierce, shall expand,
Shall hold a taper unto deeper vasts
That men may e'er stumble upon.
For womankind goeth through the valley of death
In darkness, with no taper for to lighten,
Leading men to the brink of day;
And he, finding the day made perfect
Through the agony of womankind,
Struts![7]

Genuine Retrocognition Cases?

Geraldine Cummins (d. 1970) was an Irish psychic whose work we will discuss under mediumship. She practiced automatic writing, but while retaining full consciousness, like Mrs. Curran. Through automatic writing and at top speed, she wrote a history of the New Testament, *The Scripts of Cleophas,* and a volume on the Book of Acts, *Paul in Athens.* These scripts were given to Dr. W. Oesterle, a Scripture scholar at Cambridge, but he was not told their source. He thought they were an excellent, scientifically researched, work on life in Palestine at the time of Christ. Geraldine had no special learning in this period. Yet she knew, for example, "Archon" as the name for the head of the Jewish community in Antioch, even though, only shortly before the period she described, "Ethnarch" had been the title. Only an unusually careful and profound student could have known this.

The messages claimed that they came from Cleophas who guided seven scribes and from a chronicle known in the early Church but only to a few. Geraldine said the history was plucked from the Great Memory, not as it actually happened but as it was remembered by man.[8] Cleophas, strangely, seemed unacquainted with the things on earth, for example, the invention of printing, and he did not know those parts of "Holy Writ" that have been preserved. Whatever the explanation of Mrs. Cummins' work, some element of the paranormal seems to have been involved.

Stephan Ossowiecki (1877–1944), a Polish engineer, could touch an object and be flooded with correct images about its handlers.[9] The use of objects to compute knowledge of the past is called psychometry. Ossowiecki gave details of pre-historic man, some of which were verified a number of years later. For example, he described some stones as seats from the Magdalenian period around Paris, and he seemed to be mistaken when he described oil lamps as from the same period. Yet both statements turned out to be correct, as well as countless other details. Ossowiecki was carefully studied by Drs. Richet and Geley in France. Ossowiecki predicted his own death, and he was massacred with many other Poles on August 4, 1944 at the Gestapo headquarters in Warsaw. This is a carefully studied case of genuine retrocognition. Ossowiecki gave as his source "consciousness of the one Spirit."

Maria Reyes de Zierold was tested by the German doctor, Gustav Pagenstecher, who lived in Mexico, and by Walter Prince, an experienced American psychic investigator. Given a piece of pumice stone whose origin she did not know, she vividly re-enacted the great volcanic eruption of Vesuvius at Pompeii. Shortly after World War I, she was given a piece of string which had been attached to some dog tags worn by a German soldier. She said, "It is intensely cold and the day is foggy. . . . I am in a battlefield, it smells of gunpowder. In front of me a tall man standing, with a big gray overcoat on, which reaches to his feet. Behind him I see three men standing likewise. They talk German, or better said, they shout. . . . Quite of a sudden I see coming through the air, and moving with great rapidity, a big red ball of fire . . . which drops just in the middle of the fifteen men, tearing them to pieces. . . ." Sergeant Saenger, who had worn the dog tags, verified the incident.[10]

Beginning in 1907, Frederick Bligh Bond, an eccentric curator of the Glastonbury Chapel in England, through automatic writing discovered the existence and dimensions of the ruins of part of the early monastery.[11] The existence of these ruins had been known to no living person. He gave a history of the site with much information which was verified by later digging. The scripts came through in Latin, allegedly presented by the monks who lived in the monastery. Bond believed there was a "kind of universal species memory bank" in which information is stored in "computer books" in a personality form.

Even though retrocognition has not been studied with the same intense effort as has been invested in the study of precognition, those who are interested in the real certainly cannot dismiss this apparent power as fraudulent or as of no importance. The evidence for retrocognition is impressive and growing. Furthermore, a knowledge of retrocognition is important for understanding some of the topics which I will discuss later, such as mediumship and reincarnation.

Some Theories Offered To Explain Retrocognition

1. *Cryptomnesia.* This term signifies perceptions which were once had but which are totally forgotten. They are brought back to memory by some new happening. Cryptomnesia certainly does explain many strange phenomena such as speaking phrases in unknown languages. But it is not relevant as an explanation for the cases I have mentioned.

2. *Psychometry.* This is a type of clairvoyance by which one receives knowledge of the past through contact with some physical object. This may imply that a psychic pattern exists around everything that happens. Psychometry may well be involved in much retrocognition, but it does not apply to the case of Geraldine Cummins where no such object was involved. Furthermore, as D. Scott Rogo points out, if the object is destroyed, or if the person who contributed the object dies, the contact often con-

tinues. Therefore, something more seems to be demanded to explain psychometry. The object itself seems to act only as a catalyst.

3. *A Contact with "The Great Memory" or with Some Form of the Collective Unconscious.* Ossowiecki and Bligh maintained some such position. This reminds us of the "Akashic Records" on which all that has happened is written, a concept found in many civilizations. This is one coherent explanation of retrocognition, remarkable though it is. The objection often presented is that this is to explain the unknown by the unknown.

4. *Tapping the Memories of the Living, such as Historians.* This explanation involves a prodigious type of ESP, known as "Super-ESP." It hypothesizes that the mind can comb in a paranormal fashion almost any extant source of information. However, there is no firm evidence that such a power exists as we will see in our later investigations of mediumship and of reincarnation. Furthermore, this explanation does not explain the Glastonbury Scripts where the information presented was in no known living mind.

5. *Tapping the Memories of the Dead.* In the case of Geraldine Cummins and in that of the Glastonbury Scripts, such an explanation was offered in the scripts themselves. However, it is perplexing that the "dead" in these cases seem more like psychic husks who do not know what has transpired on earth since the events they describe. They seem to be absorbed in little else than the events at hand.

Some Conclusions

It would be simplest, perhaps, to take the safe position and simply state that more research is needed. But more research is needed in almost all that parapsychology investigates. I personally believe in taking *very tentative* positions. If one tentatively chooses a hypothesis, he or she can continue to investigate and test the hypothesis for coherence in the face of new data. If one never tentatively takes a position, it is less easy to change one's mind since no tentative forming of it has occurred.

I lean toward the idea that there is some contact with a kind of universal psychic memory or a kind of Jungian Collective Unconscious. However, only one other alternative remains which fits all the data. This would be a tapping of the minds of the dead. Even if we include tapping of the minds of living historians, a theory which does not fit some of the data as they were known to any living agent, still we are left with retrocognition as an important form of paranormal knowledge. This paranormal knowledge implies a greater linkage of human beings than has generally been held. It is as if all reality forms a kind of incredible intertwined web.

I wish to stress the tentativeness of my positions in this chapter. We must be open to any new explanation which will be coherent with the data. However, the material found in this chapter has definite relevance for our later discussion. The positions presented here may seem somewhat stronger when viewed in connection with other well-investigated areas.

Chapter VII

Out-of-the-Body Experiences

An out-of-the-body experience is the experience of seeming to be separated from one's physical body, often while seeing one's body from a distance. If it were to be established that in out-of-the-body experiences (OBEs) there is a real and not just an illusory separation of consciousness from the body, this would present a major problem for many philosophers and theologians. In fact, I think it would not be an overstatement to assert that this would be a milestone in human thinking for the northwestern section of the globe.

Most *philosophers* in our culture maintain that spirit, at least in our present life, cannot exist apart from the body. Else it could not think or imagine. Body and spirit, they claim, are united as two co-principles. One cannot exist without the other. This position is espoused not only by those secular philosophers who admit to the existence of spirit, but also by religious philosophers like those of the Catholic Transcendental school, such as Karl Rahner and Bernard Lonergan, both Jesuits.

Theologians, both Jewish and Christian, find the idea of the separability of body and spirit unacceptable. With few exceptions, they find the biblical picture of man as "monistic." (The separation theory is called "dualism.") That is, the Bible sees man as a single whole composed of two co-elements, body and spirit, neither of which can exist alone. (This is true at least until the period of Hellenistic influence on the Bible, as in the Book of Wisdom.) They say that "immortality of the soul" is a Greek concept, not a Judaeo-Christian one. The theory of the immortality of the soul holds a dualism between spirit and body, and

117

according to this theory "immortality of the soul" would be a natural possession of humanity. That is, once created, the spirit will go on endlessly. Although this is precisely the view of many believers, most theologians insist that Christianity believes not in the immortality of the soul but in the resurrection of the body.[1] Accordingly, afterlife is totally a *gift* from God and not a natural possession of mankind. It includes a "resurrected" body. This, of course, does not imply that the dead bodies will arise from the grave to become the resurrected body. The term more often used is "a glorious body." Whether this body of glory is given immediately at death or at the end of time before the "final judgment" is a point of division between many Catholic and Protestant theologians. Some Protestant theologians maintain that the spirit will "sleep" until the final "resurrection." Many Catholic theologians and some Protestant theologians say that individuals will receive "a glorious or spiritual body" from God immediately after death, and this is their resurrection. Karl Rahner conjectures that immediately after death the spirit will enter into a relationship with the "ground of the universe" as a whole. This relationship will replace the person's relationship to the individual body, and it explains certain parapsychological data.[2]

The chief religious proponents of a "dualistic" theory are the Spiritualists. They hold a dualism between body and spirit, and they see immortality as *natural* to humans once they have been created by God.

Specific Topic of This Chapter

My immediate subject matter is out-of-the-body experiences which are had by the living who are not facing imminent death. Out-of-the-body experiences at the time of death will be treated in the subsequent chapter on Near Death Experiences.

The Chief Objections to OBEs

The chief empirical objections to out-of-the-body experiences are: (1) OBEs are hallucinations pure and simple; (2) OBEs are not pure hallucinations, but they may be paranormal ESP experiences joined to an exclusively subjective and psychological *feeling* of being out of the body; (3) OBEs are simply dreams. The last objection may be disposed of immediately. Many OBEs are had while awake and conscious. The other two objections are our chief concern and the reader should keep them in mind as he or she considers the data presented in the rest of this chapter.

Anecdotal Cases

Celia Green of Oxford records the following case: "I was at a dance standing with a group of friends when I felt very hot and fainted. I didn't realize I had fainted at the time; one moment I felt hot and next I was looking down at a figure lying face down on the floor. I seemed to be quite high up . . . then I realized that the body was mine. I saw my body being picked up, could distinguish clearly individual people and what they were doing. I saw the main lights go on, and then just as suddenly was back in the body again. . . . I was able to note people's actions and afterwards I told them their exact movements, which they confirmed. I was a little embarrassed by having fainted and my partner told me no one had noticed as the main lights in the hall were out; however I saw the lights go on and someone fetch a chair, etc. My partner was very surprised and had to admit that every detail was correct."[3]

Catholic hagiography has often recorded out-of-the-body experiences. One of the most famous cases is that of Alphonsus Ligouri. "In September 1774, when he was seventy-seven years old, he went into a cataleptic trance and remained motionless in his cell for five days. When he woke up he announced that he had been at the bedside of the dying Clement XIV and that the Pope was now dead. The startled monks dismissed the story as pure fantasy. Rome was at least four days away by horse and carriage, and there had been no official word of Clement's condition. The news came a few days later that the Pope had died. Was this just clairvoyance, supernormal knowledge of events taking place at a distance that Ligouri saw in a vision?

Ligouri claimed that his second body had been in Rome, and his statement was later confirmed by witnesses who were with him as he prayed at the Pope's bedside—the superiors of the Dominican, Observatine and Augustinian orders. It was not a collective hallucination. The case was documented and accepted by the Catholic Church as a true bilocation."[4]

Martin de Porres (1579–1639) who was canonized in 1962 was the illegitimate son of a Spanish colonial nobleman and a black woman. He lived in the Dominican monastery in Lima, Peru, a city which he never left. He had incredible powers of levitation and became known as "the flying monk." Witnesses claimed to have seen the "black monk" in Mexico, Africa and the Philippines. In one well documented bilocation case, Martin solved a family dispute in his sister's house in a town near Lima and then slept there overnight, while at the same time he was seen by the monks in his monastery in Lima caring for a large number of patients in the infirmary.[5]

In our own day, Padre Pio (1887–1968) is accredited with a number of cases of bilocation.[6] Similarly many witnesses have testified to the apparent bilocation abilities of Natuzzo Evola, 58, an illiterate peasant woman who lives with her husband and five children in Paravati, Italy.[7] Dr. Karlis Osis of the American Society for Psychical Research has gathered evidence from witnesses, such as housewives, engineers, judges and scientists, about the apparent bilocation of several Indian gurus. For example, the gurus Sathya Sai Baba and Dadaji were seen three hundred miles and five hundred miles away from where they were physically. Some of these apparitions were said to even speak, handle objects and leave things behind.[8]

In cases of collective witnessing, presuming that the witnesses' testimony can be trusted, the hypothesis of hallucination is considerably weakened. Collective hysteria or emotional contagion is one thing. But the seeing of the same figure by many witnesses is another. It seems to be beyond the hallucination hypothesis. However, the question which must be answered is whether these "apparitions" are genuine separations of consciousness from the body or whether they are the results of unconscious telepathic communication in which the receiver then, also unconsciously, exteriorizes the telepathic message.

Spontaneous Experimental Evidence

The reader will recall that this is the type of evidence which has some control involved, a parapsychologist is present, but laboratory conditions are necessarily forfeited because of the spontaneous nature of the event. There are a number of such cases in parapsychological literature. For example, S. H. Beard, a Victorian gentleman, tried to project his apparition to his fiancée, L. Verity. Surprised, she told him she had seen his figure. Beard then told his friend, Edmund Gurney, one of the founders of the Society for Psychical Research, that he would again try to project to his fiancée in her bedroom on a given night. Beard was seen, not only by his fiancée, but also by her younger sister, neither of whom knew of the experiment nor its time. The facts were established by Gurney.[9]

This case is not unique. C. D. Broad, a demanding philosopher and careful researcher, in his Perrot Lectures at Cambridge University in 1959 and 1960, gave the details of two similar cases from before the turn of the century, in one of which the parapsychologist Frank Podmore was involved. However, these were not collectively seen cases.[10] In the famous Wilmot case, investigated by Eleanor Sidgwick of the S.P.R., Mr. S. R. Wilmot was traveling on the S. S. Limerick from Liverpool to America. In the midst of a great storm, his wife in Watertown, Connecticut thought she visited her husband on the ship during a time of concern over him. A fellow passenger who occupied the same cabin as Mr. Wilmot, William J. Tait, saw a woman bending over the sleeping Wilmot. The figure seems to have been that of Mrs. Wilmot.[11] Experiences of such projection have also been recorded in their own cases by the experimental projectors and investigators, Robert Crookall and Sylvan Muldoon.[12] In our own day, Dr. Karlis Osis has recorded that while psychic projectors were trying to project to the room where Osis and other witnesses were present in New York City, on one occasion two witnesses saw a blue globe of light, and, on another, a Mrs. Whiting saw the figure of Alex Tanous from Maine.[13] If an agent is endeavoring to project to a percipient at a certain moment, and at the same time the percipient sees the apparition of the agent, this event may not be explained by hallucination, particularly in those cases where the percipient is not aware of the intended projection. However, one still faces the possibility that what is occurring is not a genuine OBE but a telepathic communication which is unconsciously exteriorized. Indeed, parapsychologists themselves are divided on this question. For example, Susan Blackmore and John Palmer believe that what we are dealing with are altered states of consciousness (ASC) with perhaps paranormal phenomena like telepathy involved.[14] On the other hand, investigators like Osis, Janet Mitchell and Crookall believe that we are dealing here with genuine out-of-the-body experiences.[15]

Controlled Scientific Experimentation

Charles Tart of the University of California of Los Angeles at Davis was one of the first investigators to make a thorough scientific investigation of OBEs. Tart had worked with Robert Monroe whose *Journeys Out of the Body* became a popular introduction to OBE investigation in 1971. Monroe's book suggested some genuine paranormal effects during his OBEs. Monroe seemed to have picked up the presence of a visitor in another room during his tests, though whether this was done by inference is not certain. He describes flights over various scenes and strange entities which climbed onto his back and clung to him during his OBEs. He also claimed to have caused external effects, such as a pinch felt by another person, during his experiences. However, his book is generally uncritical and may have some imaginative touches which make it less useful for our present purpose.

Tart, however, was a pioneer in registering psycho-physiological reactions during OBEs. His most famous subject, a "Miss Z," was wired to test brain-wave activity, REM, skin conductivity and circulation.[16] When she felt she was having an OBE, brain wave functions slowed to an alphoid state, one to one-and-a-half cycles slower than the alpha state, but the other tests were normal. Miss Z was wired to the registering machines in a room. High above her and not visible to her, a number was placed flat on a high shelf. After a number of efforts in which she felt that she was out of her body but unable to ascend to the shelf, she finally "saw" the number 25132. The chance of guessing this number is one in one hundred thousand. This was a highly significant result. While it has been claimed that the possibility of cheating was not ruled out in this experiment, still I believe the main problem is that we do not know whether the number was not achieved by clairvoyance, or even by telepathy, since the number was known also to Dr. Tart. Tart did set a fruitful direction in measuring the physiological correlates which accompany the OBE.[17]

However, I believe the most challenging experiments thus far have been conducted by Karlis Osis and Donna McCormick of the A.S.P.R. To obviate the difficulty of excluding clairvoyance or telepathy as explanations for OBEs, "perspective tests" were conducted in which a box is placed on a shelf in a room about forty feet from the experimentee. The box has a viewing window and a special screen which splits light beams. Various kinds of boxes are used. At the rear of some are rotatable discs divided into four quadrants. On one of the quadrants is a small picture. Each quadrant has its color randomly selected. Other images and combinations have also been used. The discs are spun by a random process. If one looks through the screen, one sees everything distorted by it, i.e., all may really be pointing in a different direction from what they appear to be when seen through the screen. The presupposition behind this kind of experiment is that if one sees the images by clairvoyance they would be seen without distortion, as clairvoyance presumably would pierce the box, not going through the screen but through the sides of the box which are in a direct line with the OBE experimentee. If the center of consciousness is really up at the screen and "looking" through it, the objects would be seen in a distorted manner. The presupposition is that clairvoyance operates like normal vision, going directly to its target, while OBE vision is capable of taking a given perspective.

Various psychics were worked with—Alex Tanous, Ingo Swann and Pat Price. There were a number of significant "hits" during these experiments, as well as many failures.[18] The "hits" reaching a significant level above chance would seem to constitute evidence offering some probability to the OBE rather than to the ESP hypothesis. The weakness in the experiment is that we are not sure that telepathy and clairvoyance operate like normal sight and that they themselves could not be manipulated into some positioned perspective. This seems unlikely in view of past experiments with telepathy and clairvoyance. Much more research needs to be done here, yet I would think that these experiments add some weight to the genuine OBE hypothesis.

Osis and McCormick also conducted experiments in which an effort was made to "see" a target in another room in which there was also a feather or a strain gauge. These experiments were conducted with Tanous and Pat Price. Target identification and PK effects have been recorded at times in both kinds of tests.[19] Again, the hypothesis seems to be that it is less likely that one simultaneously, without being out of the body, produces unintended PK effects and telepathic identification than that one is undergoing a genuine OBE. This kind of experiment has less impact than the perspective tests, yet it seems to me that in the area of probability it is not without its merits. The experiments have been criticized for not having achieved their goal in any certain way. Still, this does not mean that these experiments support the non-genuine OBE hypothesis, as is sometimes concluded. I think they make the genuine OBE hypothesis slightly more probable than its competitor.

Other pieces of evidence gather around this hypothesis in their own fashion. For example, OBEs seem to be more continuous and clearer than telepathy or clairvoyance. "OBE vision was like a movie, while . . . ESP images, in contrast, tended to come in brief snatches, like still photos."[20] Furthermore, in OBEs, experiencers report seeing around corners, behind objects, through walls and even at 360 degree angles. Some feel as if they were "engulfing objects" or fusing with them, and frequently there is the experience of seeing things as transparent and glowing. (Strangely, while correctly seeing things at a distance in OBEs, some elements are also seen which do not fit the external environment.) Most of those who have experienced OBEs contend that the vision is different from both ESP and dream imagery. The dream hypothesis is mentioned here because a large number of OBEs are experienced while asleep, but not all by any means. The OBEs often change a person's vision of the meaning and structure of life, something which is not found with general ESP. Fear of death was often lost and a new view of life and death emerged.

An interesting point about out-of-the-body experiences is that not all who experience them feel that they have a body. Some do. But some have an "a-somatic" experience, or feel as if they were a ball of energy or light, as with Tanous.

It is impossible at the present stage of research to come to any truly decisive conclusions on the veracity of OBEs. However, we must remember that we are dealing with probabilities and not with "proofs" in this area. Once again, I believe it is fruitful to take a stance, if even very tentative, on this matter. Only in this way can we form hypotheses which can be tested in the future. If one were to rank the value of OBE evidence on a scale from 10 to 0 to -10, I would tentatively give about a 2 to the evidence for genuine OBEs. But let us remember that because a point has not been "proved" is not a reason for supporting the opposite hypothesis. At present, I believe that from the anecdotal and experimental evidence, and from the convictions of those who have experienced these phenomena, we might justly infer that the evidence is slightly more in favor of the genuineness of OBEs than for the other hypothesis of an altered state of consciousness with some paranormal ESP operation but without any separation of consciousness from the body.

Aura Study

The Kirlian aura is by now a phenomenon with which most of our readers will be familiar. Using Kirlian photography, auras of light have been discovered around most objects, whether healers' hands or the hands of alcoholics, or around leaves or even around coins. Phantom leaves have been discovered in which, when a leaf is cut and part discarded, an aura remains where the discarded part of the leaf had been. This slowly fades. The auras around humans do seem to give some indication of the health of the patient, and this fact is becoming a useful therapeutic tool. But what is the aura itself? Some have claimed either that it is simply the result of moisture around an object, or that it is the result of the angle at which the object is "photographed." However, Thelma Moss in recent work has given evidence against all the usual hypotheses like these. It is something unique, she believes. We really know many things it isn't, but not what it is.

Some proponents of OBEs suggest that the aura is the form of a second or "energy" body which all humans have. If this were true, then the philosophical and religious problems which we detailed at the beginning of this chapter would be solved. One's center of consciousness would separate from the body, but there would remain with it a second "energy" or "astral" body whose presence would rule out the dualism with which so many theologians and philosophers have problems. Indeed, there is gathering evidence that there may well be some energy field which surrounds all living organisms. For example, when the leg of a frog embryo is cut off, it regrows at least until a certain time in the embryo's maturation. Similarly, in a salamander where a defect has been detected by Kirlian photography in the energy field which seems to surround it, this defect later shows up in the salamander. The principle frequently used is this: everything which has the ability to organize something else has to exist before what it organizes. This pre-existent reality is called by various names: "L-fields" (Burr), "morphogenic fields" (Sheldrake), "bioplasmic fields" (Russians). Perhaps this organizing field, according to the proponents of this approach, is not destructible at death.

There is no doubt that countless cultures in the past have believed in the idea of a second body. In fact, paradoxically, even the Platonists who are often accused of dualism in their view of the separability of body and spirit may have believed in a second body.[21] However, there is a rather large leap from the theory that all living organisms are surrounded by an energy field to the conviction that this energy field is a "second" body. This is a possibility, no doubt. But we stand at the beginning of our investigations of this question. At present, the existence or non-existence of genuine out-of-the-body experiences must be separated from the question of energy fields around the body. Still, as the evidence stands, I think it is more probable than not that genuine OBEs exist.

Ecstasy and OBEs

St. Paul once wrote: "I am obliged to boast. It does no good; but I shall go on to tell of visions and revelations granted by the Lord. I know a Christian man who fourteen years ago (whether in the body or out of it I do not know—God knows) was caught up as far as the third heaven. And I know that this same man (whether in the body or out of it I do not know—God knows) was caught up into paradise, and heard words so secret that human lips may not repeat them. About such a man I am ready to boast; but I will not boast on my account, except of my weakness" (2 Cor 12:1–5).[22] St. Teresa of Avila wrote: "Turning now to this sudden transport of the spirit, it may be said to be of such a kind that the soul really seems to have left the body; on the other hand, it is clear that the person is not dead, though for a few moments he cannot even himself be sure if the soul is in the body or no."[23]

From studying the documents of the past we may never be able to tell whether these mystics experienced what we would call an out-of-the-body experience or whether their language is couched in a metaphorical form which coincidentally overlaps with OBE language. However, the very raising of the question arouses us to a possibility in studying modern mystics. Can we not discover whether their similar language is accompanied by physiological and psychological phenomena similar to those which we find in OBE studies? Only in this way, I believe, can we then return to the past and enrich our understanding of many of our classical mystical texts.

The philosopher, Michael Grosso, has proposed a theory which might make us wonder what we mean by the word "out" in "out-of-the-body experiences." The body is more correctly seen as being in the soul than the soul in the body. Thus, a subject, instead of paranormally getting out of the body, may be conceived of as already in essence out of the body. There may be various degrees of being "out." The subject in a sense is always out of the body, and the OBE may represent one empirical type and self-certifying instance of becoming fully conscious of it. In the OBE, through an altered state of consciousness, the body gets out of the way of consciousness.[24] There are many problems here, and yet this is a rich concept upon which I do not have the space to dwell. But the out-of-the-body experience, especially where it seems to have been spiritually willed as in the case of mystics like Padre Pio, may be, in Grosso's words, "a profound submergence of the personality in a larger 'transpersonal' structure."[25] OBEs thus might be seen, at times, as mini-deaths which prepare us for a larger and deeper level of existence.

In concluding I wish to note that the reader is no doubt aware that if OBEs are genuine, then they could be considered as evidence of some sort for the possibility of life continuing into a larger world beyond death. If death swallows up the physical body in the grave, it would not necessarily swallow up human consciousness as well.

I wish now to proceed to the study of near death experiences in which out-of-the-body feelings or experiences play a large role. The evidence presented in this chapter should be kept in mind as we study these near death experiences.

Chapter VIII

Recent Studies of
Near Death Experiences

The general public first became aware of research in the area of near death experiences with the publication of Dr. Raymond Moody's book, *Life After Life,* in 1975.[1] Moody had gathered information on about a hundred and fifty cases of people who either had been declared clinically dead or had come very close to physical death. Of these he interviewed some fifty persons in great detail. He found a pattern in the cases but he does not tell us how many people experienced each category of the pattern. However, no one person experienced all of the following categories: (a) feeling of ineffability; (b) feelings of peace and serenity; (c) a noise (buzzing, click, roaring, banging, whistling, music); (d) an out-of-the-body experience or OBE from which vantage point they look back and "see" their own unconscious body; some watch an operation on their body; (e) other spirit-like persons are met, often deceased parents or friends; (f) there is a meeting of a being of indescribable light, known as personal, with whom a direct transfer of thoughts takes place; this being is not identifiable: some Christians identify it as Christ, Jews as an angel, etc.; (g) an intense review of one's life; (h) an experience of border or limit of some sort that cannot be passed; at times, a loved one who died unbeknown to the person is seen beyond it; (i) there is a generally reluctant return to one's body; (j) a change is effected in one's life view: a growth in love for others and for knowledge, less fear of death, less of a reward/punishment model of afterlife; the being responded not with anger, but with understanding, even humor; (k) a corroboration of details seen during OBE, especially of technical medical details of operations, etc.

Subsequently, Dr. Moody published another book entitled *Reflections on Life After Life.*[2] In this book, he added more material to his investigation and also endeavored to make a defense against some of the objections which now were being made to his study. These objections we will handle shortly.

Osis

Few people know that certain researchers had already been at work on these experiences long before Moody's book appeared, for example, William Barrett in England and Hornell Hart at Duke. However, I wish to center on recent research concerning near death experience (NDE) and I will begin with the studies of Dr. Karlis Osis of the American Society for Psychical Research. During 1959–1960, Dr. Osis had made a pilot survey of 640 medical personnel.[3] During 1961 to 1964, he received replies to a questionnaire from 1,004 doctors and nurses in America. Then, in 1973–74, Osis with the Icelandic parapsychologist, Dr. Erlendur Haraldsson, made a cross-cultural study in the United States and India. In the United States, he mailed the questionnaire to 5,000 physicians and nurses; 1,004 returned the filled-in questionnaire. In India, practically all of the medical personnel directly approached filled in a questionnaire, totaling 704. Thus, he had 1,708 usable questionnaires. Approximately half of the respondents reported cases which he followed up in 877 detailed interviews. The combined data for his studies appeared in the book *At the Hour of Death.*[4] Some patients had disjointed hallucinations. Some had patterned experiences. Of those who had the patterned experience, there were three types of experiences: (1) visions of people; (2) visions of places; (3) elevation of mood. Below I have placed these experiences in parallel columns for clarity of contrast, a technique which may allow some oversimplification in view of the large amount of data involved.

Near Death Experiences	*Hallucinogenic Type Experiences*
There is some ESP. People correctly mention details of the room they are in and of the environment outside of it.	There was a sick brain type of delusion. There was also malfunction of the nervous system.

Hallucinogenic Factors

The use of hallucinogens did not increase the frequency of these patterned visions. In fact, ESP decreased with drug usage.	The more hallucinogens were used, the more rambling visions. But there was no ESP.

Content

Relatively coherent. Oriented to transition; "take-away" figures appeared.	These visions portrayed only memories stored in the brain and expressed as desires—the beliefs were characteristic of the culture.

Psychological Factors

The less drugs that were used, the greater clarity of consciousness, the more patterned visions.	Clarity of consciousness was less conducive to hallucinations.
The expectation of dying didn't influence the occurrence of the patterned vision.	Expecting to recover led to this-life figures; expecting to die led to hallucinations of the afterlife.
Stress did not increase frequency.	Stress increased frequency.

Women in the United States had religious emotions twice as frequently as men, but both had elevated mood. The more educated, at least up to high school graduation, the more frequent were these experiences. Specific belief did not increase the number of visions but belief did increase the religious response.

Content Variability

Little variability. Content was of visions of another life; essentially similar for old, young, men, women, Christian, non-Christian.

There was much variability. It varied widely with disposition and culture.

(But the figures Indians saw were 77 percent male; Americans saw 61 percent female. The young experienced fewer take-away figures.)

Other Miscellaneous Data

1. The patients' normal perception of the room was clear or mildly impaired in 72% of the cases.
2. They had experiences against their expectations; they occasionally saw friends or relatives who they thought were still living but who had died. Desired living persons were conjured up only in a fraction of the cases (13 of 471).
3. Those who had the patterned type of experience saw "take-away" figures, while the rambling type of hallucinations, which the others had, manifested no purpose. The latter group took visitors for strange characters, while those who had the near death experience saw the visitors for who they were—just visitors to the hospital. (Incidentally, Kübler-Ross described a similar episode as she visited her dying father. She wrote, "My own father talked to his father, who had been dead thirty years, and then turned back and spoke rationally to me.")[5] In cases of people who died within ten minutes of seeing an apparition, take-away purpose predominated.
4. If wish fulfillment were the explanation, it is strange that the messengers[6] did not come more often to those expecting to

die and less often to those not so expecting. In India, some even screamed and were opposed to being taken away.

5. What happened was not due to their religious expectations, at least if we take these from the Bible and the Bhagavad Gita. However, Christ was not seen by Hindus, nor Krishna nor a Yamdoot by a Christian.

At the beginning of their work, Osis and Haraldsson had presented two opposing hypotheses. The first hypothesis was that the experience was a transition experience to another life. The second hypothesis was that it was the beginning of an experience of extinction. The authors claimed that the data were more consistent with the hypothesis of a transition experience, of life beyond death, than with the extinction hypothesis. However (and Moody had made the same point), the authors did not claim that they had proved that there was life after death, but only that the data were more consistent with the hypothesis of a transition to another life. Osis admitted that there were subjective differences in his cross-cultural study, but he insisted that the cross-cultural *pattern* suggested a meaningful transition experience. It is true that Osis' subjects do not specifically mention OBEs, but there is a sense of "being in another world." Cases of paranormal knowledge also are rarely mentioned. But Dr. Osis tells me that neither of these two phenomena was capable of check or verification in his survey. Thus no discrepancy may yet be claimed between his view and that of Moody on these points. Similarly, there is no specific mention of the "indescribable light" in Osis' studies. Yet, there is specific reference to religious figures such as Christ or God, the common denominator being the religious apparitions which possess qualities of a numinous experience of varying degrees of intensity.

Noyes

A different interpretation of the experience is presented by Dr. Russell Noyes, associate professor at the University of Iowa College of Medicine, who has collected 114 cases.[7] He also found the experience of the life-review and the experience of transcending the body. But he believes that the life-review could be the result of a rapid regression to prior life to escape a frustrating reality and thus reach an intrinsically pleasant state. The experience of body transcendence would be the result of a type of dissociation (depersonalization) through which the reality of death would be excluded from consciousness. This allows one to pretend he is only witnessing it as a spectator. Freud said that our death is unimaginable and we have to perceive it as a spectator, for in the unconscious everyone of us is convinced of his or her own immortality. However, this position does not account for the paranormal perceptions of the patients in Moody's work (seeing the doctor, the operation, and the deceased who they did not know were dead). Noyes admits definite mystical overtones in the experience but his explanation is similar to Freud's, who practically reduced mystical experience, the "oceanic feeling," to a regression to the security of early infancy. Many psychologists today believe that it is illegitimate to base all later "peak" experiences on the model of the young infant's pleasure-seeking instinct. However, Noyes' nuanced explanation seems to stop short of Freud's reductionism. He endeavors to remain more open and presents an excellent phenomenological description. This type of description may be very helpful as we endeavor to come to definite conclusions about the nature of the experience.

Rawlings

Meanwhile, a book by Maurice Rawlings, M.D., *Beyond Death's Door*, appeared in 1978.[8] Rawlings' claim is that he is particularly qualified to speak on deathbed experiences because he is a cardiologist who is a member of a resuscitation team. Furthermore, he recounts a number of experiences of a "hell" which were reported by patients who "survived clinical death." But he discovered that, while the "heavenly" scenes were remembered, the "hellish" scenes were *not long remembered* and were totally repressed by the patients later on. His conclusion is, "I feel assured that there is life after death, and not all of it is good." Rawlings himself had always thought of death as "painless extinction," but contact with the experiences of these patients occasioned a conversion experience. Rawlings' book has been criticized for its careless, popular and non-scientific treatment. The book is also colored by a kind of evangelical, Fundamentalist missionary tone. For example, he writes of "our need for missionary work at home." Rawlings claims, incorrectly, to be the only investigator who has actually resuscitated patients.

As an example of one of the more *positive* or heavenly scenes, he tells us of a man who is looking for Jesus and sees a huge building. The man who was with his deceased parents said to them, "What is that?" They said, "In there is God." In many of the positive experiences there is a flooding light which is identified by the person as Christ. In one of the *negative* visions of "hell," a woman who had attempted suicide saw a huge foreboding cave. Inside, "the beings had tails and slanted eyes," she says, "and looked horrible." From a philosophical-theological point of view, these scenes are certainly not literal transcriptions of the beyond. They are, at the most, symbolical. The question is: Are these symbols only one's own psyche, or are they symbols of some transpsychic reality? Secondly, some of the visions suggest that the sight of "hell" which was had may not be an experience of hell as traditional Christianity has thought of it. For example, a lumberjack in a vision stood near a lake of fire. There he sees a youth who died at thirteen with cancer of the jaw. Christ comes and beckons him out. Thus, "hell" here is not eternal. Again, a staunch Christian, the founder of a Sunday school, during cardiac arrest had a vision of hell. He then had two further cardiac arrest experiences in which, "without any apparent reason, unless some secret transformation or dedication occurred (of which I am unaware), the patient's subsequent two experiences during other deaths were beautiful." As Rawlings is unaware of any apparent conversion, the notion of an experience of hell followed by an experience of heaven without any apparent life change seems to suggest something that is symbolic only of the state of the subject's own psyche. Rawlings also mentions the prevalence of depression preceding suicide attempts. This fact should be kept in mind when we interpret death-bed experiences following suicide attempts.

Ring

In 1980, Dr. Kenneth Ring, professor of psychology at the University of Connecticut, published a work, *Life at Death: A Scientific Investigation of Near-Death Experience.*[9] This represents a well-written and seriously critical effort to investigate NDEs. Ring had 102 formal interviews with near-death survivors in addition to informal contacts with almost a hundred other persons. Forty-eight percent of the sample had experiences which conformed at least in part to Moody's model. However, Ring found that the earlier stages of Moody's experience were most common and that the later stages manifested themselves with decreasing frequency. In other words, more people experienced peace and bodily separation. More than a third of the dying had distinct out-of-the-body experiences, but fewer progressively entered the darkness, saw the light and entered the light. One-sixth of the sample mentioned that they saw the light but only one-tenth entered the light. This is the stage in which deceased relatives are seen and greeted. Ring notes that there was no conjunction between seeing spirits or relatives and encountering the light-presence. It was an either-or experience, not a combination of both. He also says that women are most likely to have near death experiences in conjunction with illness, whereas the experiences of men tend to occur in cases of accidents or suicides. Illness victims appear most likely to have near-death experiences, accident victims are next and suicide attempt victims are least likely. Many suicide victims are left with no recall.[10] Ring found that religious persons are not more likely to have near-death experiences than those who are non-religious. Religiosity may well be a determinant of the *interpretation* that the individual places on his or her experience, but religiosity does not affect either the likelihood or the depth of a near-death experience.

Ring ruled out explanations like depersonalization, wishful

thinking, psychological expectations, dreams or hallucinations, and pharmacological explanations. He found the experience to be different from temporal lobe involvement and cerebral anoxia. Basically, he holds that we do not as yet have a plausible explanation for these experiences. Ring notes that in his study, as in Moody's, people had no feeling of guilt with regard to their mistakes. It was as if they were watching their life, like an objective spectator. As with Moody, if judgment was made, it was self-judgment. But he adds an interesting fact with regard to the life review. People who experienced this not only had flashbacks but also "flash-forwards." This unusual fact eliminates many psychological theories as a total explanation of this experience. Ring holds with a number of investigators today that there is for many people a *transpersonal experience* at death. He also tentatively favors the hypothesis that in these experiences there is a genuine out-of-the-body experience or separation of consciousness from the known body. He hypothesizes that the transpersonal experience may well be an experience of another dimension of time-space. He speculates that the voice that is heard at times in these experiences is not so much the voice of God but the voice of one's total self or what some traditions call the higher self. There is no indication of loss of individuality.

Ring believes that dying brings a change of consciousness, a movement to a new "frequency domain." This shift of consciousness is gradual, the tunnel, the friends, the light, etc. To clarify his point, Ring uses as his model a hologram. A hologram is an image which is the result of lensless photography and light techniques. If a part of the image is broken off, the broken part continues to contain the whole image. Similarly, one taps into that order of reality that is behind the world of appearances. The fragmentary experience taps into the whole. Some people experience a most pleasant transpersonal experience ("heaven") because they have negotiated the change of consciousness or frequencies. Some "get stuck" as it were in the lower frequencies. This accounts for the "hellish" experience, and experiences where drooping and depressed people are seen wandering around. The reason one becomes "stuck" is not clear, but it seems to be related to the state of mind previous to the experience. Furthermore, these experiences always change from "bad" to "good," a fact which suggests a gradual change of consciousness.

Ring has presented here an intriguing and rich interpretation of the experience. Admittedly, much is very tentative. Also his concept is close to Jung's idea of the "collective unconscious" and its fate will probably be tied to the acceptance or rejection of Jung's position. But neither Ring nor Jung implies a loss of one's individuality.

Sabom

In 1982, another fine work on near-death experiences was published by Michael D. Sabom, M.D., *Recollections of Death: A Medical Investigation.*[11] Sabom studied one hundred hospital patients. Thirty-nine of these recalled nothing during the period of unconsciousness. Sixty-one had definite recollections. Surprisingly consistent details came forth and there were three types of experience: self-visualization from a position of height ("autoscopy"—16 patients); passage of the consciousness into a foreign region or dimension ("transcendency"—32 patients); or a combination of autoscopy and transcendence (13 patients). We will not analyze these data in detail but Sabom, working at times with Sarah Kreutziger, a psychiatric social worker, clearly ruled out anoxia and hypoxia, loss of oxygen to the brain, as explanations. For example, there were no illusions of people as distorted or flat, no sudden feelings of despair, no olfactory experiences. Drugs were not an explanation. Several patients indicated no drug usage. The depersonalization experience mentioned by Noyes also does not explain the experience. It requires, Noyes admits, *perception* of imminent death as with people who *consciously* face "psychological" death just before a car crash. But many of Sabom's patients were already unconscious and Noyes himself admits that this seems to be a different kind of experience. Also Sabom notes that there was no lack of emotion in his patients, lack of which is a characteristic of depersonalization. Sabom also clearly distinguishes between autoscopic hallucinations, which are described in psychiatric literature, from NDE autoscopic visions. In NDE "autoscopy" there is a perception *of* the physical body *by consciousness outside of it* in contrast to the psychiatric experience where there is an experience *by the physical body* of a self-image outside. (Celia Green has coined the phrase "autophany" to distinguish this phenomenon from autoscopy.) Sabom says that his own beliefs in this matter are leaning in the direction of a genuine out-of-the-body experience. The accuracy of the "visual" observations while a person is unconscious helps him to come to this conclusion. "The out-of-body hypothesis simply seems to fit best the data at hand." Sabom makes it quite clear that we have in no way as yet solved the meaning of near death experiences. However, he does wonder whether the split of the mind from the physical body which happens at death could be the soul which continues to exist after final bodily death according to some religious doctrines. This of course raises an enormous problem of dualism for philosophical and Christian thought, a point which I hope to treat elsewhere.

Other studies have been made on the near death experiences, as for example those done by C. Lundahl, E. Kübler-Ross and C. Garfield. For brevity's sake let me mention as typical a quotation from Dr. Charles Garfield, a clinical psychologist and assistant professor of medicine at the University of California cancer research institute in San Francisco. "About 21 percent of the people I've interviewed who had been near death had these experiences." Some of the other reports claim as high as 59 percent, but the existence of a core pattern is the common thread.

Siegel

There have been a number of serious, even vehement, attacks made on the very tentative conclusions of some of the authors I have mentioned. Perhaps the most important of these attacks was made by Dr. Ronald K. Siegel, of the Department of Psychiatry and Behavioral Sciences at the University of California, Los Angeles.[12] Siegel mentions that anthropologists cite the deliberate interments of the dead by Neanderthal man as the first evidence of humans' belief in life after death. However, he says that if deliberate burials are signposts of the belief in life after death for humans, it is very strange that many large animals such as elephants also display similar death rituals. He believes that the ritual was caused by the shaping of instinctive behaviors. After dismissing apparition study of recent times with a wave of the hand and rejecting Stevenson's incredibly detailed work on reincarnation as a study of the reveries of children, Siegel continues by comparing these near-death experiences to subjective hallucinations associated with depersonalization or dissociative experiences.

To understand Siegel's approach one must be aware that he does not accept at all the existence of ESP, "an untestable construct." Secondly, he seems eager to show that there is no life after death. "The most logical guess is that consciousness shares the same fate as that of the corpse." His article in *Psychology Today* ends this way: "But, for the living, may the life after death rest in peace." I will give a brief but necessarily inadequate summary of some of Siegel's main points in the following paragraph, and I will place an asterisk after each detail which does not correspond to a near death experience. I will also interject some of my own comments in parentheses.

There are certain "form-constants" in hallucinations:[13] a bright light in the center of a visual field, a tunnel-like perspective, cartoon-like people.* The constants are lattice-tunnel forms, red colors,* exploding rotational movements, and a bright light; a change of imagery* so rapid that it is difficult to maintain a running commentary, things often seen in cartoon or caricature,* pulsating scenes;* a floating feeling (Ed.: but no paranormal knowledge connected with it); depersonalization* during which a person feels as if he is seeing himself from a distance (Ed.: but Sabom said depersonalization is usually accompanied by automatic movements, lack of affectivity, anxiety etc., which are not in the NDEs). Also a "feeling of unreality"* (in NDEs, patients describe them as their most real moments, unless of course Siegel here means reality as he defines it). Siegel holds the light is caused by phosphenes, visual sensations arising from discharges of neurons in the structures of the eye. The experiences are due to common biological structures in the brain and nervous system. Dr. Siegel also wrote for *The UFO Handbook*[14] where he sees UFO abduction experiences as similar to

NDEs in having abduction-like phenomena, travel in tunnels, sensations of floating, sources of glowing objects* (Ed.: at least not in the forms of UFOs).

Every asterisk and parenthesis above represents important differences from the NDE experience. Each point has been handled by some of the authors describing NDEs. Still, as an expert on hallucinations, Siegel deserves a hearing. The patterns in his book on hallucinations, however, are random and haphazard and unlike the patterned experiences in NDE, except for the light, occasionally the city of lights and the tunnel effect.[15] He does point out, however, that in hallucinations the rest of the room is not always distorted, a position differing from that of Osis.

Grof

Siegel alludes to Grof and Halifax[16] as if supporting his position that these experiences "are related to stored memories of biological events that are activated in the brain." Grof and Halifax had indeed held that dying or the near-death experience, in Siegel's words, "triggers a flashback or retrieval of an equally dramatic and emotional memory of the birth experience." In the article cited by Siegel and in their later work, they present LSD experiences as at times re-enacting the birth experience: for example, "the first perinatal matrix is a kind of paradise where the child floats in the womb; the loss of paradise begins as the fetus feels a hostile pressing environment; a kind of "no-exit" experience ensues in which there is struggle and seeming death (apocalyptic images occur at this point with certain LSD subjects); finally after a psychological death of the ego, there is a rebirth and a resurrection.[17]

But Grof and Halifax do not treat the experience in a reductive fashion. The LSD experiences with dying cancer patients, they wrote, "can function as triggers of unconscious matrices." There are at times transpersonal, religious and metaphysical components in the experiences. In *The Human Encounter With Death* (1978) they claim the experience has biological, emotional, intellectual, philosophical and metaphysical dimensions.

In fact Grof later writes that "biological death is the beginning of an adventure in consciousness."[18] They see in the death experience a relationship to Jung's archetypes and his collective unconscious. They do make the point, however, that psychedelic sessions with dying cancer patients did not differ substantially from sessions with those who were not dying, e.g. alcoholics.[19]

On the other hand, Grof does not tell us, to my knowledge, what proportion of his patients who were not dying underwent an experience similar to near-death patients. For all patients, the more advanced stages such as those reached in NDEs came after the repeated administration of LSD. According to R.E.L. Masters and Jean Houston in their classic, *The Varieties of Psychedelic Experience,* one needs preparation to reach the stages beyond memory retrieval. In their study about 40 percent reached the next to the highest stage, the symbolical, which involved archetypal imagery and death-rebirth imagery. Only 11 of 246 reached the "highest" stage, the integrative-mystical stage.[20] But in neither Masters nor Grof do we find as a constant of any sort the pattern which recurs in NDEs. The percentage of people who had this exact experience with LSD would be most enlightening. On the other hand, I find no problem in principle in finding a similarity, if there is one, between LSD experiences had by people who are not dying but are advanced and ready for ego loss, and NDEs. Preparation may do for these people what near-death itself does in NDEs.

In *The Human Encounter With Death* Grof describes one man who had the same experience twice, once with LSD and once while really dying.[21] However, the man who had the two experiences knew he was dying in both cases because he was terminally ill. Perhaps proximity to death was the cause and not simply the LSD. Much more research is needed in this area.

Conclusion

I wish now, at some risk, to assay a tentative position on near death experiences, a very difficult thing in view of the mass of data which is, at times, conflicting. If, of course, one believes that life becomes extinct at death, one cannot discuss near death experiences as pointers to the beyond. However, whether life goes on after death is not principally solved by the study of near-death experiences. One's belief or disbelief in life beyond death is connected with previous philosophical or religious positions.

My own belief, shared by Christians and countless others, is that death is not the end. However, many who share this belief might still hold that the near death experience is a purely subjective hallucination. They would in my judgment be opposing much of the evidence. *Tentatively,* I judge that NDEs are *archetypal, symbolical experiences.* I will place two columns below. The first column I call archetypal theory (a cross-cultural or trans-personal symbolism whose origin is within the collective psyche). The second column I call a literal transition experience (with some subjective and cultural embroidering).

Archetypal Experience	*A Literal Transition Experience with Some Symbolism*
In the work of Osis, persons are sent back as if a mistake has been made. This seems implausible if we are dealing with a literal experience. Osis himself believes there may be hallucinatory elements in these cases.	We might well guess at some good purpose for this, e.g., a purposeful pre-experience of death for growth or insight. If these are hallucinatory, we still have the core pattern to account for.
Subjective symbolism is certainly involved, e.g., Christ appears only to Christians, Krishna to Hindus.	We admit the presence of subjective cultural conditioning, but the cross-cultural pattern suggests something objective beyond cultural conditioning.
Rawlings' account has many strange caves, unusual animals, God in a big building, etc. These all seem definitely symbolical.	We can picture what is really beyond space-time only through this-world symbols.
Rawlings speaks of a man	Rawlings seems to imply that

who had a "hell" experience, then without any apparent conversion he saw two beautiful scenes. This seems to imply an archetypal picture not necessarily connected with one's afterlife state.

Moody mentions that a few patients who attempted suicide had negative experiences. Osis mentions a case of a woman who saw "hell." But the woman had a prior guilt feeling and those who attempted suicide may have had prior depression. The prior subjective state rather than an experience of a literal afterlife may account for this. But "nasty, mean" people, in Osis' description, often view beautiful scenes. Love and ethics don't seem to affect what is seen, a strange point if this is a literal picture of afterlife.

what one sees is what one receives. But Rawlings himself seems to have missed the point that this does not come from his material. Two of his patients saw "hell" but Christ brought them out. The experience may have a purpose.
But these may have been experiences of a genuine future life. What the woman felt guilty about was an extramarital affair and illegitimate children, and the suicides learned they were trying to avoid problems which "death" did not solve.

But we don't know the inner self of these people. More research is needed on whether genuine, theological, guilt feelings bring experiences which are different from those who die with neurotic or immature superego guilt feelings.

The fact that one can go back and forth this way in the dialogue shows how difficult it is to come to a decision on this issue. However, one point becomes very clear from the dialogue. The two positions are very close to one another. The more literalist interpretation holds that NDEs are *genuine transition experiences* to another life but *woven through with symbolism.* The archetypal-experiences interpretation hypothesizes that NDEs are archetypal and symbolical experiences which *may* point to another life, but without informing us of its real nature. They are "bridge" experiences, as it were.

I tend to choose as a tentative interpretation the archetypal-symbolical position because (a) it covers all the data, (b) it does not go beyond the data as does the other position, and (c) it prevents *premature foreclosure* of the question.

Archetypes and the Real

The problem thus shifts focus to this question: Are archetypal symbols genuine pointers to the real? This question leads us, of course, to C.G. Jung and his theory of archetypes and a collective unconscious.

Many mistakenly believe that Jung in his theory of archetypes held that all people are born with innate *images*. He certainly made this point clear in his later writings. There are two elements in archetypal theory: (1) an innate patterning power which has a tendency to form motifs, and (2) specific images or experiences which are *a posteriori* and drawn from one's culture (e.g., in NDEs the appearance of Christ or Krishna). Jung has been criticized rightly for listing various images as archetypal too casually.[22] But I think the broad lines of his theory are supported, for example, by Grof's work, by studies of specific states of consciousness, by work in transpersonal psychology, by its application to dream study and schizophrenic drawings, and lastly by its evident usefulness in explaining certain paranormal events in parapsychology. (One really needs to have an acquaintance with parapsychology to get a better understanding of NDEs, as they fit in as part of a more general pattern, nor are they the best evidence for life after death.)

But do archetypal experiences and images point to the real beyond phenomena? Here one must make an option. Jung in *Memories, Dreams, Reflections* wrote, "A man should be able to say that he has done his best to form a conception of life after death. Not to have done so is a vital loss. For the question that is posed to him is the age-old heritage of humanity, an archetype rich in secret life, which seeks to add itself to our own individual life to make it whole. . . . The unconscious helps by communicating things to us, or making figurative allusions. It too has other ways of informing us of things which by all logic we could not possibly know."[23] He finally calls them "hints." But as Kelsey cites him, Jung may personally have held that they were more than hints. "He (Jung) believed that electing a course of action that results in permanent healing, in human wholeness, comes closest to living with reality as it is."[24] Ira Progoff who was influenced by Jung put it this way, "The messages (symbolical) to the ego from the larger transpersonal consciousness (the unconscious) contain larger principles which give intimations of the meaning of life to us."[25] Progoff is explaining how he interprets the work of the famous medium, Eileen Garrett.

Rollo May calls myths a "clue to reality." (NDEs can be seen as myths in the positive sense.) "Myth," he says, "is a description of a position of life arising out of the unconscious, that carries the values for a society and gives a person the ability to handle anxiety, to face death, to deal with guilt. It gives him an identity."[26]

Archetypes and Myths Bipolar

Archetypes, however, are bipolar. They can be salvific or demonic. Discernment is needed to interpret them. I find nothing demonic in NDEs. The effects of the experience are precisely the type of criteria one looks for in judging the validity and fruitfulness of a mystical experience, at least in its broadest sense: a sense of peace and joy, a change of horizon toward the spiritual, a lasting reformation of one's life, and a greater sense of charity and growth.

But might not NDEs encourage people to commit suicide? Some authors are afraid of this. Moody especially has discussed this point. Those who have had the near-death experience, and especially persons who have attempted suicide, report an absolute conviction afterward that this is not the way the Light wished them to face problems. One therapist even gives people with suicidal tendencies Moody's book to read and has reported success. But more evidence will be needed in this area.

Another negative point about near-death experiences has

been brought forth by certain evangelical writers. The Light or Presence seems so benign, so humorous, in face of the faults of so many that the experience seems to go against Scripture. But certain points must be brought out in the face of this objection. There is judgment in these experiences, but it is *self-judgment.* This fits present eschatological theory as presented by many theologians today who also believe they are scripturally based. Secondly, if one looks carefully, NDEs combine the benignity of "God" with the presence in other dimensions of great distress. This suggests the effect of self-judgment, although I think the visions tell us nothing of hell in itself or its duration. Lastly, the benignity of God is very much Jesus' picture as well as that of Paul who had universalist tendencies.[27]

The position I have presented here may be invalidated by future research. But tentatively, at least, it seems very plausible that near death experiences are symbolical, transpersonal archetypal experiences in the sense I have described. At least this position is somewhat testable by research like that of Grof. For example, one could investigate whether a person who had *very negative* experiences in a NDE was suffering from a neurotic guilt feeling built on a superego distortion rather than from a genuine conscience in the theological sense. If so, the set and setting would seem to be the catalyst and the experience of the afterlife would not seem to be a genuine one.

I wish to conclude by emphasizing one point. Most of the authors involved in NDE studies, whether they hold extinction, symbolism, genuine transition or no position, all agree on this point. The near death experience is, generally speaking, a very rich, rewarding and satisfying one which in a sense crowns one's life with a mystical experience in the broad sense. Michael Grosso who has written both on ego-loss in meditation and on near-death experiences says that this ego-loss is "not loss but letting go of control of thought processes." Ego death, he writes, concerns a release from an addiction to what Garfield calls the "logico-deductive method" or, put otherwise, a low tolerance for "ambiguity, logical paradox and paralogical process." "Death marks the boundary the theological-deductive method is experientially incapable of crossing."[28] However, Faith can cross this boundary for it is a transition in trust, not in this experience, but in the living God. Yet for some people today, wherever they are on this planet, death seems to begin as an *experience,* a mysterious experience of unfathomable realms of consciousness which we are merely beginning to investigate. Many experiences will be joyful, but a few may begin in distress. For many others we do not know what experiences await them. Only a reasoning faith helps us to glimpse "through a glass darkly" the outlines of what *follows* the near death experience.

But is the position presented here a "denial of death"? As I conclude this chapter, I wish to make a distinction about this phrase which is now so commonly used, "the denial of death." Two separate meanings are imperceptibly intertwined in the modern usage of this phrase. *The first meaning:* One observing death blithely denies the dreadful suffering, pain and grief, and sees it merely as a "stage." This acts as a defense reaction against personally feeling the brutality of death.[29] Dr. Charles Garfield who has studied NDEs and who has witnessed many deaths points out that, despite NDEs, many patients still die in great agony, debilitated by chemotherapy and toxins, and breathing with great difficulty. But, he says, a *caring* environment is an important factor in "maximizing the likelihood of a positive altered state of dying."[30] Would we say that the nurse or relative who brings to the bedside of a dying patient a loving care, despite great fatigue and great personal sacrifice, is denying death? This is certainly not to deny death with all its "obscenity." *The second meaning:* If those who bring such empathy and care to the dying patient also believe that life goes on beyond death, are they "denying death"? This second sense of denying death is often blended imperceptibly with the first sense which is an escape mechanism from the real. But the use of "the denial of death" in this second sense is an *a priori* begging of the very issue being investigated.

Chapter IX

Apparitions and the Resurrection of Jesus

Let us now advance beyond NDEs and turn our attention to the general area of apparitions. First I will describe some of the empirical work done on apparitions by parapsychologists, together with various theories proposed to explain apparitions. Then I will investigate the possible relevance of this work for illuminating the resurrection of Jesus as it is described in the New Testament.

The word "apparition" in this chapter will be used in contrast to "hallucination." An hallucination is a sense perception without sensory stimulation and whose cause is exclusively subjective. The word "apparition" will signify a paranormal sense perception involving sensory stimulation and where the cause is not exclusively subjective. The point to be demonstrated is that in apparitions there is not only a *percipient* but also an *agent* distinct from the percipient. This, of course, would involve significant evidence for life beyond death. It also is a point of central importance in the discussion of Jesus' resurrection.

The study of apparitions has been based mainly on anecdotal evidence and most of the cases are not of recent origin. The reason for this situation is historical. Apparition study was one of the main preoccupations of the Society for Psychical Research, as exemplified in the Census of Hallucinations published in 1894. After this approach had almost exhausted its resources, parapsychology, especially with Rhine at Duke and Soal in England, turned its attention toward establishing a firm foundation through controlled study of telepathy, clairvoyance and psychokinesis. This situation has continued until relatively recently when renewed study of apparitions has been undertaken.

Types of Cases

Apparitions are not uniform in appearance, circumstance or technique of observation. There are many widely differing types of apparitions. For purposes of clarity I will adhere to the classical division of apparitions proposed by G.N.M. Tyrrell in England.[1] To these I will add a few divisions of my own.

1. *Crisis Apparitions.* These are apparitions which appear at the time of crisis or death. Gurney had set a rough limit to the meaning of "crisis." Apparitions occurring twelve hours before to twelve hours after crises he called crisis apparitions.

2. *Post-Mortem Apparitions.* These apparitions appeared from twelve hours after death until many years later.

3. *Hauntings.* These are ghosts or apparitions which habitually frequent certain places. Hauntings may be divided into (a) intelligent hauntings which display some sign of human intelligence, and (b) *automatons* which repeat actions in an apparently automatic manner.

4. *Apparitions of the Living.* These include cases in which an agent has deliberately tried to make his or her apparition visible to a particular percipient. Apparitions of the living are included here under apparitions because of the great similarity to apparitions of the dead. (See also Chapter VII.)

5. *Photographed Apparitions.* These are photographs of apparitions which are obtained under some controlled conditions. The reason for including them here will be discussed below.

6. *Ectoplasmic Apparitions.* These are apparitions produced in a séance situation and which seem to be formed out of a substance materialized by a medium. Usually considered fraudulent in Britain and America, they have been more studied and appreciated by Continental parapsychologists.

Let us now consider some of the better examples in each of the above categories.

Crisis Apparitions

"Eldred Bowyer-Bower was a World War I pilot. On March 19, 1917, his plane was shot down over France. That same morning his apparition was seen by his half-sister, Mrs. Spearman, who was in India." She wrote: "On March 19th, in the late part of the morning, I was sewing and talking to baby. Joan [another child] was in the sitting room and did not see anything. I had a great feeling I must turn round and did, to see Eldred; he looked so happy and had that dear, mischievous look. I was so glad to see him I would just put baby in a safer place, then we could talk. 'Fancy coming out here,' I said, turning round again, and was just putting my hands out to give him a hug and a kiss, but Eldred had gone. I called and looked for him. I never saw him again."[2] This was an unexpected visit and occurred close to the time of the pilot's death.

The second case involves the apparition of a dying mother, seen ten hours before her death and again three months later, on the night before her baby's death. "A friend of mine named Mrs. J. died in November 1877; she had been confined just over a week. A few days before she died she said to me, 'I am going to die,' and asked me to take care of her baby which I did until three months after. The night before she died we were awakened between twelve o'clock and one o'clock by a noise like tapping on the window twice. My husband got up and went downstairs but could see nothing. So we tried to settle to sleep again, when all of a sudden we were alarmed by our little boy, who was not quite two years old, calling out 'Auntie,' by which name he used to call her, and pointing towards the foot of the bed, and there I saw her, standing all in white. She died the next morning between nine and ten. She appeared again a second time about three months after: it would be about midnight. My husband saw her standing by the fire. At first he thought it was I, until he turned round and saw I was in bed. We were very much frightened for a long time after. The baby died the next day about three o'clock in the afternoon."[3] This is a case which involved a percipient who was a young child not yet two years old, and also it involves a collectively seen apparition.

Post-Mortem Apparitions

The Sutton Case. On October 11, 1907, Mrs. Rose Sutton, a Catholic, who lived in Portland, Oregon, received a letter from her son, James, who was at Annapolis.[4] The letter was full of youthful vigor. On the evening of October 12, she felt pain and shock and said that something was wrong with Jimmy. Next day, after Mass, she told her daughter, Louise, "Jimmy is here." Thus began an unusually persistent apparition. That same day her husband phoned to say he had received a telegram saying that Jimmy had shot himself and was dead. At that moment she saw her son and he said, "Mamma, I never killed myself." He said that a man hit him with the butt of a gun, that three men jumped on him, broke the crystal of his watch with a kick, hurt his ribs and injured his forehead and then shot him. He asked her to clear him. On October 16 there was another vision in which the apparition said that they had bandaged his forehead and jaw to hide the wounds and that "Utley" had managed the whole affair. Utley was a lieutenant and fellow student. Daisy, Jim's sister, said someone showed her a face in a dream and she later picked the face out in a class picture. It was Utley. In 1909 the family had the body exhumed. They found the wounds exactly as the apparition had detailed them (they had also received the watch back with the cracked crystal). The angle of the bullet was inconsistent with the suicide hypothesis. Altogether, there were ten witnesses to verify Mrs. Sutton's earlier story about James and the visions. James Hyslop, the famous psychic investigator, had contacted his friend, George Thacher, in Oregon, to investigate the case. Rose saw the apparition frequently (she had had other psychic experiences). The daughter, Louise, felt James' presence, and Dan, a brother, saw the phantom. A letter was received later, which was anonymous but in which the writing matched that of a serviceman at the scene of the crime, which said that the son had been murdered.

This is a case in which the details were verified, where more than one person saw the apparition, and in which the apparition appeared many times. Also some careful investigation was conducted. As D. Scott Rogo has said, the anti-survivalist position might be that Mrs. Sutton, a Catholic, could not accept her son's suicide, and that she picked up the scene by ESP and then dramatized it as an apparition. The survivalist might reply that Mrs. Sutton was not alone in seeing the apparition, that Dan and Louise were involved in supportive apparitions, and that Jimmy, as a Catholic, would want to reassure the family that he did not commit suicide. However, if this case were looked at alone, an ESP tradition in the family could not be clearly ruled out, though it would have to be a kind of Super-ESP, a point which we will consider in the following chapter.

The Chaffin Will Case. James L. Chaffin, Sr. died in 1921. In his will he left everything to his third son, Marshall.[5] He disinherited his wife and his other three sons. In 1925, a son, James L. Chaffin, Jr., began having vivid "dreams" (possibly he was awake) in which he saw his father wearing an old black overcoat which he had worn in life. The apparition said, "You will find my will in my overcoat pocket." After several visions, James went to the house of his brother, John, where the overcoat had been kept. The lining of the pocket had been sewn up and inside was a piece of paper on which was written, "Read the 27th chapter of Genesis in my daddy's old Bible." James went to his mother's house with some witnesses. There he found the Bible and in the chapter mentioned he found a yellowed will made in 1919 in which the father had divided the property equally. The will was taken to court. Handwriting experts were called in and the state of North Carolina ruled that the second will was legal. (The father had died in an accident and apparently was unable to tell the family of the second will.) During the period of the court proceedings, the father's phantom reappeared asking about his will. Rogo, in a thorough treatment, gives solid reasons for ruling out all explanations other than a genuine apparition of the father. This is a case in which information is given which no one else on earth seems to have had.

The C.S. Lewis Case. C.S. Lewis would have been horrified during his lifetime if he found himself cited in such an example. He had a great distaste for what he called "the occult." At any rate, Canon J.B. Phillips, who has published a translation of the New Testament, saw Lewis twice in apparitions after Lewis' death.[6] Phillips had been undergoing a peculiar greyness of spirit which robbed life of color and to some extent of meaning.

Lewis spoke a few comforting words relevant to Phillips' state of mind. The apparition was only four or five feet away and lasted about a minute and half each time. He looked perfectly lifelike and was wearing the tweeds which he liked to wear. Phillips had seen Lewis only once during his lifetime and he was in a cassock.

The Case of Mrs. George Butler. After Mrs. George Butler's death around 1800, her apparition returned to her village of Sullivan, near Machiasport, Maine.[7] She was seen in the form of an apparition over a period of three months by some one hundred persons, including her husband. This case, even though it is rather old, is very well documented. One hundred viewers saw the apparition, thirty affadavits were collected, and a pamphlet on the subject was published by the theologian, Abraham Cummings, who investigated the case. The apparition often spoke. On occasions the remarks were rather long, and once there was an extended discourse before forty-eight witnesses. It appeared twenty-seven times between 1800 and 1806. Predictions were made about births and deaths in the family which proved correct. Sometimes the apparition spoke on religious matters. Captain George Butler attempted several times to touch the apparition and found that his hand passed through it, though its form seemed solid. At times it was seen as a luminous figure. This is an example of an apparition which was collectively seen and well documented. However, the profusion of details and the long discourses are so untypical of apparition cases that some skepticism is not unwarranted in this case.

Hauntings or Continual Apparitions

The Morton Ghost. A phantom woman with a handkerchief over her face was seen frequently in a large house in Cheltenham, England from 1882 to 1889.[8] Rose Despard, who was called "Rose Morton" in the accounts, saw the apparition six times. Rose had an experimental leaning and she kept a diary of the events which she sent daily to Miss Catherine Campbell in Northern England. She even tied strings across the stairs but the spectre moved through them. Rose saw it in daylight. She and her three sisters saw it in quick succession, and two of the sisters saw it independently on August 12, 1884. The maid saw it. Edith, her sister, saw it in July 1885 and felt a cold chill. Rose spoke to the woman. The figure gave a gasp as if to speak but it seemed it couldn't. It went into the drawing room while Rose, her sisters and her father were there, but she alone saw it. Her dogs were affected by it. Rose tried to photograph it, usually at night, but got no results. It was so solid and lifelike it could be mistaken for a real person. The lady, tall and slim, was dressed in widow's dress and her face was hidden by a handkerchief held in her right hand. Only the upper part of the forehead could be seen. She was seen in different parts of the house. Sometimes she stood for from ten minutes to a half hour. The apparition was also seen by Rose's young brother and another little boy while playing on the terrace. At that time it was crying bitterly. A friend of the family recalled seeing it as a child and the children joined hands around it. At times Rose felt as if she had lost power to the figure. (Recall the experiments with Ingo Swann and the thermistor in Chapter II.) From 1887 to 1889 the sightings were rarer, but footsteps were heard. Investigations were made about the previous tenants of the house. Rogo believes it was probably Imogene Swinhoe, the wife of the house's first tenant. Rose picked out a photo of Imogene's sister from a random group of photos and this sister looked very much like her. Before Imogene died she had been looking for jewels which her estranged husband had hidden in the house. She died of alcoholism. This was a case which was collectively seen, over a long period of time, and it was well investigated. Animals also reacted to it. The figure was unknown. Thus it cannot be ascribed to desire to see one who had died.

Experimental Projections of Apparitions

These experiments were made by living agents and the projections were made to living percipients. We have already treated this category in the chapter on out-of-the-body experiences. The category is included here because the actions and characteristics of these projected apparitions are very similar to apparitions of the dead. Thus they seem to give some backing to the influence that in some apparitions of the dead an agent is also involved and that the visions are not pure hallucinations.

Photographed Apparitions

Usually not much attention is given to photographs of ghosts because of the evident ease with which fraudulent photographs are produced. However, Fred Gettings has published some remarkable photographs of apparitions which should not be so lightly disposed of.[9] Good controls, at least for the turn of the century, were in operation. Also, some of the photographs seem to defy explanation through fraud. For example, a Chinese laundryman was photographed circa 1900 and next to his face there appeared the face of a child. When he saw it, the laundryman said it was his son who was living in China, whom he had not seen in three years. However, unknown to him, the child had died. In another photograph of a Mr. J.R. Mercer, the face of his wife appeared next to his, together with a written message about her happiness. But during the wife's lifetime no daguerreotype or screened block photograph of this kind could have been made. The only explanation for these photographs apart from influence by an agent beyond death is, I believe, thoughtography, a PK impression produced on film by the one taking the picture. But I have seen no examples of reading of another's mind together with imprinting through thoughtography on a film. In this age of instantly developing Polaroid cameras a more solid case could be made for the genuineness of apparition photography. Experiments with various instruments has begun in this area.[10]

Conclusion

In the cases I have presented, we find details which represent solid criteria for judging the non-subjective reality of apparitions. Most of the people involved seem normal and not markedly pathological. Some apparitions were seen collectively. As the psychic investigator Frank Podmore said, that two people should receive the same telepathic message is possible, but that they should both invest it with exactly the same sensory form seems most improbable. However, research should be continued in this area.[11] Animals and very young children saw or reacted to some of these apparitions. In one case paranormal knowledge was offered by an apparition (the Chaffin Will case) which seemingly was in the possession of no one on earth. Lastly, these apparitions are most similar to experimental projections in which there is an agent involved beyond the percipient. These kinds of evidence seem to me to imply that some appearances of phantoms suggest a life which continues beyond our earth dimensions.

However, the study of apparitions is an area of extreme complexity in which an excessive tidying up might not do justice to all the data. More and more the mind is seen to be a mysterious power whose potentialities we have by no means fully understood. The following case cited by Brian C. Nisbet is an example of this complexity.[12] In 1887 Canon Bourne and his two daughters went out hunting. As they began to return home, the daughters were momentarily delayed. Then they saw their father waving to them from the side of a distant hill. They recognized their father and his horse. The horse looked dirty and shaken and the coachman remarked that he thought there must have been a nasty accident. They even saw the brand mark inside their father's hat as he waved it at them, a thing which seemed impossible in view of the distance. But when they reached that point, the father was nowhere to be seen. When they arrived home, the father said he had never been in that field the entire day and that he had experienced no accident. How is one to explain a case like this?

Apparitions can appear in space or in or on something like a wall or the ground.[13] Most are not normal physical phenomena and generally leave no physical traces, though imprints are sometimes left, as in prisons where someone has been executed. Apparitions usually behave as if they are in a physical environment. They avoid chairs and tables, and they are at times reflected in mirrors. But they disappear when a person closes his or her eyes. They appear with clothes on. Some apparitions may make an effort to speak; others may really speak. A number are collectively seen, in one counting 8%. A feeling of cold and sometimes of static electricity often accompany the appearance. A feeling of presence is so strong at times that it awakens a person. Some are intangible, and one's hand goes through them; others feel like human flesh, and there are even solid accounts of apparitions which eat and drink. Sometimes animals are seen and at other times animals seem to perceive apparitions.

According to G.N.M. Tyrrell who specialized in apparition study the most coherent and probable explanation for some apparitions is the survival of an individual beyond death.

Ectoplasmic Apparitions

Until recently, most British and American parapsychologists have tended to group ectoplasmic phenomena under the heading of fraud. Many Continental parapsychologists, more biologically oriented, have been more favorable in their views. The reader is advised to refer to the appendix of Chapter III where this question is discussed.

One of the best examples of ectoplasmic apparitions has been presented by D. Scott Rogo who has an ample knowledge of the Continental literature. Franek Kluski (b. 1874) was a Polish man of letters who was prone to psychic experiences throughout his life. In 1920 he was tested by Professor Gustave Geley at the Institut Métaphysique. During these tests, "phantom limbs materialized, brilliant lights ignited in the air, luminous forms glided through the séance room" and phantoms materialized and were photographed.[14] No good evidence was ever presented which suggested that Kluski's powers were not genuine. The reason why much of the work with even apparently genuine ectoplasmic phenomena was conducted in darkness or semi-darkness was that the one who produced these materializations suffered actual pain when subjected to bright lights. (This is not to deny that many mediums utilized the dark for intrigue and fraud.) Geley described one Kluski experiment which seems to preclude fraud as follows: "Control was perfect—right hand held by Professor Richet and left by Count

Polocki. The controllers kept repeating, 'I am holding the right hand,' or 'I am holding the left hand.' After fifteen or twenty minutes splashing was audible in the tank, and the hands operating, covered with warm paraffin. Professor Richet and I had added some blue coloring matter to the paraffin, which then had a bluish tinge. This was done secretly, to be an absolute proof that the molds were made on the spot and not brought ready-made into the laboratory by Franek or any other person and passed off on us by legerdemain. This operation lasted as before, from one to two minutes. Two admirable molds resulted, of the right and left hands the size of the hands of children five to seven years old. They were of bluish wax, the same colour as that in the tanks."[15]

An American professor, F.W. Pawlowski, wrote about the apparitions which appeared and were photographed: " . . . the apparitions appear almost unexpectedly beside or behind the medium. In this case I have seen something like a faintly luminous smoke or mist accumulating above the medium's head like a small cloud. The cloud shifts sideways and in a few seconds evolves a human head; or it extends vertically and evolves a complete human apparition, which immediately begins to walk around, etc. . . . The most striking and interesting thing about the apparitions to me . . . was their perfectly human behavior. They conducted themselves as callers at a party. They made a round of the sitters, smiling an acknowledgment of the familiar sitters and looking curiously at the sitters they had not seen before."[16] As Rogo says, this kind of physical mediumship seems connected with poltergeist effects. It need not infer contact with life beyond death.

Theories

A listing of some of the main theories presented as models to explain apparitions may help the reader to make a better assessment of the evidence we have presented.

1. The *percipient* uses clairvoyance and telepathy. He or she unconsciously gathers data by clairvoyance or telepathy with

the living and then unconsciously dramatizes this is an external fashion. While this theory may have value for some cases, it does not explain cases where the figure seen is unknown to the person seeing it and is often long dead, as in the Morton ghost case—that is, unless one holds that all reality is available to us in our unconscious. This Super-ESP theory we will discuss in the next chapter. Note that this first theory postulates no agent beyond the percipient.

2. An *agent* (dead or living as in OBE projections) sends data telepathically to a percipient. In this theory the agent may be considered as really present in physical space, or else the agent may not be considered to be present in physical space but to send a message paranormally to the percipient.[17] In some cases the apparition seems to know the details of a house as if it is there in reality and not just by telepathy. If one holds the not-real-presence telepathy position, it seems best to add another element to this hypothesis. The agent sends a message but the *percipient cooperates* by unconsciously dramatizing the scene to fit the details before him or her. If it is seen collectively, then the agent reaches the mind of the group by telepathy, and they all dramatize the same apparition moving between the tables and chairs which they see. The weakness to the second or telepathic approach is that animals at times react to the vision, as in the Morton ghost case, and occasionally it is photographed.

3. The *agent,* whether living or dead, goes in an *OBE* to visit the percipient. This explains how some apparitions can be photographed and why animals react, sometimes even before the people who are present see it. The weakness is, as we have seen in the chapter on OBEs, that our evidence for a genuine, quasi-physical body is very slender.

Theory 1 above does not fit the data in many cases. In theories 2 and 3 where an agent is involved, the only agent who would make the experience coherent is one who has died, as in the Morton case, the case of the World War I pilot, the Butler and Sutton cases, the C.S. Lewis case and the case of the very young child reacting to an apparition. In many cases, the most coherent explanation is that someone who has died is communicating.

The Resurrection of Jesus

To begin with, let us divide the resurrection event into three elements: (1) the apparitions, (2) the empty tomb, (3) the belief that Jesus had entered into a new dimension of glorious life "at the right hand of the Father." What I would call conservative and moderate theologians maintain that the three elements are historical. This is the apparent meaning of Scripture. Many moderate to liberal theologians hold a qualified position. They believe that there were apparitions which were not simple subjective hallucinations, and they believe that Jesus now was and is in glory with the Father. But they find difficulty in holding that there was really an empty tomb. They do believe that Jesus arose but not necessarily in conjunction with an emptying of the tomb. They believe that the empty tomb passages in Scripture may have been later additions, not based on history, but added for apologetical purposes. This would have been deemed legitimate by the apostles after they were convinced through the apparitions that Jesus lived beyond death with the Father. Many of these theologians believe either that, incredibly to me, the disciples did not look into Jesus' tomb, or else that Jesus was buried in such a manner that he could not be found, as in a common grave. This opposes the scriptural narrative that Jesus was buried in the tomb provided by Joseph of Arimathea.

Lastly, there is the opinion of those whom I term the extreme liberal theologians, like Rudolf Bultmann. The scriptural narratives about the empty tomb and the apparitions do not depict historical happenings. They are fictive or mythical symbols used to present in popular models the only event that happened, namely, Jesus lives beyond death in union with the Father. This was their belief. Bultmann, too, affirms this belief as a Christian. He does not think that one can, in an age of electricity, radio and modern technology, believe in an empty tomb or in apparitions. For him, Jesus' resurrection means simply that the cross saves.[18]

Discussion

The earliest written account of the witnesses to the resurrection of Jesus occurs in 1 Corinthians 15:3ff.:

> For I delivered to you as of first importance what I also received, that Christ died for our sins in accordance with the scriptures, that he was buried, that he was raised on the third day in accordance with the scriptures, and that he appeared to Cephas, and then to the twelve. Then he appeared to more than five hundred brethren at one time, most of whom are still alive, though some have fallen asleep. Then he appeared to James, then to all the apostles. Last of all, as to one untimely born, he appeared also to me.[19]

The four Gospels began as oral tradition before Paul's account was recorded but they were compiled and written as complete Gospels from about 65 to 80 A.D. for the Synoptics and from 90 to 100 A.D. for John. In the Gospels there are many accounts of Jesus' apparitions but the names of those who saw the apparitions, the timing and place do not always agree. Remember, the Gospels are not history in the modern sense but faith documents based on history. The resurrection presentations apparently represent the confusion experienced at the time of the event and the various Gospels do not portray a harmonious synthesis.

In recent years many liberal theologians and scriptural exegetes have treated the apparitions of Jesus with an almost unconcealed embarrassment. Occasionally, there is an outright denial of any genuine trans-subjective apparitions. More often what is offered is an extremely subtle and confusing presentation in which the role of the apparitions is so minimized that the reader is left bewildered as to the author's actual position.

For example, the outstanding Catholic theologian, Edward Schillebeeckx, O.P., treated the apparitions in such a subtle manner in his first book, *Jesus,* that he had to publish, after also publishing *Christ,* a subsequent work, *Interim Report on the Books Jesus and Christ.*[20] Schillebeeckx was not interested in so stressing the objective elements in the appearances that the faith and conversion experience in the face of the apparitions would seem to be of secondary importance. This is indeed an important move. But the parallel data from parapsychological research about apparitions warn us not to allow Jesus' apparitions to fade away into an excessively existential and purely subjective experience. Schillebeeckx, in his *Interim Report,* rejects a purely existential and subjective explanation of the apparitions, yet there is such a wariness about treating them in any critical way that his support of the apparitions as actual occurrences is extremely general and leaves the reader with little regard for their importance. This emphasis on interpretation with only a minimal notice taken of the events is also true of the recent work of Hans Küng.[21]

The confusion in the Gospel presentations of the apparitions, their locations and percipients, is understandable if we see, as even the official position of the Roman Catholic Church now proposes, three levels in the formation of the traditions about Jesus: (1) the actual events, (2) the oral tradition and (3) the editing by the evangelists which underlined and stressed certain theological motifs.[22]

On level 1, the level of actual events, if one studies the Gospels apart from certain "modern" philosophical and theological presuppositions, I think one must say that something *within the realm of history* happened, some genuine apparitions occurred. Can we imagine Paul listing the various individual and collective witnesses to the apparitions in 1 Corinthians 15, and writing that "if Christ has not been raised, then our preaching is in vain and your faith is in vain. We are even found to be misrepresenting God that he raised Christ whom he did not raise . . ."—but meanwhile he was presenting only a kind of "symbolical concretizing" to support the belief in Jesus' presence "at the right hand of God"? Charles Martin in *Christian Origins and History* puts the point very well:

> They slunk out of Jerusalem while Jesus was nailed to the cross. They went back to their houses and their fishing. Yet, six weeks later, (suppose) they were found on the steps of the St. Paul's Cathedral of the day, telling the clergy that they were talking nonsense, and were moreover guilty of

conspiracy in Jesus' death. . . . Instead of being laughed into
silence by the crowd, they won the crowd over. These Jews,
with centuries of privileged pedigree behind them, threw it
all away and became Christians. The whole system of Judaism was rocked to its foundations by their preaching. Does it
seem likely if nothing out of the ordinary happened at
Easter?[23]

Few exegetes or theologians make any use of parapsychological data when they investigate the apparitions of Jesus. One
of the few whom I have found to refer to these data is Wolfhart
Pannenberg:

> Recent studies in the field of parapsychology (extrasensory
> perception) [he cited Joseph Rhine's *New World of the Mind*],
> including such things as prophetic intuition (precognition),
> clairvoyance and telepathy, have reopened the question of
> the objective reality of unusual occurrences. One should be
> on one's guard against drawing direct conclusions for our
> question about the reality of the Easter appearances from
> such investigations. Up to now they show nothing more than
> the possibility of visionary experiences that are not merely to
> be judged as subjective projections but—in satisfactorily
> demonstrable numbers—involve something to which they
> coincide; that is, they lay hold of extrasubjective reality.
> Nevertheless, in any case one conclusion may be drawn:
> precisely in the area of the history of religions, where only
> exceptional phenomena are handed down, the psychiatric
> concept of "vision" may not be postulated unless a more
> specific point of contact for it is given by the tradition.[24]

Apparition experiences, Pannenberg rightly suggests, may
not be *automatically* extrapolated as a univocal base for understanding the resurrection appearances. The tradition has always
considered these experiences as a unique irruption of the divine
in human life. On the other hand, he sees parapsychology as
supporting the idea of "objective" apparitions. But can we not
go further?

Karl Rahner, S.J. published his remarkable *Visions and Prophecies* in the English version in 1963.[25] In this work he shows a very
broad knowledge of parapsychological literature and he demon-

strates a deep grasp of the issues. Yet in his studies on the resurrection he makes little or no use of these data, although his explanations of the *total meaning* of the resurrection are important for theological students of parapsychology. For example, " . . . the resurrection must be understood not as any kind of coming to life of a man, or even as the return of a man to the plane of temporal and biological existence, but rather as a unique event, though one that still takes place within the unfolding of our time, as the seal of God upon the reality of Jesus. . . ."[26] Similarly, he writes, we must "pose the question of how in all seriousness the first disciples could have arrived at their Easter faith if they had known nothing beforehand about Jesus from his understanding of himself, except that he was a wandering religious preacher preaching a message which was totally independent of his person and his own faith."[27]

At the same time, Rahner writes, "We certainly should not imagine it [the resurrection] in terms of the way spatio-temporal realities of this world confront us in our everyday experience. Such a practice would not show deep faith; it would simply be wrong."[28] Again, "It is obvious from the outset that we cannot weigh and measure the risen Lord, cannot photograph him with our cameras, that even a team of television reporters could not make a documentary about him. He does not belong to the world of experience."[29] We must be careful to understand these citations within the total context of Rahner's theology. He is speaking about the global complexity of the resurrection as a faith event and not just about apparitions. As to the apparitions, it is most probable that, even when seen as produced through the divine initiative, the general "laws" and patterns of human creaturehood are still respected. This is a point which Rahner as much as anyone has stressed, especially in his studies of the incarnation and Christology.

That the apparitions could not be seen by everyone seems obvious to many authors. This is often based on Acts 10:41 where it is said that God caused him to be seen not by all the people but by "us who were chosen by God as witnesses, who ate and drank with him after he rose from the dead." This theological motif of Luke, whose point is to stress the divine initiative in the resurrection appearances, cannot become a generalized statement about who could see Jesus' apparitions. At least this is the warning which arises from the study of recent parapsychological research. In Matthew 28:17 it is said, "And when they saw him they worshiped him; but some doubted." This passage does not imply that the doubters did not see Jesus. Who could or could not see the apparitions of Jesus is by no means clear. However, from a theological point of view, this at least is clear. Apparitions should not be considered as isolated slide-specimens separated from the total context of the resurrection. The resurrection event must be seen in its proper context, that of unlimited love present in human existence.

Some Questions about Jesus' Appearances

There is no question but that we must avoid a Fundamentalist approach to the words and actions of the resurrected Jesus as presented in the Gospels. We have learned that there are theological motifs in operation which demonstrate that the appearance stories are not straight history in our modern sense. For example, in regard to Matthew 28:19, "Go therefore and make disciples of all nations, baptizing them in the name of the Father and of the Son and of the Holy Spirit," modern exegesis has made it reasonable to assume that these are not the exact words of Jesus but the coloring of Jesus' words by later liturgical formulae and theological conclusions. In the Book of Acts, baptism is given not in the name of the Trinity but in the name of Jesus Christ (Acts 2:38). The quotation in Matthew seems to reflect a later liturgical formula. Similarly, if Jesus in his resurrected life gave the disciples an *explicit* command to teach *all* nations, then discussions about this precise point in Acts 10 and 15 as well as in the letters of Paul become unintelligible.[30]

We might make the same judgment about the story in Luke 24:13–35 about the two disciples on the way to Emmaus. They did not recognize Jesus as they journeyed along with him, but "their eyes were opened and they recognized him" only at the meal when he took bread, blessed and broke it and gave it to them. Many exegetes have made a solid case for the position that this episode may not have been a specific historical event but a faith sermon to the early Christians to recognize Jesus in the eucharistic meal.[31]

However, parapsychological data may be of some assistance in interpreting a number of the apparition stories, even despite the obvious theological coloring of the narrative. Let me make this point very specific and concrete by, first, asking the following questions: (1) Could Jesus in his resurrection appearances speak? (2) Could he be touched and could he eat?

Many theologians and Scripture scholars seem to presume that it is evident that little if anything that is placed on the lips of Jesus as he appeared to his disciples came from Jesus himself. They see these words simply as the interpretations by the disciples of the (mute?) apparitions of Jesus. But the anomaly in this position is seen by the fact that we have excellent evidence for verbal expression by apparitions. Merely to refer to the cases I have cited, mention could be made of Mrs. Butler, James Chaffin, Sr., C.S. Lewis, and James Sutton. Why such evidence should be considered totally irrelevant to the understanding of the resurrection appearances is by no means clear. It should not at all be taken as self-evident that the risen Jesus never gave instructions to his disciples.

Secondly, many scholars believe it is self-evident that the scriptural passages in which Jesus is touched, as by Mary Magdalene (Jn 20:17), or where Jesus says he may be touched (Lk 24:39; Jn 20:27), or where he eats (Acts 10:41; Lk 24:42) are obviously not historical episodes at least with regard to these details.[32] However, we have a goodly number of cases in parapsychological literature where apparitions are touched.[33] Similarly, we have modern evidence in which apparitions are said to have eaten.[34]

I trust that the reader will understand that I am not driving toward a Fundamentalist position here. I am merely considering parallel evidence from parapsychological investigation which unsettles positions which seem to have become frozen into certainties on given points. From these points, at times, conclusions are drawn that seem very shaky in the light of evidence from a different discipline.

A Problem

Undoubtedly, the reader will see a problem arising from the previous discussion. If other people besides Jesus have appeared and even spoken in apparitions, how then is Jesus' resurrection unique? I do not have the space to elaborate fully on this point, and I am sure that those who later consider the data presented will improve on what I have to suggest. However, I wish to stress two points. First, in the total resurrection event of Jesus there is also an empty tomb. Second, Jesus' life, teaching and implicit claims (cf. Chapter III) cannot be separated from his apparitions.

(1) Many theologians and Scripture scholars downplay the empty tomb episodes, even among those who accept them as historical, as if they were of no account. However, in our present context they take on considerable theological importance. Jesus in his glorified life is a unique new creation, a new Adam, as St. Paul said. The old body-life has disappeared. He lives in a new dimension.

Historically, the empty tomb fits coherently into the total picture. I have never seen it explained how St. Paul could have preached Jesus as resurrected while some of his hearers knew that Jesus' body was still in Palestine. Most scholars admit the tomb was empty. Even the Jewish leaders seem not to have denied this. Some scholars speculate that he may have been buried in a common grave and the exact place of burial was unknown. (Yet all the evidence we have claims that he was buried in the tomb of Joseph of Arimathea.)

Here I do not intend to elaborate on the old debates. Who could have taken the body? Not the Jewish leaders certainly. Nor the disciples who proceeded to venture forth, preaching vigorously about the resurrection and often dying for their beliefs. The reader may find this point discussed in many books and articles. My point is that in view of what I have said previously, the empty tomb takes on added importance. Rahner and Schillebeeckx are undoubtedly correct when they say that the empty tomb alone would not give rise to belief in the resurrection. Neither writer denies the empty tomb, but I believe that both greatly underrate its significance.

(I doubt that those writers enlighten us very much about the empty tomb who understand it analogically to cases of well-attested materialization and dematerialization phenomena. The processes in these strange phenomena are themselves most mysterious. They may be merely reflections of a higher power operative in Jesus' resurrection, or the resurrection may be of a completely different dimension of unique divine operation. However, the recollection of the existence of such powers may aid some people in their *imagination* of the resurrection.)

(2) Jesus' life teachings and implicit claims (an "implicit Christology") cannot be separated from his apparitions. This is the impact which the apparitions had on those who first witnessed them. There was no discontinuity. The apparitions may have heightened or made explicit what was there in an implicit way but they did not create a Christology out of nothing. Jesus' apparitions, as Rahner and, to a lesser extent, Schillebeeckx claim, are like a seal on Jesus' *whole* life.[35] They cannot be seen as isolated events. Thus, Jesus' uniqueness is seen not only in the fact that he appeared and perhaps spoke to his disciples, but in a life lived and in an interpretation acted out. Jesus' implicit Christology is bound up with the apparitions and it is never restrained or checked by them.

A Recent Treatment of the Fatima Apparitions and a Possible Application to Jesus' Resurrection

The official Church has always been most circumspect about judging the validity of the apparitions seen by saints and mystics, and rightly so. For example, Fr. Herbert Thurston, S.J. (1856–1939) compared the visions of Jesus' life had by Anne Catherine Emmerich with those of St. Bridget of Sweden and Maria de Agreda of Spain, all highly esteemed visionaries.[36] The discrepancies are overwhelming in detail, and telepathy seems to have been at work between Anne Catherine and her amanuensis, Clement Brentano.

However, one of the most intriguing series of apparitions in recent times had been that at Fatima. I presume that many readers are already acquainted with the major details of the apparitions. Three Portuguese children were involved—Lucia, 9, Jacinta, 8, and Francesco, 6. At the first vision of May 13, 1917, they saw a flash of light and then a young girl dressed in white.[37] The apparition asked them to return to the Cova da Iria on the thirteenth of the month for the next six months. Also, the prediction was made that the three children would go to heaven and that another child, Amelia, was in purgatory. (Francesco had not at first seen the vision, and in later episodes he would hear nothing.) They were told to say the rosary for peace in the world and for the end of World War I.

Afterward, on July 13, a sound like the buzzing of a house-fly in a bottle preceded the vision. A secret was told, "Good for some, but for others bad." Before the August apparition, the air grew noticeably cooler, the sunlight dimmed, there was a flash of lightning and the sunlight took on various colors.

On September 13, 1917 (as well as on May 13, 1918 and in 1924) there was a shower of white objects like snowflakes or rose petals which could be photographed.[38] On the culminating day, October 13, 1917, about 70,000 people gathered at the Cova da Iria. A few came to mock and some were from the anticlerical paper, *O Seculo*. A sort of mist surrounded the tree, or, some said, the children. The apparition asked that a chapel be built on the spot in honor of "Our Lady of the Rosary." People were told to ask pardon for their sins and that they must not offend our Lord any more. Mary was seen with Joseph and the child Jesus.

There then followed the famous solar apparition. Rain which had been falling stopped, and the sun, "dull silver like an eclipse," pierced through the diaphanous clouds.[39] It had a giddy movement and wheeled about wildly. This caused a moment of apprehension that it was about to descend and crush the specta-tors. Various colors spread through the atmosphere.

A strange aspect of the apparition was that it is known that a few who were present did not see it. Martindale mentions two ladies who saw nothing. On the other hand, I.L. Pereira, later a missionary in India, saw it while at school six miles away. And the poet, Alfonso Lopes Vieira, saw it while twenty-four miles away.

The "secret" which was given in July had three parts.[40] The first part was a vision of "hell." Apparently there was also a prediction of the end of World War I and of a worse war during the reign of a later Pontiff. The second part referred to the devotion to "the Immaculate Heart of Mary" and to the request that the Pope consecrate the world and especially Russia to the Immaculate Heart of Mary. The third part of the secret was written down in 1943. "This part, which has not yet been made public, is in the sealed archives of the Vatican."[41]

This is a most perplexing apparition and one which is still puzzling today after so much analysis. A Catholic astronomer at the time suggested to Fr. Martindale that layers of air at different temperatures and densities acted like a series of lenses and could cause apparent motions in the sun. This, of course, would not explain all the phenomena. The Catholic paper, *A Ordem,* doubted a miracle. A group claimed to have seen the same phenomenon the next day. Karl Rahner in *Visions and Prophecies* had some hesitations. Why would God reveal something concerning the whole world but then order it be kept secret until after its fulfillment.[42] Puzzled, he mentions the many visions in the past in which incorrect information had been given. As far as I can determine, Rahner seemed to lean toward the idea of a private revelation in children's words mixed with religious imagination.

Recently, D. Scott Rogo has studied the Fatima events. He sees them as a group PK phenomenon produced collectively and unconsciously. He points out that it centers around children.[43] "There are really only two basic theories that can account for the Marian visitations. The first is that these apparitions are psychic projections, something akin to thought forms, which are produced by the minds of spectators or by the Catholic community at large in the countries in which they appear. The alternative is that they represent actual visitations by a spiritual being or presence deliberately sent to instruct us. The first of these seems to be the more cogent. It was suggested earlier that Marian apparitions might be the result of a projected archetype that occasionally emerges from a universal collective unconscious in times of spiritual crisis ... only a week before the apparition revealed itself for the first time, Pope Benedict XIV had issued a statement to the effect that only the Blessed Virgin could intercede to end the First World War, and he urged the world to pray to her. The figure of the Virgin Mary may indeed have been an archetype projected either by the children themselves or by the entire Portuguese people in response to overwhelming national chaos . . . this creation then may have taken on a temporary life of its own."[44] As corroboration Rogo mentions a revival meeting in 1905 in North Wales in which spectators noticed orbs of light which would suddenly appear in the sky and zigzag about. On March 29, 1972 he mentions a similar event in the Dominican Republic. Before more than a thousand people a dark cloud appeared and opened in the sky, "revealing a glowing disc that illuminated the entire courtyard. The cloud then folded up and the object vanished."[45]

Is there any supporting or parallel evidence for such a view which seems at first glance so outrageous? The "Philip" group in Toronto (see Chapter II) through unconscious group collective PK power effected table rappings which spelled out a fictitious story which the group had concocted about an imaginary Philip. Similarly the Batcheldor group in Exeter, England produced significant group PK activity with a table. However, neither group produced an apparition of what was in their consciousness.

Recently, in *The Story of Ruth*, psychiatrist Morton Schatzman tells of a patient who experienced a persistent hallucination of her father.[45] (The father had raped her and is now living in another country.) Once her husband Paul saw an apparition she had conjured of herself and he addressed it as if she were sitting on a sofa instead of where she actually was a few yards away. (However, this seems similar to OBE projections about which we have already spoken. It does not help us directly with cases where there is an alleged projection of reality which is not simply the self.)

Alexandra David-Neel who studied Tibetan mysticism in depth published her findings in *Magic and Mystery in Tibet*. She speaks of *tulpas*, "magic formations generated by a powerful concentration of thought."[48] When endowed with enough vitality to be capable of playing the part of a real being, it tends, she wrote, "to free itself from its maker's control." She herself, by conscious effort, created a *tulpa*, a monk, short and fat, of an innocent and jolly type. Once a visiting herdsman saw it in her tent. She tried to dissolve it but she succeeded only after six months of hard struggle. "My mind creature was tenacious of life." However, this *tulpa* did not speak.

Rogo's hypothesis deserves further investigation. However, the phenomena of Fatima were so complex and so many-faceted that I do not at present feel that this is the full explanation of the events (the visions, the solar phenomena, the predictions). For the moment I prefer Rahner's theory of a private revelation through a superhuman agency but couched in children's words and concepts.

Before leaving Rogo's hypothesis about Fatima, let us approach a much more delicate question, that of the relevance of Rogo's position to explanations of the resurrection appearances of Jesus. Could the disciples have unconsciously projected the image of Jesus whom they believed reigning with the Father beyond death? This would not be a hallucination in the traditional sense. The resulting apparition would have been caused subjectively but there also would have been something perceptible in physical reality. The projection would result in an image which had a quasi-physical quality. It could be seen by others, say the five hundred of whom St. Paul spoke. Whether the image would be true to reality (i.e., whether Jesus really was alive in glory and at the right hand of the Father) could be decided only by faith. It would not necessarily be a false representation.

Some Christian theologians who seem to be almost embarrassed by the apparitions and the empty tomb may find some attraction in such a theory. After all, they say, despite stories about the empty tomb and apparitions, conviction about Jesus' resurrection can come only through faith, and this alone is to be stressed. However, this kind of a projection theory cannot account for the empty tomb. Neither, as far as I can see, can it account for apparitions had by *groups* (e.g., the five hundred mentioned by St. Paul and the apostles as a group) as well as by *individuals* (Cephas, James, Mary Magdalene) on *different* occasions. We do know from parapsychological literature that all apparitions are not simply conscious projections from the mind of the percipient. This is certainly true of some of the cases I have mentioned as well of the OBE experimental projections in which there obviously is an agent involved beyond the percipi-ent. While this sort of theory will undoubtedly enter into future discussion of the resurrection of Jesus, and while one might well remain a Christian and embrace such a view, I believe it is not a satisfactory explanation.

In conclusion, my judgment is that it is fully consonant with parapsychological literature that it was the agency of Jesus (or God) which produced the resurrection apparitions.[49] Further-more, the empty tomb is an essential part of the resurrection event and its downplaying has been unfortunate. It is one aspect of the uniqueness of the Jesus event. The other aspect is the implicit Christology found in Jesus' life. Neither of these two elements should be forgotten in endeavoring to understand the meaning of Jesus' existence. Lastly, parapsychological literature, in adducing cases of materialization and dematerialization, may act as a devotional aid for some people in *imagining* the process of the bodily resurrection, but it probably will also be misleading in that it encourages a literal imagining of an event without parallel in human history.

Chapter X

Mediums: The Unconscious or Life Beyond?

Perhaps nowhere does the word "fraud" jump to mind so quickly as in the discussion of psychic mediums. Indeed, history has uncovered many mediums who were dishonest.[1] But if one is animated by desire to know the real, fraud becomes a too easy escape in the study of a large number of mediums. In most of the cases which I will cite, balanced critics have found no reasonable suspicion of fraud. There may be alternate explanations for handling the data but fraud is not one of them.

In the study of mediums, four elements should be distinguished: the medium, the control, the sitter and the alleged communicator from the beyond. The medium is a psychic or sensitive who appears to communicate with those who have died. The medium often enters into a deep trance, but some mediums are conscious, operating only in a light trance or merely in a deep state of concentration. The "control" acts like an other-worldly master of ceremonies, summoning those who are to communicate from dimensions beyond. Most parapsychologists consider the control to be a kind of unconscious "persona," in the Jungian sense, a fragment of the unconscious personality which takes over the medium's consciousness.[2] The "sitter" is the person who comes to attend the medium's effort at communication and addresses questions to the "discarnate," a word cherished by many psychics. However, at times the "sitter" may

175

not be present at all. He or she may mail questions, even from another country. The existence of the alleged communicator is, of course, the point at issue in medium study.

Medium work often has begun through the instrumentality of the ouija board with its gliding planchette or pointer. The more accomplished mediums frequently present the messages in the form of automatic writing. They may feel that their hands are directed or they may write down a message heard, "clairaudience." Of late, as befits a technological age, automatic writing has moved to the typewriter, as with Ruth Montgomery and Taylor Caldwell.

Communications Which Are Actually ESP

Let us first consider alleged mediumistic communication where it is clear that no communication from beyond this world is taking place.

Richard Hodgson (1855–1905) had been a research officer at the American Society for Psychical Research before he died in 1905. He then allegedly began to act as the control for Mrs. Leonore Piper (1857–1950), the Boston medium of great fame and integrity. G. Stanley Hall, a psychologist, went for a sitting with Mrs. Piper. He asked the control, Hodgson, to contact Hall's niece, "Bessie Beals," so that he might speak with her. Miss Beals was duly introduced and proceeded to communicate with Hall through Mrs. Piper. Actually Bessie Beals did not exist. She was a figment of Hall's mind.[3] "Hodgson" in embarrassment tried to wriggle out of the situation, saying that he had been mistaken about the name. He said the person brought was a Jessie Beals, related to another sitter.

S.G. Soal, afterward famous for his card-guessing tests, visualized incidents with an imaginary friend, John Ferguson. He then went for a sitting with the medium, Blanche Cooper. The incidents he visualized came forth as though communicated from beyond death.[4]

At another time, Soal received communications through Blanche Cooper from a Gordon Davis. Davis had been an acquaintance of Soal during his school years. Soal had last met him in 1916 and later heard Davis had been killed at the front in France. Soal thought he recognized the tone of the voice with its fastidious accent. Davis spoke of the school they had attended, Rochford, and details of their last conversation. He even described pictures and furnishings in the house in which Davis had lived. As a matter of fact, Davis was not dead and Soal visited him in 1925. During both of Soal's sittings, according to Davis' diary he was consulting with people as a real estate agent.[5] During the sittings Davis first inspected the house described. But only about a year later did he move into the house, and the furnishings of the house had not been planned in advance. Yet, the details mentioned in the sitting turned out to be correct: a large mirror, lots of paintings, glorious mountain and sea scenes (two of the paintings were done after the sitting), very big vases with funny saucers, two brass candlesticks and a black dickie bird.[6] This last case is remarkable in that it involved some form of precognition.

Here are three cases of alleged communication with the dead which are examples of telepathy. But despite these examples, it can readily be shown, as we will see, that simple ESP is not the general explanation for cases of mediumistic communication. As with the explanations of the interior of the atom, all is not so simple. More processes and elements are involved than one would have imagined.

Cases Demanding Further Explanation

A Swedenborg case. Let us begin with Emanuel Swedenborg (1688–1772).[7] Swedenborg was a busy engineer who worked for the Swedish bureau of mines. He was dedicated to the intellectual pursuit of science and economics and to political causes. He was also a remarkable psychic. In a famous anecdotal case, he was asked by a widow to contact her husband in order to find a receipt for a bill she had paid. She was being pursued for non-payment of a very expensive piece of silver. After three days, Swedenborg returned and told her that her husband had said to look in a secretly designed drawer in a bureau upstairs. The widow and her guests went upstairs and the receipt was found.

Is this a case of communication with the dead or is it to be explained by Swedenborg's clairvoyance? I cite this case in order to set up the problematic which will be discussed in what follows.

James-Hyslop. Laurens van der Post, a biographer of C.G. Jung, relates an experience involving William James (1842–1910) and James Hyslop (1854–1920), a professor at Columbia University and a psychic researcher who investigated Mrs. Piper. Hyslop and James, according to Jung's account, promised each other that whoever died first would endeavor to give the survivor evidence of individual life beyond death. James died first. Hyslop waited, apparently in vain. But one day he received a letter from Ireland, a country he had never visited. It was from a husband and wife whose experiments with the planchette had become dominated by a certain William James, insisting that they contact Professor Hyslop of whom they had never heard. Finally locating Hyslop, they delivered the message, "Remember the red pajamas?" Hyslop could remember no red pajamas. The message seemed banal, but he began to reflect on the possible objectivity of such a point of trivia. Suddenly he remembered that on a trip to Paris, he and James had arrived ahead of their luggage and they had to shop for necessities. Looking for sleepware, Hyslop could find only some "really fancy red pajamas," and James teased him for some days about his dubious taste. Jung, in recounting the event, said he himself had never been bothered by the apparent triviality of such messages. "If there were a life beyond death, it would be an idiom which we could not possibly possess in the here and now and as such utterly incapable of transmission in terms we could understand. What was surprising, therefore, was not the insignificant nature of these intrusions but that they should take place at all. . . ."[8] Did the couple read Hyslop's mind, a man they never knew?

A Cross-Correspondence Case. Three famous psychical researchers and founders of the Society for Psychical Research died around the turn of the century—Edmund Gurney (1847–1888), Henry Sidgwick (1838–1900) and Frederic W.H. Myers (1843–1901). Shortly thereafter various women began to produce scripts through automatic writing and mediumistic communication which claimed to originate principally with Myers and Gurney. For the most part, each of the participants was unacquainted with what the others were doing. The mediums were the following. Mrs. Margaret Verrall (1859–1916), wife of Dr. Verrall, and a classical scholar like her husband; her daughter, Helen Verrall (1883–1959), later married to W.H. Salter who thoroughly investigated the Chaffin Will case; Alice Kipling Fleming (1868–1948), known as "Mrs. Holland," a sister of Rudyard Kipling and living in India, who began her scripts in 1903 (she was told in a script to send it to 5 Selwyn Gardens, Cambridge, which turned out to be Mrs. Verrall's address though at the time she knew neither the city nor the lady); Mrs. Coombe-Tennant (1874–1956), known as "Mrs. Willett," well-known for public services and a sister-in-law of Myers, who began her scripts in 1908; Mrs. Leonore Piper in Boston (1859–1950) who was studied by William James among others; Mrs. Stuart Wilson who began after 1915; Dame Edith Lyttleton (1872–1948) who joined in 1913; and some others.

Over a period of thirty years a system of "cross-correspondences" appeared in the scripts. Scattered allusions to classical myths, e.g., Ovid or Virgil, and to English authors like Browning and Keats, became coherent when linked with messages from other mediums. It was like an elaborate jigsaw puzzle which was reminiscent of the style and knowledge of the three men. For example, puns abounded, a feature characteristic of Myers. Some phrases came across in Greek and Latin words. Only two of the mediums knew Latin or Greek, Mrs. Verrall and Helen. The scripts were signed, mostly by "Myers" or "Gurney." There were some cross-connections between a few of the mediums, but not enough to explain the cross-references.[9]

The scripts were read by Gerald Balfour (1851–1945), as well as by others. Balfour, a fine classical scholar, accepted them as genuine communications. Gardner Murphy, a careful scholar and once president of the American Psychological Association has written that in the scripts he was studying the best working hypothesis is that we are in direct contact with "some part" of the surviving personality of F.W.H. Myers.[10] The brilliant and critical investigator, Eleanor Sidgwick, the wife of Henry Sidgwick, said, "I myself think that the evidence is pointing towards the conclusion that our fellow workers are still working with us."[11]

The reader might wish to consult some of the lengthy samples of these scripts published by W.H. Salter, H.F. Saltmarsh and Gardner Murphy. The evidence is overwhelming that some designing mind lies behind these scripts. However, even if one knows Latin and Greek and is acquainted with English literature, piecing together the evidence and clues is so demanding amidst such a mass of evidence that it would take months if not years to reach the level of appreciation attained by the original researchers. However, in all learning we depend upon the research of others. Thus this difficulty is not unique to the scripts. The chief problem, for our purposes, lies elsewhere.

The real problem is whether an alternate theory can explain the facts. Thus we are thrown headlong into the "Super-ESP-theory." W.G. Roll, an excellent parapsychologist and the editor of the journal *Theta*, has presented the Super-ESP case recently.[12] Briefly, if these cross-correspondence cases are to be explained by the hypothesis of Super-ESP (a type or scope of ESP which is never found in experimental work), then Mrs. Verrall and/or Helen were the most likely candidates for the designing mind behind the tests. Notice that this is not to claim that fraud by "the designing mind" is operative. Fraud can be eliminated without too much difficulty as an explanation for the scripts. Whatever went on, it proceeded on a subliminal or unconscious ESP level (though one might then wonder about the mischievousness of the unconscious). Both Mrs. Verrall and her daughter Helen knew the classics. Mrs. Verrall's husband had conducted experiments with her before his death in which some of the key words later to appear were used. In the Gordon Davis case, as Alan Gauld points out, some form of a Super-ESP power seems to have been in operation. Again the psychometry tests mentioned in Chapter VII seem to display some Super-ESP activity. As Gauld puts it, "The continuity hypothesis and the super-ESP hypothesis appear to have reached a virtual stalemate."[13]

"Mrs. Willett." Mrs. Willett was the pseudonym for Mrs. Coombe-Tennant. Her husband was the brother-in-law of My-

ers, but she had not known Gurney or Sidgwick. She had read an abridged version of Myers' *Human Personality and Its Survival of Bodily Death*, which, however, did not contain the philosophical discussions. She did not know Latin or Greek. Apart from classical allusions, her scripts contained intricate and coherent discussions with "Gurney" about the mind-body problem, the structure of the human self, and the relation of the self to the Absolute in Hegelian fashion. She herself was not at all interested in philosophy, and critical observers have been struck by the conversations had through her between "Myers," "Gurney" and the sitter, Gerald Balfour, on Hegelian theories. The dialogue included Myers' and Gurney's phraseology and characteristics. Balfour was Hegelian but he held different views than Myers and Gurney.

In the famous "Ear of Dionysius" case Mrs. Willett produced scripts purportedly from the classical scholars, Butcher and Verrall, in which abstruse classical allusions were discussed, knowledge of which Mrs. Willett certainly did not have. There were also many touches characteristic of both men. Gauld sees this case as one in which matters unmistakably beyond the grasp of the medium are referred to. This type of case seems unexplainable by the Super-ESP hypothesis and suggests that the mind of the medium is somehow controlled by an outside agency. Could it be that various processes are in operation in mediumistic communication, at times Super-ESP, at other times contact with a trans-earthly agent?

Geraldine Cummins. Mrs. Coombe-Tennant died August 31, 1956, still known in mediumistic circles only as Mrs. Willett. She had had four children, Christopher (1897–1917), Daphne, a "very loving child" who lived only from January 1907 to July 1908, Alexander (1909) and Henry (1913). Henry had become an atheist or an agnostic, and after his mother's death he got W.H. Salter to write to the now famous Irish medium, Geraldine Cummins (d. 1970) to try to get a message "from a dead mother to her son" who had doubts about life beyond death. Geraldine was given only the name "Major A.H.S. Coombe-Tennant" and scraps of his mother's writing. No "sitter" was present, unless we think of the absent sitter as Major Tennant in England. Geraldine Cummins worked in Ireland. After six sessions Geraldine became practically sure that the "communicator" for the messages she was receiving was Mrs. Willett, and this was then confirmed by Salter.

Geraldine gave an almost exact description of Mrs. Coombe-Tennant's personality, a woman who was a bit haughty, utterly honest, forthright and very strong-minded. She gave details about how she brought up her children, about her regrets after the death of her baby Daphne, and her unconscious rejection of the subsequent son Alexander when she wanted another girl. She gave indications of an afterlife change in Mrs. Coombe-Tennant as to her compensatory possessiveness toward Alexander which brought about a negative reaction in him. Even the sons did not know about this and other details until they found an old diary of their mother of which they had been unaware. The twists of phrase, the idiom and personality were all verified as being exactly that of their mother. Some of the details revealed were known to some few but they did not become public until two years later.

The scripts claim to adduce evidence from before the birth of Henry specifically to avoid the ESP difficulty. Interestingly, Miss Cummins did poorly in quantitative ESP tests. The scripts are meticulously analyzed by C.D. Broad, a scholar who had done careful research in parapsychology as well as philosophy at Cambridge. The resultant book, *Swan on a Black Sea*, is one of the most impressive works in mediumistic research.[14] Either this is a case of genuine contact with Mrs. Coombe-Tennant, or else it is an incredible example of Super-ESP. If it is the latter, it involves not only locating and reading the minds of the sons, but also locating and reading a diary whose existence was unknown, as well as an impersonation of the mother so exact that the sons could scarcely find a discrepancy. In the Gordon Davis case, we do find a possible duplication of Davis' voice with its affected accent, but that seems possible through telepathic processes. Is a total impersonation of an unknown person possible through Super-ESP? At present this does not seem possible, and I tentatively would accept these scripts as a message from Mrs. Coombe-Tennant.

The Airmen Who Would Not Die. Eileen Garrett (1893–1970) ranks with Geraldine Cummins as being one of the greatest mediums of modern times.[15] She has always desired that her talents be scientifically investigated. Her daughter, Mrs. Eileen Coly, told me that to the end of her life she wavered about life after death "depending on which side of the bed she got out of." In 1926, while walking in Hyde Park, London, she "saw" a great silver ship moving westward. Again in 1928 she saw an airship in the sky. It wobbled, dipped, gave off smoke and disappeared. She was surprised to see nothing about it in the papers the next day.

In 1928 Eileen had a sitting for the wife of Captain Raymond Hinchcliffe who had just died in an effort to make a transatlantic flight from London to America. "Hinchcliffe" tried to warn his close friend Ernest Johnson, who was to be the navigator of one of two dirigibles recently announced as to be built by Britain, that it would crash. These dirigibles were named R-100 and R-101. Johnson was to navigate the R-101.

In 1929 Mrs. Garrett again saw the ship over London, burning and giving off clouds of smoke. She warned Sir Sefton Brancker, Director of Civil Aviation, that the R-101 would crash.

Three days after the crash which occurred on October 4, 1930, Mrs. Garrett was asked to give a sitting.[16] Harry Price, a critical psychic investigator, and Ian Coster, a journalist, among others, were present.

First, Coster received a message from an old woman whom he thought was his grandmother. Then Eileen's control, "Uvani," a supposed Arab soldier from the fourteenth century, changed its voice from an Arab-English accent to one of a clipped English accent. Uvani announced that Flight Lieutenant H. Carmichael Irwin, captain of the R-101, was speaking. The alleged Irwin began to give a detailed account of the crash: "the bulk of the dirigible was too much for the engine . . . engines too heavy . . . useful lift too small . . . elevator jammed . . . oil pipe clogged . . . flying too low altitude . . . ship badly swinging . . . severe tension on the fabric which is chafing." Many complicated details were given. No one present knew anything about dirigibles.

Will Charlton, chief supply officer at the plant where the R-101 was built, after seeing this account in the paper, asked for a copy of the medium's remarks. He called it "an astounding document," replete with a mass of technical detail and expert observation about dirigible construction which only an expert could possibly have known. William H. Wood, a pilot friend of Irwin, noted the use of terms like "strakes," the nautical name for the plates used to make the sides of an airship. He wondered how Mrs. Garrett could have said, "Gross lift computed badly— inform control panel." This later was confirmed as one of the causes of the crash. The assertions that the fuel injection had not functioned properly and that the air pump failed were also confirmed. The statement that we almost "scraped the roofs of Achy" was also confirmed, though Achy did not appear even on good maps, but only on those used by professional railway and military people. *Forty items* of technical and confidential information were correctly given and at great speed. Pilot Wood who was a friend of Irwin noticed the quick, jerky delivery of Irwin, a noted eccentricity.

At the end of October, with the sitter being Major Oliver Villiers, a close friend of many officers on the flight, "Irwin" again came through together with Major George Scott and Squadron Leader E.L. Johnston. Many technical details were offered about wind velocity, gas bag pressure, girders and electrical work, and that the diesel engine explosion was the final cause of the crash. In succeeding sessions Villiers received more details from "others" on the flight.

Is this an example of genuine contact with those who have died? The two strongest hypotheses are either genuine contact or else Super-ESP. But how could Super-ESP have worked? Very rapidly, correct details were given about the cause of the crash which were not known until later. Can a clairvoyant diagnose unconsciously a piece of wreckage and, though unequipped to do so, correctly give the engineering and functioning defects? I lean in the direction of direct contact with those beyond death.

Arthur Ford. Arthur Ford (1897–1971) was an ordained minister of the Disciples of Christ. His many paranormal feats are well known but I wish to center on one episode, his séance for Bishop Pike. Pike's son, Jim, Jr., committed suicide in London, February 1966, at the age of twenty. Strange phenomena followed his death. In Pike's apartment clocks stopped at 8:19, the precise time of his death. Postcards with his son's handwriting on them mysteriously appeared in Pike's quarters. His son's shaving mirror performed movements on its own power.

In 1967 Ford, then 71, conducted a séance before TV cameras on a Toronto station with Pike present. A large amount of verified material came forth as if from James Pike, Jr. However, while writing Ford's biography, Allen Spraggett and Canon William V. Rauscher discovered obituaries in Ford's notes, obituaries from the *New York Times* which gave details of some of Pike's friends who were correctly identified in the séance.[17] Ford's former secretary claimed that he carried a suitcase with notes on prospective sitters because, as Ford said, "no one could perform 100 percent of the time." Harmon Bro, a noted clergyman-therapist, told Spraggett that Arthur Ford once confided to him that "during the darkest days of his alcoholism he had resorted to cheating in public clairvoyance."[18]

However, on December 16, 1967, three months after the televised séance, Ford gave a private sitting to Pike and his secretary, later his wife, Diane Kennedy. Many apparently unsearchable details were given, such as that James, Jr. met up with a crowd in New York, that a friend in California could confirm this, that drugs were not his chief difficulty (Stringfellow and others suggest that it was homosexuality), etc. Spraggett presents strong evidence that Ford really had paranormal powers.

Here is a case of a medium who certainly seems to have had psychic powers but who dishonestly tried to bolster them through private research. The séances with Pike may have been accomplished, in part at least, through ESP as Pike had many of the details in his own mind.

Summary

The cases which we have surveyed have various explanations. One involved some fraud, two clearly are to be explained by simple ESP, some may be explained either by contact with a person who has died or by Super-ESP. The cross-correspondence cases push us in the direction of genuine contact, I believe, but enough parapsychologists hesitate on this to make one wary of ruling out Super-ESP. The Geraldine Cummins scripts seem to point more clearly in the direction of contact with the dead than of Super-ESP. Otherwise we must postulate an incredible power of spontaneous impersonation. The same seems true of the Airmen case.

Some Thoughts About Super-ESP

Super-ESP would enable a person to move anywhere in the world, it seems, to gather information paranormally from people's minds and objects, to know where to find these people and objects, to computerize the data, as it were, and then to dramatize the data in an impersonation of one who has died. This may seem incredible to some readers, especially those who at the beginning of our study wondered whether such a thing as even simple telepathy existed. However, apart from genuine contact with the dead, there is no other rival theory to explain the data. We do not know whether Super-ESP exists. I have, however, given some evidence, such as that found in psychometry, to supply a basis for belief in it.

Allen Spraggett writes: "If a Super-ESP faculty exists, of the scope required for mediums to ferret out facts from every obscure nook and cranny in the universe, then why cannot a medium simply tell anybody anything they want to know? Super-ESP is really a pseudonym for omniscience."[19] However, this may not be the case. Perhaps there are kinds of links, rhythms, bonds of affection, etc., which limit our ability to gather information. Super-ESP need not imply omniscience. C. Ducasse, a probing philosopher and psychic researcher at Brown, used to say that if Super-ESP existed, then how could it distinguish between information from the living about the dead and from the living about themselves? But we have found that this is indeed a problem with ESP as in the Gordon Davis case.

I do not believe advance in research will come through a total elimination of the Super-ESP hypothesis. Instead, a broader approach is needed which would include three points. (1) Different mediumistic cases may have different explanations.

The evidence suggests that we cannot reduce all to one single law of economy. As I said previously, as with the core of an atom, there may be incredible diversity within the mediumistic area. (2) The Super-ESP hypothesis should not be cavalierly forced on every case as if it were of equal value to the survival theory. In the Cummins-Coombe-Tennant case, for example, as well as in the Willett-Ear of Dionysius case and in the Airmen case, the Super-ESP theory seems to be stretched beyond the breaking point to explain some of the data. Recall that in the Ear of Dionysius case, Mrs. Willett did not have in her mind the very recondite Greek and Latin references which even afterward were extremely difficult to find.[20] In the Cummins-Coombe-Tennant case, impersonation would be so thorough that Super-ESP would not simply involve gathering data, but bringing across a personality so perfect in detail and mannerism that one would come close to holding that one could telepathize another's automatic movements of personality—"telepathizing a skill," it is called. We will touch on this in our brief treatment of xenoglossy. This is deemed impossible. Remember, we are dealing here not with proof, but with probabilities. The reader may say, "But contact with the dead has not been proved." This is true. We seek logical, historical and experimental convincing evidence wherever it may be found. But we are not asking simply, "What can be proved?" We are asking, "What seems to be the real?" Probability is the subjective result of evidence which leads one in a certain direction. Evidence that leads in a consistent direction toward a point but not *to* it, not to total conviction, evokes a sense of probability. I, and many others more competent than myself in these areas, believe that in some of the cases I have listed the most coherent and probable explanation is contact with those who have died. (3) The very holding of Super-ESP would be an *indirect* support, philosophically, for survival of some kind beyond death. Philosopher Hoyt L. Edge writes: "However, to argue this, i.e., that survival is not proven, we must realize that we have to argue not only for the existence of ESP, but for its existence in a fantastically extended fashion. To say we have no proof for survival is to assert the existence of [Super-] ESP. And to say that such ESP exists is to say that we have evidence which undercuts the naturalistic view of man, which, in turn, is the main reason for one to reject the possibility of disembodied survival. If it were not for our physicalistic biases, I do not think that one could intelligently argue the logical impossibility of disembodied survival."[21] Philosopher H. H. Price puts it this way, ". . . the more you *deflate* the survival hypothesis, the more you *inflate* the powers of the human unconscious—the unconscious stratum or level of the minds of physically-embodied human beings."[22] And from this concise positing of the situation, inferences may be drawn similar to those of Edge. Some researchers wring their hands when they feel we are at an apparent impasse between survival and Super-ESP, a kind of Catch-22 situation. But this would be like a person who wins a contest and who had expected to win a house but who wins $100,000 instead. He would not wring his hands. He should think what he could do with $100,000. As William G. Roll says, "On closer examination, the counter-hypothesis to survival, ESP, is actually itself a survival hypothesis."[23] Roll holds the notion of a "field consciousness." After death, he suggests, a person may identify himself or herself with this field to a greater or lesser extent.[24]

At this point in our discussion, let us not forget that medium work is not the only parapsychological evidence which is relevant to the question of survival beyond death. Recall what was said about the possible ramifications of precognition and retrocognition, our discussions about OBEs, deathbed visions and apparition study. These are not merely links in a chain in which the weakness of one link weakens all the others. Some of our pieces of evidence are independent units which stand on their own, and when combined they increase the strength of the whole. Before adding a few theological considerations, let us look at two further types of cases which must be handled rather briefly here.

Xenoglossy Cases

"Xenoglossy" means to speak an unknown language. Recitative xenoglossy is the ability to repeat phrases in a language which one has never learned. This is easily accounted for by the incredible memories which some people have to recall phrases—

a "flypaper memory," someone aptly called it. Even if the source is completely forgotten consciously, the unconscious has incredible memory powers. This power is called "cryptomnesia," the unconscious recalling of forgotten memories.

However, what we are interested in is what is called "responsive xenoglossy." This is the ability to *converse* in a language which one has never learned. Ian Stevenson has produced a lengthy monograph on the case of a woman, a thirty-seven year old housewife in Philadelphia, who in a trance spoke intelligible Swedish with a "Jacoby Jensen" persona. The dialogue was intelligent, though rather simpleton-like. Swedish words of the period when Jensen was supposed to have lived were used. Tools spoken of were those known at the time. Strangely, "Jacoby Jensen" asked no questions of the investigators and sounded like a person with organic brain damage. The husband and wife were given the Minnesota Multiple Personality Inventory, a polymath test for lie detection, and a word association test for language cheating, and acquaintances who were Swedish or Norwegian were questioned about previous contacts. Very detailed research on the couple's life was pursued. All tests suggested honesty.

Magician Milbourne Christopher jumps to the conclusion that this xenoglossy case was obviously fraudulent. Four years after the Stevenson case, the lady gave some séances. But she was discovered with notes in her purse and once with a book from a library with passages which were reproduced in a séance. Stevenson says she was suffering from involuntary dissociation at this time, and fraud seems to have been ruled out in his previous investigation of the Jacoby Jensen case. Such a finding, however, makes this case less acceptable for genuine xenoglossy than is true for some other cases. I deliberately mention this case to demonstrate the care with which such cases must be investigated.

However, there is another case with which Stevenson was associated. A contemporary woman, Dolores Jay, spoke German as the persona Gretchen who supposedly lived one hundred years ago in Germany, although she was never identified. Stevenson says she spoke German intelligibly and gave sensible answers in German to questions spoken to her in German.

Stevenson's efforts to ascertain whether Mrs. Jay had ever learned German were so thorough that he became an annoyance with his persistence. But no fraud was found. [26] There are some other cases of xenoglossy, and Louisa Rhine is not correct when she claimed in *What Is ESP?* that there have been no authentic cases of xenoglossy. Stevenson presents a thorough study of the notion of "skill" and offers good evidence that while one can telepathize words, phrases, ideas and images, one cannot telepathize a skill. One can learn from a book, e.g., how to ride a bicycle, or one can even perhaps telepathize this knowledge from a rider's mind. But one cannot telepathize the skill needed to ride a bicycle. Stevenson believes that the survival of personality after death "is a major hypothesis to be considered in its interpretation." I believe that this position by a brilliant and meticulous investigator is valid. However, I feel rather perplexed about the meaning of these cases, especially because of the quasi-passivity of the communicator. Are these people drugged wanderers in another dimension, as it were?[27] Also the personae who manifested themselves in the cases mentioned were never identified as individuals in past history. For the moment, I take xenoglossy cases to be another example of that great and mysterious nucleus which is the human mind.

Drop-In Communicators

A drop-in communicator is one whom the medium does not know or is not expecting. In August 1972, Stevenson conducted experiments with the Icelandic medium, Hafsteinn Björnsson. The medium sat behind a thick curtain and Icelandic subjects from around New York City were brought in one by one. Each student wore earphones which played music, thus blocking out the medium's voice as he gave the reading. He was not in a trance.

Björnsson gave the full personal name of the drop-in communicator, e.g., "Alex Jonson." This is unusual because most mediums give only the first name. Usually the communicator was reported as being two or more generations older than the student sitter, e.g., a grandmother, or a great-grand uncle. The sitters were young people who knew very little about their relatives who had died many years ago in Iceland. Ian Stevenson and Erlandur Haraldsson cooperated in the investigation by contacting the sitter's parents. Many times the older people would recognize the names which the youngsters had not known, and they would verify what the medium had said about the personality of the "communicator." This, therefore, does not allow for the sitter-telepathy theory.

The results were rated as beyond probabilities. Neither Björnsson nor the experimenter in the room with him knew the order of the students as they entered. Afterward the students were given all the transcripts and were asked to pick out the ones they thought referred to them. Four out of ten picked the correct ones. Two students were surprised to learn that an ancestor who they knew had died, but this was correct. (Some incorrect details were given by Björnsson.)

Many of the cases were victims of violent deaths. This is true also in reincarnation cases. The medium never described living persons as dead or vice versa. Concrete pictures were given. For example, Björnsson said: "A man is there who went suddenly; a man of average height, rather slim, both around the body and in his face, with long-drawn facial features, a finely made man who says his name is Gunnlaugur Jónsson, a very resolute personality. He went very suddenly. I feel choking and suffocation . . . something happened to his breathing organs and he died as a result." When contacted, members of the family immediately recognized a prior person mentioned in this sitting but not Jónsson. However, the investigator later located a Gunnlaugur Jónsson as a man who lived 1894–1962. He died from a piece of food that got stuck in his throat. The student sitter's grandfather vaguely remembered him in Iceland. In this session all the communicators were identified.[28] Note that five of the students had been to a sitting with Björnsson in Iceland. In that country the medium often gave readings for a thousand people in an auditorium. The supposed communicators came in groups. They had been friends of each other during life. Sometimes Björnsson mixed up people from one questioner to the next.

These cases clearly involve some paranormal process. Once again, the best working hypotheses are contact with persons active beyond death or knowledge through Super-ESP, perhaps with the student as a kind of psychometric object. This latter might be the better hypothesis in these cases.

A Few Theological Remarks

I will devote a separate chapter to possible transformations in Christian eschatology because of research such as that done with mediums. However, I wish to add here a few concluding remarks. There are passages in the Bible (e.g., Deut. 18:10; Lev. 19:31) which condemn consulting the dead or soothsaying. Also, the Catholic Church in decrees of 1898 and 1917 condemned the practice of automatic writing and communication with the dead.[29] However, the biblical prohibitions apparently were directed against aims and motives which are quite different from the aims and motives of modern researchers. Rev. Donald Bretherton of London University writes: "Whereas clearly seventh-century [B.C.] psychism sought to undermine the moral authority and credibility of Yahweh, modern practice seeks to do just the reverse. . . . 'Seeking after the dead' in ancient times was designed to show Yahweh as either incompetent or untrustworthy, whereas modern mediumship seeks to show the reality of the claim that 'underneath are the everlasting arms.' "[30]

Many modern parapsychologists might not put it precisely in this way, but they would insist that they are attempting to gain a deeper empirical understanding of the nature of man. A change is beginning to manifest itself in theological circles in connection with survival study. It is now recognized that there is a genuine effort by some scholars to approach these studies with a scientific attitude, at least in the wide sense. There still may be dangers in using ouija boards and automatic writing where one toys with a powerful unconscious at the very least.[31] Insofar as something is not understood nor approached in a discerning manner, great danger is present. This seems to be the spirit behind the Church's decrees.

Some theologians believe that there is no need for this type of study if one has faith. One might question this position in the face of loss of adherents to Church organization and decline in belief in the afterlife, especially in Europe. However, there seems to be a presupposition operative here which is not valid. It implies a vast dichotomy between faith and knowledge. Yet, all faith must involve some knowledge or it is not a human virtue. Faith is knowledge going beyond itself but not in contradiction to prior knowledge. As Tillich put it, faith is reason grown courageous. Why it is perfidious to make use of knowledge gained through parapsychology, and not against faith to use knowledge from disciplines such as scriptural exegesis, history, psychology, sociology and (an often latent) philosophy is impossible to understand.

Marjorie Suchocki has written that some theologians have joined secular thinkers in renunciation of immortality, adding theological reasons to material evidence against this hope. Some theologians believe, she says, that "aspiring to an immortal condition" is "the sin of idolatry, of self-centeredness rather than God-centeredness."[32] The reader will understand the importance of this warning. There is a self-centered seeking in some psychic writing for "immortality and me." On the other hand, we read many works where the emphasis is on a transpersonal "selfless" relation to "the One." In some of the literature it is clear that the lover of the eternal kingdom is aspiring for the presence of God. I believe that theologians should turn an eye to the evidence and be more hesitant in labeling human aspirations as sinful. Perhaps we are being offered another chance to look through Galileo's telescope. The charge of "narcissism" too often is based on an uncomprehending insensitivity. In "In Memoriam" Tennyson wrote:

Ah Christ, that it were possible
For one short hour to see
The souls we loved, that they might tell
What and where they be.

This is a very human and loving emotion and it is compatible with one who, like Tennyson, placed it within the context of a Power of whom he said, "Closer is He than breathing and nearer than hands and feet" ("The Higher Pantheism"). As Rahner says, our interest in life beyond death may also involve hope *for others*.

One's world view always enters to some extent into one's apprehension of Christian revelation. Before Jesus' resurrection, the apostles themselves held the Pharasaic belief in final resurrection beyond death, and this allowed them, many think, to enter more wholeheartedly into the experience of Jesus' resurrection. A world view which is a leftover from a more mechanistic model of science seems today to remain a controlling influence on a few theologians' understanding of the Gospel message. But parapsychological studies are without doubt acting as a solvent on this older, congealed world view.

On the other hand, theology has an important point to make in our present context. Parapsychology offers many very strong signs, indications and intimations that life continues on beyond the grave. Indeed there is more here than merely "rumors of angels." Still, Christian theology warns us not to presume that we know exactly what that life beyond is like. As Rahner wryly says, "it does not mean that things continue on after death as though, as Feuerbach puts it, we only change horses and then ride on. . . ."[33] If the world has ultimate meaning, it is because it has its source in the Nameless Mysterious One. If life beyond death is to fit into this world, it must be in relation to that One. Some treatments of parapsychological data hypnotize one into considering the little fragments of other-worldly vision as if they were tiny computer chips whose total message is contained in crystallized isolation. The true meeting point of parapsychology and theology comes at that numinous moment when the investigator is momentarily blinded by the awesome splendor of this cosmos in which we live. United in a vision which is both disciplined and religious, a precise and cold investigator might even be led to feel unknown emotions. For a theologian, the alleged messages from the dead are always to be kept in relationship with larger perspectives.

Both the theologian and the parapsychologist would insist that one be constantly aware of the danger of taking literally the pattern of detail in the messages from the beyond. As we have mentioned, the medium, the control, the sitter and the alleged communicator are all involved in the transmitting of the message. When all these elements are taken into consideration, it is clear that even if there is genuine communication, and as I have shown in many cases, this is no better working hypothesis, it is very difficult to distinguish what is contributed by each element in this constellation. As "Myers" is once reported to have said, communicating with the living is like trying to dictate through frosted glass.

The religious philosopher Gabriel Marcel (1889–1973), together with some friends, had a number of remarkable experiences with a ouija board in 1917. For example, accurate information about a soldier killed in World War I was brought forth which until that time was not known but which was later verified in the regiment's records. In discussing efforts to communicate with the dead, Marcel, at first cool to such practices, later saw them as perhaps means to enable the closed philosophical mind to become permeable to the infiltrations of the invisible.[34] One danger Marcel pointed to was the tendency to materialize or reify the presence of the departed one, to reduce the person who has died to the level of an object. Marcel (who believed in an astral body) developed an existential philosophy of the notion of "presence." Speaking of contact with the dead, he said that the techniques of "objective" investigation merely aggravate the situation. "Real presence is had when everything happens within the interiority of love, a sphere which is inaccessible to 'objective' knowledge. The mystery of death cannot be separated from the mystery of love. Faith in the permanence of the loved one is, in sum, a transcendent prolongation of friendship and love. This communion in creative fidelity may be had in faith and hope but not in the 'objective' proofs of metapsychical research. . . . Immortality transcends survival."

The point about reification or materialization is important and it recurs in Karl Rahner's treatment of statements about the dead. Rahner believes that if the dead appear or speak, they could only do so as *we* are, not as they are. "Spiritualist séances display the spirit of the earthbound, with their crude ideas and manias, not the tranquility of an eternity filled with God. . . . We do not meet the dead as they are now before God . . . but their as yet unredeemed and limited, confused and obscure past. . . ."[35] Rahner's position does not fit some of the data, such as those presented in the Geraldine Cummins' scripts. However, there is an interesting point here. In many alleged messages from the departed, they frequently speak in the present tense, as if they were presently undergoing a past event, or as if their life afterward is a kind of blank. Is it possible that, in some cases, even in genuine communications from beyond, we are picking up a psychic husk, as it were, an emotional form present at the time of death? The evidence suggests, indeed, that there is an intelligence still living behind this form. But in those cases it is as if we are not contacting the person directly but through an "earth-form" animated by one living beyond death. This theory is well worth investigating. It would demand that notions of growth, as found for example in the Cummins' scripts about Mrs. Coombe-Tennant's development of insight about her possessiveness during life, would be extrapolations which belong to the medium's mind alone.

At any rate, theology, and especially Fundamental theology, which in Catholic circles investigates the presuppositions behind the ground of all Christian doctrine, Christian revelation, must in the future take into consideration science in all its forms, and this includes parapsychological data. Edward Schillebeeckx says that, as the domain of scientific phenomena became enlarged, ". . . theology had to retreat more and more, first relinquishing the cosmos, then the world of evolution, then society and the depth dimension of human behavior. By giving up phenomena, theology lost almost everything. . . . No one seemed to realize that the sciences form a part of our developing history, a subdivision of the story of mankind. In any case, theology cut itself off from these sciences. But by this dissociation from the empirical sciences, theology became marginalized; it was isolated from concrete history in which it had always discovered God's saving activity. . . . Theology finds its identity not alongside of or above other sciences, but in and through them. Like the Gospel, theology must exist for the other sciences as well as for itself."[36] At the same time, I wish to stress, as he does, the difference between this activity of theology and faith: "Although acquaintance with the sciences is needed for 'theological rationality' (the old *ratio theologica*), theology must remember that it lays no foundation underneath the Christian faith. Thank God, religious faith does not stand on a rational, safely controlled foundation. Theology advocates what man can become and be beyond the describable and analyzable."

Analysis of the parapsychological evidence about life beyond death demands great maturity. Maturity will depend not only on what sense we make out of life but also in what we have become. William James believed that "fitful influences from beyond leak in" from a continuum of cosmic consciousness, but he remained baffled as to their structure and individuation. In 1904 he answered a questionnaire in which we find: "Do you believe in personal immortality? (Answer) Never keenly, but more strongly as I grow older. If so, why? (Answer) Because I am just getting fit to live."[37]

Appendix: Descriptions of Life After Death

A number of accounts have been published which present detailed accounts of life after death gathered from the writings of mediums.[38] One of the most famous of them was supposedly communicated from Myers through Geraldine Cummins. There are seven stages. Stage one is the earth plane. Stage two is a kind of intermediate stage, the condition of the individual immediately after death. This is called "Hades," a strange coming-to, like a baby emerging from the womb. Myers called it "the journey down the long hall." Stage three is the plane of images. Materials are so pliable that they can be shaped by the direct action of the imagination. One can remain in this stage as long as one wishes. Some prefer to return to stage one (reincarnation). Each further stage is preceded by a voluntary death. Stage four is the plane of the breaking of images and a stage of intense color. All rigid intellectual structures are left behind. There is a sorrow but not earth sorrow, ecstasy but not earth ecstasy. Some hostilities may still be present to a degree. Stage five is the plane of flame. Imperfections have been purified. The spirit can now range widely. Stage six is the plane of light. Spirits are matured spirits, having lived through the conscious apprehension of all the aspects of the created world. Plane seven is the plane of timelessness. The spirit reaches a full partnership with God which baffles description. It is joyful and heartbreaking. Even great saints hesitate to take this last step into plane seven.

What is one to make of such pictures? Actually we would not pay too much attention to them were it not for the general excellency of Miss Cummins' mediumship. At the same time, pictures of afterlife by various mediums, despite a certain coherency, do not always agree. For example, different messages take opposing sides as to whether reincarnation is a reality or not. "Myers" himself said that he did not have the power to express in words, which he must borrow from earth minds, the amazing character of life after death. "No echo comes from behind the dark curtain which will even faintly convey the music of that other life."

I believe that Miss Cummins' picture is largely a construction of her unconscious imagination. Perhaps what we have is a picture of a kind of archetypal journey.

If one, on religious or philosophical grounds, affirms the reality of life beyond death, I suggest that the above picture, while it should not be taken in a literal sense, may have a function. It can give zest and body to a conviction that one already holds on other grounds. Actually it resembles a demythologized view of the doctrine of purgatory. Those Protestants who do not believe in an intermediate state between death and the final goal may have unsurmountable difficulties with this picture. Many Protestants today, however, are more open to it at least symbolically because of the idea of gradual growth in an evolutionary world. And if we live beyond death, does the law of evolution cease?

Many theologians reject all pictures about afterlife. Perhaps they are reacting to the damage that certain pictures from Dante have done to the Christian psyche. However, I believe that their reaction is a mistake on psychological grounds. Religious psychologists have found that when people lose all symbolic images connected with beliefs, the result is not so much that there is a direct denial of the beliefs, but that it ceases to have any affective and effective meaning. I am suggesting, then, that we may allow ourselves such pictures as operative images while remaining skeptical about the literal truth of the details. In sum, the picture is stating in symbolical form the belief, put so dramatically in Jane Roberts' *Seth Speaks*, "You are as dead now as you ever will be" (p.491).

Chapter XI

Reincarnation

Only when one is fully aware of the evidence presented in the previous chapters is a sound approach to reincarnation possible. We will now attempt to assess that topic and our two principal questions will be: (1) Is reincarnation a reality? (2) How might Christian theology face the reincarnation data?

Hypnotic Regression

The two chief methods for exploring reincarnation are hypnotic regression and field study by a trained parapsychologist. In our own day we are witnessing a remarkable confluence of cases in which evidence is brought forth as if from a previous life through hypnotic regression. Studies have been published by Helen Wambach, Edith Fiore, Peter Moss and Joe Keeton, Morris Netherton and M. Gerald Edelstein, among others.[1]

At times subjects are hypnotized with the express purpose of regressing them to a "previous" life. In other cases, patients come for hypnotic sessions who are suffering from phobias or unexplained physical illness. The aim in these latter regressions is to return to one's early life in order to discover some forgotten traumatic cause of the problem. In both types of cases, patients begin to experience an apparent previous existence. Patients suffering from unexplained symptoms are often freed in a remarkable manner from their illness through the discovery of some damaging incident in a supposed previous life. Whether reincarnation is a fact or not, these sessions often work. They are effective aids for the recovery of the patient's health. (Occasionally, however, they cause an upsurge of guilt feelings.)

In what follows I will center on the hypnotic regression work of Helen Wambach while adding some enlightening details from other researchers.

Helen Wambach is a clinical psychologist at Monmouth Medical Center in Long Branch, N.J. She conducts group sessions in hypnotic regression whose purpose is to probe into possible previous lives. In preparing her books, she used 1,088 data sheets which had been filled out by subjects after the hypnotic sessions. In her judgment, only 11 data sheets out of the 1,088 showed clear discrepancies from known past history.[2] For example, one subject reported playing the piano in the 1500s, when in fact the piano was not developed as a musical instrument until the 1700s.

Items which seemed to match history were as follows. Class: less than ten percent belonged to the upper classes. Race: included were Caucasian, Asian and Indian, black and Near Eastern. Clothing: the claims to be wearing animal skins, draped cloth, tunics or pants matched what we know from history. So, too, footwear mentioned was consistent with history—hides, sandals, rags, boots, shoes or slippers. Food: whether cereals or meat were staples in the diet was not inconsistent with knowledge of the past. Eating utensils: wooden spoons, three-pronged or four-pronged forks showed the same consistency, as well as the types of wooden plates, leaves or gourds. Much of this, of course, could be accounted for by one's knowledge of history, whether explicitly remembered or long forgotten. Population increases on earth were also reflected in the samples, though this could be related to the fact that the subjects had more data available from recent times from which to construct their fantasies. The strongest demographic evidence, psychologist Wambach believes, was that in two samples 50.3 percent and 50.9 percent were male in another existence, while 49.7 percent and 49.1 percent were female, though the subjects in the sample had no such equal balance.

Subjects who were regressed to the time of their birth experience felt, in the main, that they chose their own birth circumstances. Most were in no hurry to join the fetus. Only 1 percent were in the fetus before the fourth month and only 15 percent were exclusively in the fetus before the ninth month. (Using such possible fantasies as a basis for making ethical decisions about abortion would, of course, be quite irresponsible.) If we are to believe these subjects, getting born is like walking out on a high diving board and much more apprehension was present in being born than in the experience of dying.

Not many cases about previous existences were specifically verified as to the personal details of the lives mentioned. However, one remarkable case was that of "Anna." Details given about a life in the small town of Westfield, N.J. from 1884 to 1917 were checked and they proved to be correct. A puzzling detail about a fire bell in an old schoolroom was solved. A description of a Captain O'Neill of the police department was verified through a photograph. The name of the town druggist was confirmed. A "Mud Lane," at first unlocated, turned out to be the previous name of Crestwood Drive.

One of the best subjects, "Robert Logg," drew hieroglyphics while in the hypnotic state. These were analyzed by an Egyptologist who reported that eighty percent of them were used in ancient Egyptian scripts but "the style of writing was that of someone who was drawing a picture rather than writing the way a scribe would have written them."

Most of the authors we have mentioned did not make the same effort at verification as was made by Helen Wambach. What are we to make of the data? Let us reserve judgment until we piece together an overall picture, including evidence from field research. Meanwhile, it should be mentioned that there are pieces of counter-data to take into consideration. For example, Peter Moss and Joe Keeton in *Encounters with the Past* present a case in which there is "a bizarre intertwining of two personalities of the same name and living at approximately the same time."[3] This is inconsistent with the reincarnation hypothesis.

Ian Stevenson mentions a study by E. S. Zolik (1958) who showed that people could be regressed to some previous life suggested by the hypnotist. They "recalled" another life with incredible imaginative creativity. Upon being awakened, they recalled nothing of this. (Wambach's subjects did recall what they had said.) D. Scott Rogo writes of a psychologist-parapsychologist, Dr. Reima Kampman of the University of Oulu in Finland. In his studies he found that people who were capable of past life recall were different psychologically from those who could not make such a recall. They were less neurotic or repressed, they handled stress better, and they were less threatened by fantasy. Dr. Kampman then rehypnotized his subjects, asking them to go back in their present lives to the moment when they first came upon the information out of which the past-life memory was created. One girl recalled a novel whose plot matched her past life. Another who sang a song in Old English discovered that once she had run through the pages of a book whose authors she correctly remembered. The song was found in that book. Another recalled a photograph in a newspaper of a seven year old girl who had been killed during an air raid.[4]

These facts, of course, do not explain all cases of supposed reincarnation, including ones to which we will turn in a moment. However, as Rogo says ". . . reincarnation is a treacherous phenomenon to investigate."

Field Investigation

Evidence from research in hypnotic regression is not a sufficient basis for reincarnation study. A much more satisfactory approach is field study, that is, cases which are carefully investigated by a professional parapsychologist. The outstanding figure in this field is Ian Stevenson, M.D., a psychiatrist at the University of Virginia. The scholarly meticulousness of Dr. Stevenson is evident in his large volumes, *Twenty Cases Suggestive of Reincarnation* and *Cases of the Reincarnation Type, I and II.*[5] Let us examine a few of the cases Stevenson investigated.

The Shanti Devi Case

Shanti Devi was born in Delhi in 1926; from the age of three she began to recall details of a former life in Muttra, 80 miles away. She stated that her name was Lugdi. Born in 1902, she said she married a cloth merchant named Kedar. She gave birth to a son and died ten days later. As she continued to make statements, her family wrote, when she was nine, to see if her "husband" existed in Muttra. Kedar answered the letter and confirmed her statements. Later he sent a relative and finally came unannounced himself. She immediately identified both of them.

The following year (1936) it was established that the girl had never left Delhi, and a committee was appointed to witness a visit by the girl to Muttra to see if she recognized a relative of Kedar's amid a large crowd of persons. She recognized him. She was then directed to a carriage, the driver of which was instructed to follow her directions. These led to the district and house of Kedar which she recognized even though the color of the house had been changed. In the area of the house an old Brahmin appeared and she identified him correctly as Kedar's father (i.e., her previous father-in-law). Upon entering the house she answered correctly a number of questions put to her regarding the arrangement of the rooms, closets, etc.

She then went to the house which she claimed belong to her previous parents, whom she correctly identified out of a crowd of more than 50 persons, and she correctly called them by name. Shanti claimed to have hidden some money in another house, the one which was the home of Kedar's family. In this house she pointed to a corner of one of the rooms as the place where she had buried some money. When a hole was dug, the witnesses came to an arrangement for keeping valuables, but found it empty. Shanti Devi insisted that she had left the money there, and eventually Kedar acknowledged that he had found the money and removed it after his wife's death. Shanti Devi used idioms of speech familiar in Muttra before she had been there. Her use of this dialect was a further feature of the case impressive to witnesses.

Stevenson says that the accounts available to him indicate that Shanti Devi made at least 24 statements of her memories which matched verified facts. The reports indicate other verified statements, the particulars of which are not given. No instances of incorrect statements are recorded.

Note: Kedar often traveled from Muttra to Delhi and went

to a sweetmeat shop a few yards away from Shanti's house. She saw him there one day as she was passing by.[6]

Ravi Shankar

On January 19, 1951, Munna, the six year old son of Sri Jageshwan Prasad, a barber, was enticed from his play and murdered with a knife or razor.[7] The motive seems to have been the desire by one of the murderers who was a relative to inherit his property.

In July 1951 Ravi Shankar was born in another district of the same city about a half mile away. A few years later word reached Sri Jageshwan Prasad that Ravi described himself as his son. Ravi named the murderers, described the murder, and gave many details from Munna's life. Between the ages of two and three he asked for the toys which he claimed he had in his previous life. When he was four, on July 30, 1955, Ravi gave Sri Jageshwan Prasad an account of the murder which corresponded with what he himself had been able to put together from the retracted confession of one of the murderers. Ravi's father beat him in order to force him to stop making such statements. Apparently he was afraid that the boy would be taken from him. Ravi's mother testified that the boy had a linear mark closely resembling the scar of a long knife wound across the neck. She first noticed the mark when he was three or four months old, but apparently it was congenital. In 1962 parapsychological investigation was begun. However, Ravi had largely forgotten the events of the previous life, a common feature in such cases. Stevenson entered the investigation in 1964. He found that the two families had only "a nodding acquaintance" with each other, though two witnesses thought that Ravi and his father had once visited the home of Sri Jageshwan Prasad.

Ravi mentioned having had a wooden slate, a school bag, a toy pistol, a wooden elephant, a toy statuette of Lord Krishna, a toy ball attached to an elastic string, a watch and a ring. He correctly identified Chatun, the alleged murderer, and Munna's maternal grandmother as well as his father. Munna's mother became mentally ill after the loss of her son. "She was trapped in past memories of her son Munna, had preserved all his toys and other belongings and attempted to deny the passage of later events."

Birthmarks are important pieces of evidence but they must be combined, as in this case, with other verifiable information to take on appreciable value.

Corliss Chotkin, Jr

Victor Vincent, a Tlingit Eskimo, died in 1946 in Angoon, Alaska.[8] He had predicted that he would return as the son of his niece. He said he would return with identifying birthmarks matching scars on his back, from a lung operation, and on the right side of his nose. About eighteen months after the death of Victor Vincent, Mrs. Corliss Chotkin, Sr., the niece, gave birth to a boy and named him Corliss Chotkin, Jr. At birth he had two marks on his body corresponding to those predicted by Victor, including what looked like stitch marks on his back.

When Corliss was thirteen months old, his mother tried to teach him his name, but he said, "Don't you know me? I'm Kahkody." The latter name was the tribal name of Victor Vincent and the boy uttered it with an excellent Tlingit accent. When he was two, he spontaneously recognized a stepdaughter of Victor Vincent and correctly called her Susie. He also recognized William, Victor's son, and other people. He also correctly narrated two episodes in the life of Victor Vincent which his mother thought he could not have acquired normally. By nine, Corliss' memories began to fade, and by fifteen when he was interviewed by Stevenson he said he remembered nothing. Many similar attachments and tendencies were found in the two lives. Stevenson obtained corroboration of 16 items and failed to do so for 5.

It is worth mentioning that Stevenson has investigated cases not only from India, but also from Burma, Italy, England, Belgium, Greece, Cuba, Mauritius, Japan, France, Syria, Canada, Lebanon, Turkey and Alaska.[9] Furthermore, he rates less highly cases where less than six items of information are matched between memories and verified facts, or where two persons were born into the same family or where the families were neighbors, so that communication of information might have been possible in a normal fashion.

Theories

Let us now investigate some of the theories which have been proposed to explain reincarnation data. Fraud and family suggestion immediately come to mind as possible explanations. However, in view of the incredible care and energy which Stevenson invested to test such possibilities, it seems extremely unlikely that such theories could explain all reincarnation cases. The reader would have to verify this by reading Stevenson's works. Fraud and suggestions implanted by the family seem to be subterfuges to avoid the problem.[10] Let us look at some other possibilities.

1. *Cryptomnesia.* Cryptomnesia is the power to recall forgotten memories of past events embedded deeply in the preconscious or the unconscious. Many people have had the experience of walking through the streets of a city, for example, and having the eerie feeling that they had been there before ("déjà vu"). Some apparent cases of reincarnation memories can be explained by cryptomnesia. This was pointed out in our discussion of hypnotic regression. However, serious investigation by Stevenson has ruled out cryptomnesia as an explanation for many reincarnation cases.

2. *Super-ESP and Impersonation.* The Super-ESP theory, which was discussed in the chapter on mediums, involves gathering information paranormally from living people and then dramatizing this unconsciously. In reincarnation cases, the dramatization would be an interior one. Impersonation involves an identification with a previous life so close that one experiences the same spontaneous reaction to situations and even similar skills. (It would be practically impossible to train a very young child in such spontaneous reactions.) While the Super-ESP theory might explain some cases, in general it suffers from serious weaknesses. (a) Apart from the reincarnation experience, most of the

people investigated did not seem to have had paranormal ability otherwise, though admittedly more research is needed here. (b) The theory demands that one hold not only that the subject had paranormal ability but also that its use was restricted to communicating with persons who had the data on a single person's life.[11] (c) This theory cannot explain the ignorance of changes after the first person's death. In the Shanti Devi case, she did not know that the compartment where she had hidden the money was empty. Also she did not know that the color of her house had been changed. Super-ESP, if it included clairvoyance, would have picked up these details. (d) This theory cannot explain birthmark cases. (e) In our discussion of Super-ESP with impersonation in the chapter on mediums, we never found that these mediums identified with the person from whom messages were supposedly received. In reincarnation cases there is such identification. It is true that such identification with an interior phenomenon is more acceptable with young children, but the Super-ESP theory does not account for such *continued* identification, together with similar and spontaneous likes and dislikes, until the time when the memories begin to fade.

3. *Retrocognition.* Retrocognition is paranormal knowledge of the past. Retrocognition as an explanation for reincarnation cases suffers from the same weaknesses as the Super-ESP theory, of which it is a variant. Retrocognition might be consistent with a person's not knowing changed details in the present, but otherwise, point by point, it has the same deficiencies as the Super-ESP position. And, most importantly, in retrocognition one may experience the past in the same way another person experienced it, as with Maria Reyes de Zierold's experiences of the soldier's battlefield terror, but one does not identify with the person in the past to such a degree that one is certain one is experiencing one's past life.

4. *Benign Possession.* Benign possession differs from the demonic possession which we discussed in Chapter II. But as we have not previously treated this type of possession, it will be necessary to relate some examples of the phenomenon in order to see why it even should be proposed as a possible explanation for reincarnation cases.

The Watseka Wonder Case.[12] Mary Roff of Watseka, Kansas

died on July 5, 1865. From early years she had frequent fits. She could also read letters blindfolded. Lurancy Vennum was born April 16, 1864 in Watseka. Thus she and Mary Roff were both alive at the same time for more than a year. At thirteen, Lurancy complained of feeling queer and she went into a cataleptic state lasting five hours. On January 31, 1878, "Dr." Stevens, a spiritualist minister, came to observe. Lurancy was possessed successively by certain distasteful personae but finally a "good angel" came, Mary Roff.

The next day Mr. Vennum came to Mr. Roff's office and said that his daughter claimed she was Mary Roff and wanted to go home. Some days later she went and lived with the Roffs. She was perfectly happy. She knew every person and almost everything that Mary had known twelve to twenty-five years before. Hundreds of incidents from Mary's life were recalled. For example, she remembered a trip to Texas and a collar she was "tatting." But she did not know or recognize her own family, nor neighbors nor friends nor anything about Lurancy. This state lasted three months and ten days. Lurancy came out of the state she was in and returned to her real home. She married and had ten children. Occasionally when she visited the Roffs, the Mary personality came back for some little time as if to visit her parents.

Mr. Roff had spiritualist interests. He had put Mary in an asylum before she died. The Roff and Vennum men had a formal "nodding acquaintance." But they were close neighbors for a part of a summer when Lurancy was six. Also Mrs. Roff visited Mrs. Vennum for a few minutes when Lurancy was seven. While they were close neighbors during the summer mentioned, some might wonder whether Lurancy could not have picked up information on Mary telepathically from the family. However, during the time of the possession Lurancy acted in every way as Mary had. This similarity was so strong that the Roff family believed that Mary had come back in Lurancy. Even in her letter writing, Lurancy had a different style of writing than she had when she wrote as Mary.

The well-known parapsychologist J. G. Pratt claimed that the possession hypothesis merited attention here rather than just some pathological explanation because psi phenomena were present and these are not present in cases of multiple personality. Secondly, he suggests that such cases may help us understand mediumship and reincarnation.

Other possession cases have been researched and recorded.[13] Might reincarnation cases be attributed to something like benign possession?

Benign possession cases as explanations for the reincarnation data suffer from the following deficiencies. (a) In possession cases the subject's own personality is temporarily blotted out. This is not true in reincarnation cases. (b) In possession cases the other personality seems to be possessing the subject's body. In reincarnation cases the other personality is seen as belonging to another time and place. (c) In possession cases the possession ends abruptly, whereas in reincarnation cases the memory of the past life gradually fades away. As Stevenson says, ". . . it is difficult to understand why 'possessing spirits' would all (or mostly) withdraw themselves in such a fashion and when the subjects were of about the same age." However, some apparent reincarnation cases may be possession cases, as, for example, in the xenoglossy cases which we have discussed.

5. *Unconscious "Tuning-In" on a Personality Still Living Beyond Death.* This is similar to the Super-ESP theory above but it differs from it in that one does not gather information paranormally from living relatives and existing documents. One gathers it directly, but unconsciously, from the "wave length" of a person still living beyond death. It is similar to benign possession but it allows for a distinction between reincarnation cases and possession cases. Possession would be a "tuning-in" which is so strong that the subject's own present personality is "jammed out." Reincarnation would be a weaker tuning-in which allows for the maintenance of the subject's own personality. The metaphor "wavelength" is used to allow for the suggestion that similar personalities gravitate to each other. Recall the similar fits and psychological patterns in the Mary Roff–Lurancy Vennum case and in many reincarnation cases.

This theory seems to be less vulnerable to the criticisms offered against the Super-ESP theory. Yet it seems to remain basically unsatisfactory as an explanation for all reincarnation cases. (a) Why does the possession experience end abruptly while the reincarnation experience fades away? (b) It does not explain birthmark cases, unless one is to hold that the "wave length resonances" operated from the time when the fetus was in the womb, producing similar marks and scars.[14]

6. *Genuine Reincarnation.* For many cases this is the most plausible theory at the present time. This is particularly true in those cases where there are many verified items of information, impersonation by a very young child, and where there is the added detail of matching birthmarks.

Theological and Religious Commentary. Should a Christian theologian deny outright that reincarnation might be a reality? Must he reject reincarnation because of Christian doctrine? This would seem to me to be most inappropriate. First, faith and knowledge are not dread adversaries. Second, history should teach us to be careful in areas of apparent conflict between Christian doctrine and some newly emerging hypothesis backed up by gradually accumulating evidence. It was once thought that belief in the Bible precluded belief in the heliocentric theory. Similarly, it was previously believed that the doctrine of original sin was incompatible with all but monogenism, the doctrine of an original couple. For a long time it was thought that biological evolution was not in harmony with Christian faith. Similarly we have changed on doctrines such as "no salvation outside the Church," and no salvation without baptism. Slavery, it was once thought, was compatible with the Gospel.

If we are to be faithful to Bernard Lonergan's principles about theological method, we must persevere in the unrestricted desire to know and love as far as is possible, while preserving the central aspects of Christian tradition. The question for the theologian to pursue is whether reincarnation is necessarily opposed to the central Christian revelatory experience centered in Jesus.

Christian Tradition. Only rarely in the Christian tradition has reincarnation been a large or explicit problem. It is true that eddies from Gnosticism have existed in almost all periods of Church history, especially during the Hermetic influence on the alchemists. Still the two chief movements in the past which brought the problem into focus were the Origenist movement in the sixth century, and the Albigensian and Cathari movement in the twelfth and thirteenth centuries.[15]

Some theologians believe that Origen (ca. 185–254), the great theologian from Alexandria, held a doctrine of the pre-existence of souls, of reincarnation and of universal salvation. Other theologians deny that Origen held reincarnation. For our purposes, we need not delay on this debate. However, Origenism which followed after Origen's time seems to have held these positions. A local synod at Constantinople in 543 passed a decree which rejected the doctrine of the pre-existence of souls and the position that the punishment of demons would cease. The Ecumenical Council of Constantinople II in 553 simply placed Origen's name on a list of heretics. Specific rejections of Origenism seem to have been made at an extra-conciliar session. The question certainly was peripheral to the Council's central purpose.

According to the hermeneutical principles for the interpretation of Councils which are generally accepted by Catholic theologians, the decrees of local synods are not universally binding on the faithful.[16] The meeting of 543 was a local synod. Only ecumenical councils are so binding. Constantinople II was an ecumenical council. But in such Councils only the central and essential points (understood from the text, the context and the history of the period) are binding in faith. This requirement was not fulfilled at Constantinople II. Many authors debate whether the decrees at Constantinople II were politically motivated, etc. But this is not the most important point for our present discussion. No formal or solemn decree centering on reincarnation has issued forth from the collective centers of the Christian tradition. The Councils of Lyons (1274) and Florence (1439) evidently *presumed* that reincarnation was untenable, but they never handled the question in an explicit or solemnly formal manner. Even though the general Christian tradition has been opposed to reincarnation, at least implicitly, an absolutely binding position on reincarnation cannot be found in this tradition.

At the same time, modern theological investigation is beginning to stress that conciliar decisions are "second-level" expressions, important but inferior to the first-level expression found in the original witness to the Christian revelatory experience, the New Testament. Councils were attempts to protect or reinterpret the original experience as presented in the New Testament. Therefore, according to this insight, the focus of theological debate on reincarnation should move to the domain of the New Testament if we are to reach the heart of the matter.

The New Testament. The most formidable theological objection to reincarnation is that Jesus did not teach it and it is not proposed in the New Testament (nor in the Old Testament). This is a strong objection.

Recently efforts have been made to circumvent this objection by attempting to show that Jesus himself accepted reincarnation.[17] For example, in John 9:1, Jesus sees a man who has been blind from his birth. His disciples ask him, "Rabbi, who sinned, this man or his parents, that he was born blind?" Despite Ezekiel and the Book of Job, many Jews still saw physical defects as a result of the sin of the parents. But how could this man have sinned before his birth? Many reincarnationalists present this episode as evidence of Jesus' acceptance of reincarnation, for Jesus answered, "It is not that this man sinned, or his parents, but that the works of God might be made manifest in him." Jesus, they say, seems to accept the possibility that the man could have sinned before his birth in this lifetime.

But the major commentators on Scripture do not see evidence here that Jesus accepted reincarnation. Actually some rabbis thought that there could be ante-natal sins, as, for instance, when a pregnant woman commits idolatry, involving the child in her womb in the act of bending in idolatry.[18] A syncretistic belief in reincarnation may indeed have crept into some Jewish circles of that time, but Jesus does not here accept reincarnation.

Again, in Matthew 16:14 (Mk 8:27, Lk 9:18) Jesus asked his disciples, "Who do men say that the Son of Man is?" And they said, "Some say John the Baptist, others Elijah, and others Jeremiah or one of the prophets." A case might be made that, although it was not official teaching in Israel, some Jews might have held a vague notion of reincarnation. But generally New Testament commentators take these references to the return of Old Testament figures in a symbolic sense, that is, the new figure takes on the functions of the former person, like Elijah, for example.

In the Old Testament, Malachi (4:15) had said, "Behold I will send you Elijah the prophet before the coming of the great and terrible day of the Lord comes." Jesus (Mt 11:14) said, "And if you are willing to accept it, he [John the Baptist] is Elijah who is to come. He who has ears to hear, let him hear." Yet, in John 1:21, John the Baptist is asked, "Are you Elijah?" He said, "I am not." This suggests that Jesus' language is to be taken symbolically. (Once again, it is possible that this question put to John by the priests and Levites might imply belief on their part in reincarnation, at least in a mitigated sense, since Elijah according to 2 Kings 2:11–12 never died but was carried by a whirlwind into heaven.) As William Barclay says, religious Jews expect Elijah before the Messiah and "to this day they leave a chair vacant for Elijah when they celebrate the Passover."[19]

It would be inconceivable that Jesus implicitly accepted a doctrine of reincarnation. In the New Testament we have the parable of the last judgment (Mt 25:31) where no second chance is implied, and the parable of the rich man and Lazarus (Lk 16:19) where the rich man is unable to return to earth to warn his five brothers about the way they are living.

Furthermore, texts in the New Testament which seem to imply individual pre-existence do not teach reincarnation. Apart from Christ, in the case of ordinary people, they imply existence as ideas in the mind or plan of God. No other explanation is allowed by the context.

We seem to have met the great obstacle to the doctrine of reincarnation: neither Jesus nor Scripture teaches this doctrine. However, one approach to this question must be plumbed, and that is the theological understanding of Jesus' inner psyche. Of course we cannot psychoanalyze Jesus. But some inferences about Jesus' human psyche can be drawn, based on the evidence found in Scripture.

In the past, many orthodox theologians presumed that Jesus, uniquely united to the eternal Logos but in a state of *kenosis* or self-emptying as St. Paul had said, gained his knowledge of doctrines about God from a supernatural infusion of specific knowledge by God. However, most theologians today see no evidence in Scripture for such a direct infusion of knowledge. Jesus "grew in wisdom, age and grace," and he was "like to us in all things save sin." Today, theologians like Karl Rahner and exegetes like Raymond Brown and Bruce Vawter speak of two levels of consciousness in Jesus: (a) an existential, ever present unique experience of Self, i.e., of the Logos as his center; (b) a reflective, growing consciousness based on learning and the events of history.[20] The theologian Gabriel Moran holds that Jesus' union with the Logos did not provide any *objective communicable knowledge.*[21] This came from his experience of history. Many Scripture scholars see the center of Jesus' person as his exclusive burning passion for "Abba." This was the existential center of his experience. Theologians add that this was based upon an ontological unique union with God. It was not merely a psychological feeling.

Following this line of thought, it seems reasonable to assume that if no doctrinal teaching was infused into Jesus' mind, then doctrines arose in his mind insofar as something was consonant with or repugnant to his burning numinous center of experience. For example when he castigated the Pharisees, when he modified the law, and when he forgave sin, these actions arose from his judgment of world ethics or practices when measured against his numinous experience. He did not know all things (cf. Chapter V).

Jesus also shared the world picture of his time. During that period there was an expectation that life as they knew it would soon end with the coming of the Kingdom. Jesus seems to have shared that view implicitly, even though he set up a small community to carry on his work and established a ritual memorial meal. (Recall that, as I suggested in Chapter V, Jesus foresaw the Kingdom with many layers of meaning, one element of which was complete victory through his agency by the Father. The event of bodily resurrection may not have been seen explicitly by Jesus. This was God's surprise. But there did occur the ending of history as they knew it in one sense.)

As the philosopher Geddes MacGregor points out, in a world where the end is expected relatively soon, there would be little interest in reincarnation.[22] There would be only a short future in which it could occur.

According to this theory, Jesus' idea of heaven was God or the Father, and the experience of him. Hell would be non-God. Both in this life and in the world to come this would be true. If doctrines were not infused into Jesus' mind as a result of the "hypostatic union," all of Jesus' teaching would come forth from his central existential experience of a unique ontological union with "Abba."

Accordingly, the doctrine of reincarnation was never formally considered by Jesus. Except for certain small groups, it had not become a central issue in Judaism. Its religious validity would have to be judged according to its harmony or disharmony with Jesus' central burning experience, somewhat in the manner in which Moses devised the commandments out of his experience of the "burning bush."

Let me not make this suggestion without emphasizing the extreme tentativeness of such a position. I leave it to others to judge whether such an approach can be legitimately adopted by Christian theology. Certainly, Christian theology at present is strongly opposed to the doctrine of reincarnation. And even the Indian parapsychologist C. T. K. Chari is opposed to the doctrine on empirical grounds. Canon Michael Paternoster points out that reincarnation is very difficult to fit into a modern understanding of genetics. The traditional Christian understanding of the uniqueness of each individual is, scientifically speaking, much more tenable. Furthermore, the propensity to remember past lives may, to some degree, be culturally conditioned, and, lastly, there are no absolutely decisive criteria for deciding what evidence counts for reincarnation as against some of the other theories.[23] Yet, each of these points must be balanced off against the apparent strength of reincarnation evidence.

Notice that after New Testament times, the Catholic tradition, basing itself merely on a few hints in Scripture, developed the doctrine of purgatory. The ethical idea behind this evolution seems to have been that since life is so short, we do not all reach the goal at the end. Think, for example, of infants who die. We need a slow process of maturation. Whether this would be on this earth or in the next world would not seem to be the major point. Later, as the doctrine of evolution moved into religion, as with Teilhard de Chardin, the slow processes of the universe are seen by many, even by Protestant thinkers today, to continue after death. Why should this law of slow maturing in the evolutionary process operate everywhere in the universe but end suddenly with a person's death?

According to this process, the doctrine of reincarnation might be compatible with Christianity. This is definitely a minority opinion and it is presented here merely as a hypothesis. It is interesting that Karl Rahner in his major work, *Foundations of Christian Faith,* writes:

> Let me call attention to the question whether in the Catholic notion of an "interval" [he is speaking of purgatory] which seems so obsolete at first, there could not be a starting point for coming to terms with the doctrine . . . of reincarnation. . . . This is a possibility at least on the presupposition that this reincarnation is not understood as a fate of man which will never end and will continue on forever in time.[24]

The question has scarcely begun to be discussed by mainline Christian theologians. But it certainly is in the air today within some Christian circles, and theologians must begin to address it without, however, being unaware of the empirical evidence. Notice that if there is truth in the doctrine of reincarnation, this does not imply that all people reincarnate. Perhaps it is a rare event and perhaps very few reincarnate. Perhaps it is reserved for some who do not wish to grow in another dimension and wish to return to this earth for some reason which we do not know.

General Theological Objections. Apart from the points we have mentioned, there are other objections which Christian theologians might have against reincarnation. One objection is that it would trivialize the work of Christ if persons do not come to reconciliation with God in one life, and Hebrews 9:27 says, "And just as it is appointed for men to die once, and after that comes judgment, so Christ, having been offered once to bear the sins of many, will appear a second time. . . ." Furthermore, vicarious salvation or at-one-ment through Christ is done away with in reincarnation.

(We should notice that these questions are approached in a strictly Christian context and no mention is made of the relationship of Christ to world religions. However, one cannot handle everything at once!) In reply to the objections proposed, it can be stated that in a doctrine of reincarnation individuals still make their way to God through the grace of Christ (or through the grace of the Logos as non-Christians might put it). Jesus' life is not made vain. Furthermore, the citation from Hebrews is really stating that we no longer need the repeated sacrifices of the Old Testament since Christ lived and died once and that was enough. Furthermore, "vicarious salvation" or at-one-ment through Jesus has never meant, at least in the Catholic tradition, that we are saved or at-oned with God without any cooperation on our part. As cooperation was demanded in this life, why could it not also be demanded in another subsequent life?

A major Christian theological objection to the doctrine of reincarnation is the doctrine of "karma." Karma is the law of cause and effect: "As one sows, so shall one reap." Karma operates like the law of gravity. We return to this life according to the way the scales have balanced. But if there is one thing central to the message of the Gospel which arises from Jesus' experience it is this: the Father whom we serve is a Father of mercy. He is the one who goes out to meet his prodigal son with open arms. From Jesus' inmost depths comes the conviction of the experience of grace. God is a giver, all is grace, the scales are not precisely weighed. Even though the thief who died with Jesus was to be with him that day in paradise, what is that to God, the Father of mercy? (What the thief would want to do thereafter, of course, we do not know.) However, perhaps we misunderstand the East on this point. Some Hindus and Buddhists accept a doctrine of grace just as some modern reincarnationalists combine reincarnation with a Christian doctrine of grace. But I believe that if one presents a doctrine of karma bereft of grace, then reincarnation is totally incompatible with the God of Christianity.

Philosophical Objections. Many thinkers object to reincarnation on the grounds that most people don't have any memory of a previous life.[25] Yet one cannot infer that without memory there could be no previous life. We don't remember our earliest years, yet we did exist. And it is quite possible that only those who have memories reincarnate. (This answer implies that many apparent cases of reincarnation are not real reincarnation, as in the hypnotic regression cases; these would have to be explained in some other fashion.)

However, this objection contains a serious problem which needs to be considered on a deeper level. If one does not remember a previous life, then how can there be ethical growth? Without memory of one's actions, nothing is learned from their evil or good consequences. I believe that this is one of the chief philosophical objections to reincarnation. It might be answered, again, by supposing that only those reincarnate who have conscious memories of another life. But if reincarnation is more widespread, the objection becomes formidable. Perhaps we might say that there is an unconscious part of us, like the long winding roots under a small flower, which itself can profit from former lives. But the evidence we have from empirical psychology does not suggest, I believe, that the unconscious itself can learn. If consciously we cannot remember the way we have lived, we cannot consciously correct past defects. One reply to this major objection might be that there is more to the unconscious than comes forth in the work of empirical psychology. There is some evidence to suggest the existence of a "higher self," a position which Dr. Ring used in his work on near-death experiences. Perhaps this higher self may influence us silently, somewhat like the way in which ESP motions touch us.

In conclusion, it must be said that reincarnation is incorporated into Christian theology only with great difficulty. But I have made the tentative suggestion that this incorporation is not impossible. At the same time, I cannot understand Christians who become "reincarnationalists," that is, people who, as it were, "root" for the doctrine. All humans need meaning in life. But meaning may be found apart from reincarnation. Therefore, judgment on reincarnation can be made only after a long and searching investigation as we follow out the unrestricted and non-biased desire to know and love. It seems to me that even after one has endeavored to make such an investigation, the puzzle about reincarnation remains. But if what I have said is true, there is no reason why a Christian cannot remain open to the data.[26]

Chapter XII

Eschatology:
Theology and Parapsychology

Christian theology is the heir not only of the Jewish tradition but also of two thousand years of Christian thought and spirituality. It has made a rich contribution to human culture. Despite its admitted defects, time and human suffering have seasoned it in its richest depths. Parapsychology is young and heady, but it is the heir to modern methods of investigation and verification. It must both contribute and learn. The dialogue between theology and parapsychology can only enrich both.

Problems in Paranormal Studies:
Escape from This Life?

Modern theologians seem somewhat wary of the investigations of parapsychology, especially when they touch "eschatology," the Christian doctrine of the last things. This attitude might be summed up in a concrete example. Bishop James Pike, who became interested in post-mortem existence after the death of his son, used to cite the words of the dying Thoreau to Emerson, "One life at a time." And he wore a button which read, "I believe in life after birth." Christian history has shown that a passionate interest in a future life at times has starved the passionate interest due in a future life and bleached it of its colors.[1] Furthermore, an excessive emphasis on future life can magnify our egoism. It has often led to a "sophisticated type of sheer self-centeredness."[2]

A heavy eschatological emphasis is indeed a danger. However, one should not take a one-sided view. If one reflects only on a few of the psychics we have mentioned, a neglect of this world does not seem to have been prominent in their lives. Mrs. Coombe-Tennant was deeply involved in social issues, whether it be the arts, the care of criminals, women's rights, or the League of Nations. Geraldine Cummins wrote twenty-two books, many of them plays, even though she was deaf and delicate. Elisabeth Kübler-Ross maintains an incredibly active schedule of talks and workshops in order to help those who grieve or those who help the grieving. Recall the number of medical doctors and psychiatrists engaged in these studies, as well as those psychologists who carry full teaching loads.

The value in eschatological studies (and we have not limited ourselves to these in this book) is akin to what Martin Buber said was the value and purpose of man's concern with God: "The encounter with God does not come to man in order that he may henceforth attend to God but in order that he may prove its meaning in action in the world." A theologian considers survival studies not simply to become concerned with the afterlife, but in order to prove its meaning in action in the world. In other words, psychical evidence may support but it cannot take the place of active religion. Nils O. Jacobson, M.D. puts it this way, "If belief in life after death enriches life, then it has fulfilled a great task."[3]

Spiritual Immaturity?

Without spiritual maturity, absorption in psychic experiences can cause spiritual stagnation.[4] In the last analysis, what really matters is faith and love. However, in view of the awesome issues investigated, research in this area may abet growth in spirituality. Research in parapsychology today is manifesting a reserved interest in religious issues. Furthermore, research is not the same as a craving for the experiences. Such an excessive craving can lead to a deeper narcissism than we already possess.

(In what follows, I will distinguish between careful and critical parapsychological research and popular psychic works which describe life after death. The latter one often uses uncritical approaches to what is probably unconscious material presented as communications with the dead. Spiritualist, spiritist and theosophical approaches, though not mentioned as such, frequently color both data and interpretation.)

H.D. Lewis has put the matter well. While warning that an unholy alliance between religion and the paranormal can be extensively harmful, he writes, "In oblique and mediated ways the 'beyond' which eludes our proper understanding in itself may be reflected in the limited world of our own experiences in various ways which religious life and the study of religion discloses to us. Proper account of these intimations of God in present experience and history is a considerable topic in itself. But it should not be hard to see that considerable scope may be found for the paranormal awareness to ally itself with these intimations and disclosures of God, and be brought into their service. It could well be, for example, that the glory of God is reflected in some distinctively enriching ways in modes of existence and awareness surpassing those available to us now but of which we may have occasional glimpses. As the expression of religious insights understandably takes markedly figurative forms, the peculiar mode of experience encountered in some paranormal states could provide new and stimulating symbolism for the enrichment and communication of religious discernment. . . . The religious person disregards the evidence of paranormal phenomena at his peril."[5]

Parapsychology Eclipses Faith?

Some theologians stress that a natural certainty about life beyond death which some parapsychologists seek is not an unalloyed good. On the one side, it seems to be true that the conviction that life is extinguished with death has led to great catastrophes for mankind. I believe with Gabriel Marcel and Viktor Frankl that the nihilistic convictions of some philosophers contributed to the horrible practices of the death camps in

Nazi Germany and in Stalinist Russia. Yet, at the same time, there are not a few fanatics in this world who, if they are convinced that life goes on beyond death, will more easily facilitate one's transition to the other world as a kind of favor. I am not thinking only of Charles Manson and Jim Jones, but also of religious groups prone to violence. All things which are good and true, it seems, have some danger attached to them.

Parapsychological study does not issue precisely in a natural certainty about life beyond death, but it does offer some powerful clues. To insist on faith, as if it were opposed to such research as some theologians do, is obscurantist. Faith and knowledge, as I have stressed, are not two opponents. Faith is a kind of tacit knowledge and all knowledge involves faith of some sort. Faith is a primordial thrust which goes beyond, but in the direction of, what we know. The Catholic tradition in theology generally has not believed in sweeping away knowledge to make room for faith. Faith leads us into dark, trans-rational dimensions of this mysterious world. It does not take our hand and lead us into an irrational sphere.

Our only solution to the tension between faith and knowledge is to sound the depths of what is rational, insofar as this is possible, but without sealing off a world divided into neatly separated, logically distinct and rationally analyzed boxes. Faith touches our whole being in its rational depths. Reason, which is never without some faith, tries to rest in the mind alone. Faith and reason are friends, or they should be.

If faith scorns knowledge or some probability in any area, it becomes vulnerable to Freud's charge that faith is an illusion. An illusion is a conviction which feeds not on evidence but exclusively on our wishes. It breeds Eric Hoffer's "true believer," the obsessed fanatic. It is the child of superficial aspiration rather than of intelligent conviction.

No doubt, one needs to make a distinction between Freud's "wishes" and the deepest hopes of human beings. Wishes are childish desires. Hopes are mature convictions, seasoned by love and suffering. Our primordial aspirations can indeed be pointers to meaning. But the consolations (and terrible demands) of faith must be tested, when such tests are possible, by the drive to know. Primordial aspirations, in contrast to superficial wishes, do not arise in opposition to what we think. As Arthur Koestler puts it, in the final analysis the only consolation is truth. Or as Friedrich von Hugel put it in a more religious context, we do not seek the God we want but the God who wants us. In sum the evidence from a disciplined parapsychology is as germane to faith as the evidence from astronomy or psychology or history.

Parapsychological studies offer strong clues about some kind of a survival of consciousness. But without a brain, what can such survival be like? Some parapsychologists suggest a most tenuous kind of post-mortem existence. Others offer a view of survival much like the Christian view. But they are very probably influenced silently by their own religious beliefs. Christian faith tells us that we rise as persons. St. Paul said, "Just as we have been the image of the man of dust, we shall also bear the image of the man of heaven. . . . Death is swallowed up in victory" (1 Cor 15:50, 54). The life of those who rise in glory cannot be an attenuated existence. It is a victory.

Let us now briefly review some specific points of Christian eschatology and endeavor to see how parapsychological evidence touches these areas.

Immortality of the Spirit or Resurrection?

In the chapter on out-of-the-body experiences we discussed the problem of dualism which would arise if it were established that consciousness does in fact separate from the body. The evidence, while it is very meager, points slightly in the direction of such a separation. One conclusion to be drawn is that theologians should not use "dualism" as a kind of negative tag which prevents further thinking.

Some participants in the OBE experiments felt as if they were in another body whose form they could manipulate at will. Others felt that they were in an "ecsomatic" state. It may be that there does exist a second mysterious body composed of some form of energy, but we have very little evidence for this at present. (See our discussion of this point in Chapters VII and IX.)

St. Paul in 2 Corinthians 5:1–4 wrote, "For we know that if

the earthly tent we live in is destroyed, we have a building from God, a house not made with hands, eternal in the heavens. Here indeed we groan, and long to put on our heavenly dwelling, so that by putting it on we may not be found naked. For while we are still in this tent we sigh with anxiety; not that we would be unclothed, but that we would be further clothed, so that what is mortal be swallowed up by life."[6]

As I see it, Christian theology is open to the idea that we may receive another kind of body immediately after death. I think it could also be open to the idea that what we receive is really a manifestation of what we already possess in this life. If either of these approaches is true, then dualism ceases to be a problem, for we would never be without a body. Admittedly, the evidence for this second is extremely slight from parapsychological and biological studies. (See the discussion of "life fields" in the chapter on OBEs.) But it represents a valid theological opinion. It would also aid in reducing the bewilderment often produced in the reader by some theological treatments which insist that Christianity believes in the resurrection of the body and not in the immortality of the spirit. Few theologians today would hold that the body in the grave will be resuscitated at the final judgment. If we believe as a theological opinion and not as the result of parapsychological evidence that persons at death immediately possess a second body, a major problem disappears. However, I think that we should speak of the resurrection of persons rather than of the resurrection of the body.

No Intermediate State?

The outstanding religious philosopher Maurice Nedoncelle says that the mere continuance of life as such has no religious value, for the quantity of life does not determine its quality.[7] Let us see if we can shed some light on this question through a dialogue between theology and parapsychology.

Karl Rahner believes that there is no need to postulate an intermediate state between death and the final destiny of the person. "The idea of the intermediate state contains a little harmless mythology."[8] This position he supports with some profound religious and philosophical thinking. One hesitates to differ from a great theologian with such deep religious sensibilities.

However, if survival studies do indicate some contact with those beyond, this position cannot stand. To cite only two cases, if there is no intermediate state, what are we to make of the communications with "the airmen who would not die" or of the incredible communications in the Willett-Cummins scripts? The Super-ESP hypothesis is unbearably strained if used to explain these cases. One might have recourse to the theory which holds that, at death, a kind of psychic husk of memories is left behind which is then animated by an agent in the beyond who has reached his or her final destiny. Here we would have a little pious deception about an intermediate state! Who knows what we may learn in the future about such possibilities? But for the moment our evidence indicates that there is an intermediate state of some sort.

Sleep After Death?

In the traditional positions about the state following death there are two divergent opinions among Christians. Some Church Fathers and many Protestant theologians believe that after death there is a "sleep." The dead do not arise from this sleep until the final or general judgment, at which point the dead arise to join God in heaven or to be excluded from God in hell. The other view, held by many Protestant thinkers today as well as by most Catholic theologians, is that after death there is an individual or particular judgment, followed by a stage of slow growth (purgatory), and that the final or general judgment will occur at the end of time as we know it. Survival studies present evidence which is more in harmony with this latter position. Many apparition and mediumistic cases have as their most plausible solution that we occasionally are in genuine interaction with those who have gone through the dark night of death. "Sleep" does not at all seem to be an apt word to describe this state. If the dead sleep, they are also active. "Sleep" might indicate an attenuated but relatively joyful intermediate state but it would not signify sleep in any literal sense.

Judgment as Self-Judgment

While critical parapsychological investigations give strong
indications of an active afterlife, they offer us little evidence,
beyond the idea of growth, of the nature of the afterlife. This is
true with regard to the judgment of individuals after death. In
near-death experiences, there seems to be a kind of judgment,
but it is self-judgment. However, if the reader follows the
position I have outlined in Chapter VIII on NDEs as symbolical
journeys with paranormal touches, we cannot use NDEs as
evidence for judgment beyond death. If one moves to the wider
area of popular psychic reports of communication with the dead,
the notion of self-judgment is very widespread. Yet these studies are remarkably uncritical and they may portray merely automatic writing issuing from the unconscious.

Still, the notion of self-judgment is not at all out of harmony with Christian theology if it is seen as part of God's plan. The
notion of self-judgment is in harmony with the law which
Teilhard de Chardin found at work in evolution: "God makes
things make themselves." Similarly many theologians today interpret "judgment as a kind of judgment on self made by the
person in the light of a new consciousness of the nature of God
and reality."[9] Judgment, then, might well be conceived as self-
judgment in the light of a new and startling clarity about oneself
and a universe of love.

Purgatory

Scripture does not give any clear evidence for the existence
of purgatory. In the past, Catholic theologians searched out the
few hints which we find and used them in a rigid way as "proof
texts" to support Catholic teaching on purgatory. Still, these
texts can generate some light on the matter. In 2 Maccabees
12:40–46, Jewish soldiers, wearing pagan amulets, died fighting
for God's cause. To make atonement for this idolatry, Judas
Maccabeus took up a collection to make a sin offering. "Therefore he made atonement for the dead, that they might be deliv-

ered from their sin." Here there is belief in cleansing from sin after death.[10] In Matthew 12:32, the sin against the Holy Spirit is said not to be forgiven, either in this age or the age to come. This suggests that other sins may be forgiven after death. In Matthew 18:23 ff., the parable mentions a servant whose debt was forgiven by his master but who refused to forgive the debt of a fellow servant. He is handed over until he pays the debt he owes to the master. Jesus concluded, "So also my heavenly Father will do to every one of you if you do not forgive your brother from your heart."

I have no intention here of presenting a thorough discussion of these texts on purgatory. Suffice it to say that the Church gradually developed the doctrine of purgatory after New Testament times. The doctrine of purgatory as it is presented today would contain the following characteristics. Purgatory must be demythologized of fire, and other Dante-like pictures. It should be thought of as a state rather than a place. It involves purification and slow growth, somewhat similar to life on earth. It is generally a happy place. Persons can choose their own means and rate of growth.[11] If survival study and medium work have any validity as to contact with the dead, it would seem to support this idea of purgatory. Joy pervades most of the communications. And in some xenoglossy and possession cases where joy is absent, individuals seem to be allowed to satisfy their desires to linger near the earth and not to evolve for the moment. It seems very unlikely that such joyful communications are from the first stages of heaven, although the whole process should be viewed rather as a continuum than as boxed-off places.

A Problem About Growth

Christian theology, and especially Catholic theology, has traditionally held that one's essential direction is fixed with death. In fact, Catholic theology has held that all "meriting ends with death." ("Meriting" implies a cooperating with God in growth.) But this view creates an overwhelming ethical problem.

There can be no growth without free cooperation with God, or "meriting" in technical theological language. Otherwise there is only "satisfaction," a kind of passive suffering for sin. But this position on meriting is not an unchangeable position in Catholic theology. St. Bonaventure held that there is a type of free personal growth with regard to smaller sinful ("venial") attitudes.[12] One could actively cooperate with God in growing beyond these. However, he and most theologians held that there could be no essential reversal of direction in purgatory. This latter statement presents great difficulties if we consider the case of infants and very immature people who die. What has their essential direction been? Theologians today hold that infants who die, even without baptism, are saved through the grace of Christ (non-Christians might say through the power of God or of the Logos). But it is very difficult to say what essential direction has been chosen by immature people who die young, if this direction is to be measured by their affirmation of charity and love. The New Testament, the earliest witness to the revelation in Jesus, has not settled this question about the different types of growth in the beyond, or even about essential reversals of direction for immature persons. One might say that the completely immature have never taken an essential direction. Growth for such people might be the equivalent of finding a direction. This remains an area for deeper theological reflection.[13]

If we turn to the more critical studies of afterlife evidence, the idea of growth appears consistently. For example, Mrs. Coombe-Tennant supposedly went through a conversion process with regard to her possessiveness toward her children. In many of the more plausible and well-researched cases, there is a picture of a happy state where there are growth tasks as one moves deeper into the evolutionary plan of God. No doubt, we need to be careful in assessing such data in view of what I have said about the many subjective factors involved in such communications. But amidst the welter of data presented in such communications, the ideas of free growth and joy are constants. The least we can say here is that the best studies of afterlife communications and Christian theology are not in essential disagreement on this point.

The Final Option Theory?

Ladislaus Boros, S.J. has worked out a "final option" theory concerning the moment of death.[14] At death every person sees his or her own life and in an instant makes a decision about it. This decision is consistent with one's life patterns and grows out of these. It is not arbitrary. But it is instantaneous and it can be very searing. It brings us either to God or to the loss of him.

This position is very similar to the quick review of one's life as found in the near death experiences recorded by Moody and others. After meeting the Light, and apparently affirming the Light in awe, there emerged a new resolution to grow in love and knowledge. However, Boros' theory is based on the idea that this decision and its final outcome, union with God, all occur in a flash. Time and slow growth vanish. This is not at all the view we receive from the studies we have investigated. Apparition and medium study contradict the final option theory.

Time of some sort seems to exist beyond death. Perhaps we should develop another word for this kind of time which is so different from earth time. But if time is defined as the measure of change and not as the measure of the earth's turning and its circling of the sun, then time or succession of some sort continues after death. Boros' position about the final option would have to include this notion. Else it is incompatible not only with the traditional notion of purgatory but also with survival evidence.

Hell?

In studies of NDEs, some few people seem to be depressed and moving about as if in a dream. Neither Dr. Ring nor I have interpreted these experiences as literal experiences of an afterlife. However, if one chooses to interpret them as such, it is not at all clear that these are experiences of hell. They may be experiences of less evolved dimensions of existence.

Theologically hell is essentially the absence of God, and probably the absence also of any positive human relationships.

One thinks here of Jean-Paul Sartre's *No Exit,* where "hell is other people." The Christian Church has always insisted that hell exists as a possibility, but it has never declared that any person is in that *state,* except Satan. (See my comments on Satan in Chapter II.) Since hell is a state of being and not a place, and since the Church has never defined that anyone is permanently fixed in such a state, a Christian might hope that, while such an outcome of life is possible, God's mercy always wins. One must live as if it is, at least, possible to lose the game, that is, the God of love. But it is conceivable that, because God's nature is one of love, no one finally loses self or finally fails to make the journey to God.

Some Christian theologians today speak of God's continuing to give persons utter freedom in the beyond. In the afterlife, people are allowed to "do what they want." No one is forced. Else human freedom is not respected. No one would be bound by some *external* force to hell.[15] One could leave this state if one wished. But by definition, no one in this state wishes to leave it. Even here, judgment is self-judgment under God's plan.

A minority of theologians today tend toward the idea that one can become extinct or opt out of the game of love. However, in the extinction theory, Infinite Love finally loses in its chief desire. Also, the consequences of human freedom are not respected. The previous positions which I have enunciated are supported by the Christian tradition. I think they solve the problems which those who hold the extinction theory wish to avoid.

Heaven and the Problem of Images

Only in a few of the scripts which have been investigated by parapsychologists do we hear of heaven. One of the best of these is Geraldine Cummins' *The Road to Immortality,* where we hear of Myers' alleged communications about the stages in the afterlife. However, I wish to make a few comments here on heaven and to use these as a springboard for discussion of the problem of images.

St. Augustine spoke of heaven as an eternal sabbath.[16] "The repose of the soul will be ineffable and cannot be explained." He goes on to mention the objections of some of his contemporaries that heaven would be a place of ennui. "It is said by some that we will always be awake yet with nothing to do." Scripture, they say, states that our activity will be in saying "Amen" and "Alleluia." Some feel that if they remained standing saying this, they would fall asleep uttering these sounds and would prefer silence. But Augustine adds, "Amen and Alleluia are said not with mere passing sounds but with the devotion of the heart." I mention this passage, not in order to present Augustine's teaching on heaven. Few thinkers have surpassed him in depth of metaphysical or religious richness. But the passage makes clear the problem engendered by imagining the deepest realities of life.

Should we rid ourselves of all images of the afterlife? Theologians have written, "Believers today have reached a high degree of maturity and have no need of images of afterlife."[17] But I wish to stress here, as I have done previously in the discussion of mediums, that a neglect of images leads to loss of belief. "A religious picture loses its hold on a person's life because a rival picture wins his allegiance."[18] The rival picture is often the picture of erasing pictures of an afterlife. This may be a minority view at present but I believe it is correct. The real art in Christian spirituality is the act of discerning images. One chooses images which animate one's life without unduly distorting a doctrine, while keeping these images in tension with what St. Paul says, "No eye has seen nor ear heard, nor the heart of man conceived, what God has prepared for those who love him" (1 Cor 2:9).

Theologically heaven is seen not as a place but as a state of being. St. Augustine said that heaven is nothing else but God. St. Thomas said that after death God is our place. Karl Rahner has shown that this is what we are always seeking in life, in particular when we are drawn to seek utopias, or when we seek perfection in art, work or friendship. In one sense, heaven begins in potency now.[19]

The picture we have offered of afterlife is one of growth. Is there a possibility of growth in heaven? If there is a possibility of growing in love of God, there must be a possibility of "growing" in heaven. (This has been a disputed theological doctrine.) Since the human person remains finite in uniting with God, and since the finite cannot simultaneously possess and experience the Infinite totally and instantaneously, it would seem that there is growth in heaven.[20] In fact, this is part of the essence of a person's joy, an infinity of discovery of what one loves. There even may be time in the sense of a measure of change. Some succession of experiential states is at least a probability. That is both the agony and the ecstasy of being finite.

Church documents speak of seeing God "face to face" in heaven.[21] When told that this is a symbolical image, as God has no face, many believers are shaken to their depths. When these believers hear about Moody's subjects who spoke of "seeing the Light," many felt relieved. Notice the power of images and the importance of discernment in their choice. The expression "face to face" means that we will intuit God directly and apart from all intermediate realities as on earth.

In view of this problem of images, it is not surprising that many popular psychic works speak of God in many different fashions in their discussions of the afterlife.[22] Patience Worth, in a very homely expression, spoke of "the magic of his being which hangeth all things together." Some speak of the Absolute, or Consciousness, or Cosmic Consciousness, or Absolute Energy. Some simply call God "He Who Is." I have not found these works pantheistic, but in their descriptions of God there is often an infiltration of certain Gnostic, spiritualist, theosophical or anthroposophical currents. I do not mean to imply that simply by placing a tag on certain writings we thereby show that they are false. But the reader of these works should become aware of certain presuppositions or influences. Often the writer himself or herself may not be aware of these influences. It is also interesting to note that very rarely does a supposed communicator from the beyond speak of God as "she," though God may sometimes be spoken of as "it" as a kind of transpersonal expression. The absence of the feminine pronoun underlines the subjective and cultural element in these communications.

One should be very wary of these works. Yet, whatever their value, one cannot say that God is absent. As with Teilhard, all things happen "within God." God is the haunting influence which hovers in or above all things. One reason why these popular works have had such a following is, I believe, their power to concretize non-material realities. Are theologians right who favor getting rid of all such images? Is the popular attraction to such images simply to be attributed to "the weakness of the masses"? I believe not. Paul Tillich said that all statements about God are symbolical. Theologians themselves, however rarefied may be their expressions, are still speaking in symbols. But this is not to embrace a complete relativism. Some symbols are more relevant and more apt than others to express the transcending reality of God, at least if one is speaking of the God found in the Old Testament or in Jesus' revelatory experience. The point is that one must learn to use discernment with regard to the images to which one is attracted.

Christ Eclipsed?

One last theological objection both to the critically investigated cases we have studied and to the popular psychic literature is that Jesus does not appear in them. Apart from near-death experiences and from some apparition cases, I have never read of alleged communications from the afterlife in which Jesus, the Christ, is seen. To the best of my knowledge, I would say that he is spoken of, though not very frequently. He is not seen. If what we have said about the slowly evolving states after death is true, then the lack of a vision of Jesus would not seem too strange. Jesus is "at the right hand" of the Father. Those who evolve may feel his presence and power, but they do not yet have a vision of Christ.

I do not mean to pass by this last point in an offhand manner. Indeed, precisely here may be the emotional crux behind the objections of many theologians to research an afterlife. And there seems to be a sound theological caution behind the emotional reaction. Such studies, if centered upon in isolation from one's religious life, tend to create a new center of gravity. This center of gravity could become one's own narcissism. We have already warned about this problem. Or it could become one's continued evolution rather than God. This would then run the danger of becoming a higher kind of narcissism. Or, lastly, it could become the Absolute, the All, Consciousness, an approach to God in which Jesus Christ seems to vanish.

This problem is not solved by pointing out, paradoxically, that the very discussion of God found in many of these writings originates in an unnoticed way from Jesus. While this is true, there is a deeper religious problem involved here. One solution would be the suggestion that Christians take no part in such investigations. But this would go against all that we have said about faith and reason. We can no more give up parapsychological investigation than we can give up astronomy. The other solution is the one I have endeavored to follow in this book. Make use of parapsychological investigation to illuminate, if we can, the life of Jesus himself. After all, parapsychology, as we have shown, does not merely investigate post-mortem survival. Secondly, let us admit that parapsychological investigation is but one humble approach to reality. It does open up new vistas in a closed scientific world. But it cannot substitute for religious life or for theology. If I may inject a word from my own experience in teaching this subject for the past ten years, I have found that it reanimates many students who are beginning to lose all their religious moorings. It tends to make them want to begin to study Scripture in depth. It starts up a new interest in theology. Questions which had bored them become alive. My approach to parapsychology in this book has been that of the Catholic fundamental theologian. But there is more to Christian theology than fundamental theology. I believe these students have seen this. It is my hope that the reader will feel the same urge to investigate the Christian tradition, as well as other religious traditions, in greater depth.

Let us now move to the final chapter in which we will look at some broader theoretical perspectives.

Chapter XIII

Consciousness, Parapsychology and Theology

In this chapter we will consider the changing paradigms of "consciousness" and the pertinence of the dialogue between parapsychology and theology to consciousness study. Although we will listen to specialists in various areas, our treatment of necessity must be somewhat selective. There are opposing voices. These dissonant sounds, like ominous French horns, warn us about aspirations arising out of premature syntheses. However, as William James said, our passionate nature, too, can be a guide to truth. Even scientific syntheses involve passion as well as thought. Yet the tentative nature of many of the following statements must be stressed. We are in no position to make some final synthesis from the mushrooming clouds of new data. Undoubtedly many processes are involved whose understanding will one day surprise us.

Consciousness and Religion

My colleague, Thomas Berry, C.P., has been speaking and writing for years on the need for a consciousness change in our modern religious experience. Christian spirituality, he says, will not abandon its roots. But, in the Western world, influences from India, Hinduism and Buddhism will continue to be strong. "Taoist influences will increase. The mystical quality of Chinese humanism will be understood more profoundly. Cultivation of trance states in a revived shamanistic context will also take place on an extensive scale. . . . This immediacy of man with himself is founded ultimately on the experience of the numinous within, on the consciousness of the indwelling divine mystery beyond all comprehension of which Augustine says somewhere that it 'is closer to use that we are to ourselves.' As this interior identity increases, the Oriental-Western differentiation in religious experience will be seen as more a differentiation in the human modes of consciousness than simply as a differentiation based on geographical and cultural factors. The convergence within man of the complex aspects of his being is coextensive with the universal convergence of peoples and cultures and modes of experience. Man, cosmos and history become totally present to each other." Fr. Berry believes that there is a larger human and Christian world into which we are entering. We do not as yet see fully how the smaller Christian world functions in relation to the larger world which surrounds it. It is to this larger Christianity that we must turn our attention. "Within this larger world of mankind, the multiple spiritual and humanist traditions implicate each other, complete each other, and evoke from each other higher developments of which each is capable."[1] But, with Teilhard de Chardin, he believes that we are witnessing a radical change in the mode of human consciousness. "There is now incontrovertible evidence that mankind has just entered upon the greatest period of change the world has known. The ills from which we are suffering have had their seat in the very foundation of human thought. But today something is happening to the whole structure of human consciousness."[2] "Man has no proper understanding of himself until he sees himself not as a mechanistic function of matter but as the ecstasy of the earth."[3]

Another colleague, Dr. Ewert Cousins, using the historical schema of Karl Jaspers, suggests that we are entering a period of global consciousness. Jaspers claims that prior to about 500 B.C. mankind existed in a state of a kind of mythic consciousness. It was characterized by primitive, naive and participatory thinking. But around 500 B.C. "a remarkable transformation of consciousness occurred in Greece, Israel, Persia, India and China, without discernible influence of one area upon another. [Jaspers] calls it the Axial Period because it 'gave birth to everything which, since then, man has been able to be.' "[4] The move was from mythic to self-reflective thinking, from fusion with the cosmos and the tribe to independent individual identity which is distanced, even alienated, from nature and the collectivity. At this time the great religions were genuinely born and our fundamental categories of thought arose. Dr. Cousins believes that what we are witnessing today is a Second Axial Period which is producing global consciousness. He thinks that a major dynamic of the Second Axial Period is the recapitulation of the cosmic modes of consciousness from the Pre-Axial Period, but with the preservation of the subjective, reflective consciousness of the First Axial Period.

Bernard Lonergan, S.J., more specifically applying the stage approach to Christian theology, pinpoints the stage from which we are moving today as having begun in 1680. "For that, it seems, was the time of the great beginning. Then it was that Herbert Butterfield placed the origins of modern science, then that Paul Hazzard placed the beginning of the Enlightenment, then that Yves Congar placed the beginning of dogmatic theology. When modern science began, when the Enlightenment began, then the theologians began to reassure one another about their certainties."[5]

That the views just presented are not the pipe-smoking reveries of a few scattered thinkers will be obvious from what follows. These writings are part of a pattern so widespread that it suggests a paradigm change vast in its implications for mankind and religion. Teilhard de Chardin saw the "new synthesis" of the future as involving not only deep contact between Christianity and such religions as Buddhism and Hinduism, but as something which involved a third element which had not yet been incorporated, the full meaning of evolution.[6] Let us now consider recent specific work on consciousness.

Cognitive Maps

Maps are not literal pictures. They are models which bring out or "disclose" one or two main points of something which is beyond spatial picturing. They "work" in getting these points across to our imagination. They are not "scale models" which, apart from size, match the original point by point. Rather they are called "disclosure models." Disclosure models center on one or two major points and not on the details.

Maps are sometimes called "paradigms." Maps of the mind are usually of a "polyparadigmatic" nature.[7] The reason for this is that the psyche is so rich that many points and not just one or two must be "disclosed." It is worth stressing that some faith is usually involved in the choosing and acceptance of a map. In their formation there is a dialectics of life and thought.[8] Reductionist maps depend on a faith or a life philosophy just as much as do religious maps.

Maps as Story

Experiencing is first articulated in the form of a narrative or story. The story issues forth from a "gut feeling" about life.[9] Rolf von Eckartsberg holds that professional psychologists create "stories about stories," that is, meta-stories.[10] Michael Polanyi claims that in attributing truth to any methodology we make a non-rational commitment. We perform an act of faith.[11] Rationality plays a role, he says, after the knowledge has been obtained "viscerally."

However, I think we must be careful of extreme statements about the non-rationality of story. Stories may begin in the "gut" (philosophically this would be from a pre-reflective union of the cognitive-affective-intuitive elements in psyche). But stories are at times *abandoned*. When some stories are unraveled discursively, they are found to be at odds with another paradigm which we accept, and this latter may be based on evidence. There is a non-fit. For example, we could cite the example of the non-fit of the story of an original single couple and evolution. Thus stories may begin in the "gut," but they must finally face judgment on the part of reason. Lonergan calls the combination of story and critical reasoning "authentic subjectivity." Its formation is one of the main goals of theological method. Because it is subjective, story is hard to change. But because there is also critical intelligence, we have paradigm change.[13] That we are at the beginning of a new story in our time is, I would think, not simply the outcome of "gut feeling." It is also the result of critical reasoning.

Specific Maps or Paradigms of the Mind[14]

Let us take a brief look at some of the maps of the mind available in our time. First, we have Reductionist Maps, like those of B. F. Skinner. These maps deny all free ego states and genuine transpersonal states. It reduces all to physico-deterministic elements.[15] This map is to be rejected on many grounds. Then we have Cognitive Growth Maps like those of Jean Piaget, Field Maps like those of Kurt Lewin, and Depth Psychology Maps like those of Freud and Jung. But we also have Height Psychology Maps like those of Assagioli and Frankl. We have Split Brain Maps which are proving their usefulness.[16] We have Growth Maps like those of Erich Fromm and Abraham Maslow. Finally, we have States of Consciousness Maps such as those proposed by Charles Tart and Ken Wilber. The variety of these maps may cause some bewilderment. However, apart from the reductionistic and deterministic maps, many of the "disclosures" arising from these maps are in no way contradictory. Rather they seem to be complementary. But there is one point which issues from a large number of these maps, and to this point we will now turn our attention.

Isolated Ego as Culprit

Some writers speak as if the ego is the cause of all our problems today. I would qualify this by using the phrase "the isolated ego." A collage of various books on consciousness today offers this kind of picture. "All sacred traditions begin from the idea of an ordered, intelligent universe, where the idea of hierarchy is central and where each level is related to others in reciprocal dependence. . . . Though [psychology] might recognize and show some serious interest in some of the experiences previously called religious or mystical, man is still perceived as being the center of things: his ordinary desires, ambitions, hopes and plans, whether selfish or altruistic, are taken at face value and used as a basis for action, for planning utopias and eupsychias. There is no concept of a second purpose to which man can give himself, and because of this, no real questioning whether the first could be illusory. Ordinary psychology then becomes *another elaboration of the delusion itself,* providing more blindfolds, another ring through the nose, more 'hope' to keep us turning the treadmill."[17]

Washburn and Stark assert: "The premise of egocentricity states that identity and worth are established by winning recognition and approval of other people. This assumption, which stresses the indispensability of the other, is properly an overall outlook that is called *ego*centric, because in all cases the individual uses other people to achieve something for *himself.* [But consciousness] is not so much an entity with qualities as it is a *medium* for the reflection of qualities. . . . Consciousness is thus never identical with what it identifies with."[18]

Medard Boss mentions an Indian philosopher who came to Europe to improve his knowledge of European psychotherapeutic methods. "Whereas formerly he had accepted the vicissitudes of life, like illness in the family, with great calmness, now every trifle made him nervous, restless and pessimistic. Now he thought he had always to do this or that at once and he made everything worse with haste. Obviously, from his training in Western psychotherapy, he had learned to see himself as a 'psyche.' . . . Now he had to make his way through the bustle and tumult of an external world, based on nothing but a fundamentally unknowable, anonymous, id-like 'unconscious.' "[19]

Morris Berman stresses the same point: "Of course the ego has its positive aspects. It certainly existed in the West from about 800 B.C. to 1600 A.D. without massive alienation as its corollary, but it is hard to avoid the conclusion that in its modern form the ego is the product and expression of pathology." Berman continues, " . . . the triumph of the Puritan way of life, which concomitantly repressed sexual energy and subliminated it into brutalizing labor, helped to create the 'model personality' of our times—a personality that is docile and subdued in the face of authority, but fiercely aggressive toward competitors and subordinates."[20]

Whatever may be the exaggerations in these statements, and they seem to unduly underplay the value of genuine ego states like charity and love, for example, they do witness to a possible turning by Western man toward a consciousness of the transpersonal.

Transpersonal Maps and Maps of States of Consciousness

Before I discuss transpersonal maps, let me mention a physiological description of states of consciousness. Beta, the normal ego state, is considered to be a state of about 15 brain waves per second or higher. The Alpha state is situated roughly in the area of 8 to 13 brain waves per second, the Theta state and the Delta state 5 to 7 and 0 to 4 brain waves per second respectively.

A rich mine for recent psychological research has been found in Altered States of Consciousness (ASC). Altered states of consciousness are states which are beyond the normal Beta stage. The Beta stage is the domain of our normal waking and working consciousness. The Beta state accompanies our ego planning, our striving, our working. When we plan a trip, take tests in school, work out our income taxes, compete in business or choose an insurance policy, we operate mainly in the Beta state.

A number of researchers of late have been attempting to map out stages in altered states of consciousness. Ken Wilber has worked out a map of ASC which is widely cited.[21] The original stage is that of the shadow and the persona or mask. It is the stage in which our masks and repressed elements in consciousness dominate us. The ego state (the Beta state) is that state in which develops our primary self-image. But there is more to life than the individual ego. There is a social world of persons and other realities around us, and thus we are called to social consciousness, which he calls the biosocial stage. Then there is a state which brings healing to the split between ego and body, a split which we gradually become aware of. Wilber calls this the existential stage. Then consciousness may be altered to the transpersonal stage. This is the stage where humans are not yet aware of their identity with the "All," and yet neither is their identity confined to the ego stage or any other previous stage. This is the level on which archetypes are formed. This stage may be reached in dreams, in creativity, or during meditation. Finally there is the stage of Mind. This is the experience of union with the All or cosmic consciousness. Other researchers have worked out different models. In many centers around the world a great deal of time and energy is being dedicated to such research.

A Transpersonal Model: Holism

One model of the mind which has received a great deal of attention of late is the holistic model. As we discuss this model, let us recall what we said of models. No model will explain the mind in its totality. Models "work" in that they facilitate the gathering of fruitful insights around them. At times, they assist our imagination more than our intellect.

David Bohm, a physicist-philosopher, has presented a "holokinetic" paradigm of the mind.[22] He also calls his picture "the holocosmic paradigm." He says modern physics has no philosophical foundation for its own findings. Hence it avoids facing the issues altogether, confining itself to pragmatic goals, to the prediction and control which Bohm charges have all but preempted the endeavor of physics. Such a limited approach is unacceptable to Bohm, who terms "incomplete" any theory of the cosmos "that fails to take consciousness into account. . . . Second, the more modern physics approaches the twenty-first century, the closer it seems to get to the cosmology of the remote past."[23]

A fundamental feature of Bohm's cosmology "is the claim that reality is *one,* an unbroken, undivided wholeness which is the background for everything in the universe, underlying both matter and consciousness, providing the raw material for all manifest entities." This non-manifest matrix Bohm terms the *enfolded* or *implicate* order. It manifests itself in time in various states of matter-energy or the explicate order.

Karl Pribram, a brain psychologist, has presented a "holographic paradigm."[24] Pribram makes use of the hologram. A hologram is the result of a process of lensless photography in which the resultant picture is three-dimensional, has perspective, and can be looked at from all sides, and when a piece of the image is broken off, the fragment again contains the whole picture, though in a less clear state. This model, and let us remember that it is no more than that, helps us to imagine processes which we have discussed throughout our present study.

Both Bohm and Pribram hold, like some of the Church Fathers, that the entire universe is in some way contained in the individual, not in his ego, but in the transpersonal domain. Our ego, which perceives reality in three dimensions, squanders much energy to maintain the self-deception and illusion of *autonomous* stability. There is an ultimate "empiricism" which leads to the experiential certitude that the ultimate source of nature in the universe is an energy of love. But the experimenter himself must know that he is in the experiment. He cannot observe the whole and leave himself out. Berman puts it this way: "Although the denial of participation lies at the heart of modern science, the Cartesian paradigm as followed in actual practice is riddled with participating consciousness. . . . The deliberate inclusion of participation in our present epistemology would create a new epistemology, the outlines of which are just now becoming visible."[25] No longer is it a question of a knower observing the known across the gulf of knowing that separates them. That model of consciousness has failed us during the centuries in which we have stubbornly clung to it. Bohm had said that it must be replaced by "the austere paradigm of a unified field of being, a self-conscious universe realizing itself to be integrally whole and interconnected."[26]

Many books are now appearing with a like message. For example, George Leonard writes: "But when we look at the individual as a series of waves or patterns summed up as a single wave function or inner pulse, the dualism of mind and body dissolves. The inner pulse is stable or permanent at the most fundamental level. The physical body is but one manifestation; so, too, the fields around the body and the putative field in the astral body. This pattern is not erased at death but persists in the everlasting web of rhythmic relationships that constitute a meaningful universe."[27] Kenneth Pope says that there is no mind-body problem since both are different hierarchical levels of the same system.[28]

Evidence from Other Sources
for the Transpersonal Paradigm

C. G. Jung is well known for his theory of the collective unconscious. His theory was the result of work on dreams, fairy tales, myths, religious doctrines, art, especially by schizophrenics, and the work of the alchemists. He has been criticized for being too casual in finding universal archetypes throughout the world, and this is a legitimate criticism. But recall that, as against many psychologists, he did not hold that we are born with archetypal images. They are not innate. We are born with a patterning power to form motifs, while the specific images are gathered from culture. Jung's notion of a collective unconscious is gathering support from many areas.

LSD work, especially that done by Grof, Masters and Houston, and Walter Huston Clark, has shown that there is an ASC structured into the psyche itself.[29] Their work gives backing to Jung's idea of a collective unconscious and the existence of archetypes. The same is true of John Lilly's work done in isolation chambers.[30]

Some physicists have begun to inspect the relation of consciousness to physics. Eugene Wigner believes that ultimately consciousness must become part of what physics observes.[31] According to "the Bell theorem," no theory compatible with quantum physics can require a spatial event to be independent from every other event. It must allow for the connectedness of distant events in a way that is contrary to ordinary experience. We must be careful, however, of becoming flip and cavalier at this point. Many physicists feel that much speculation in this area is a yet premature, and the intricacies are such that the layman can scarcely become competent in mastering them. My only point is that some physicists are beginning to attend to a domain which corresponds in a loose way with the study of consciousness and its interconnectedness.

Secular philosophy also has begun to investigate a level of consciousness deeper than ego consciousness. For example, Peter Koestenbaum in *The New Image of the Person* uses throughout his book the distinction between "the transcendental and the empirical ego."[32] He criticizes even humanistic psychology for making the empirical ego the ground of the psyche. The same is true in the study of mystical experiences in theology. The theology of mysticism believes that beyond ordinary asceticism or ego life, there is a deeper ground in the spirit. Contact with this deeper ground results in what we call today an altered state of consciousness. But there are at least two forms of this ground in the spirit. First, there is the ground point or apex of the spirit where God is the deepest point of the self. But also there is a state of "consciousness of the All" which may be a soul or a nature mysticism, an immanent altered state of consciousness in which all reality is interrelated, but which is not God, who is both immanent and transcendent.[33]

Theology has always warned that this immanent state of consciousness is not precisely God. In the Judaeo-Christian tradition, God is always transcendent to any state of consciousness. This consciousness may be a fruitful, though dangerous, symbol for God. God is known only through faith, which is an experience of transcending all other experiences.

Lastly, we turn our attention to what has been the subject of this book—parapsychology. Perhaps here we have the most powerful evidence both for altered states of consciousness and for the existence of a corresponding level of "objective" reality which transcends individual subjectivity. This seems to be a spiritual level of reality which is incompatible with ordinary materialism. However, the probable existence of animal psi (anpsi) should caution us about the scope of our claims here.[34] Should the probable existence of psi in animals cause us to lessen our claims about the spiritual ramifications of psi experience or should we transform our notions of the nature of animals? My own tentative position is that there are different levels on which psi operates, and some of these levels can be described only in spiritual terms.

Precognition, which is supported by very strong evidence, suggests that there is an aspect of man which either goes beyond or else dwells beyond time as we know it. Out-of-the-body experiences obviously involve altered states of consciousness, and there is at least a slight probability that consciousness actually separates from the body, whether with an energy body or not, we do not know. Near-death experiences are admitted by all experts on the subject today to involve ASC in which paranormal contact is made with a deeper dimension of existence. Verification of details in this state implies that one is not in contact simply with one's own consciousness but with something much larger. With regard to apparition study and medium work, the two best explanations for the correct information given in these experiences are (a) a genuine contact with the realm beyond death which is the best explanation for some cases, and (b) an incredible ability of the human mind to scan some kind of cosmic reservoir and to pick up information about people one does not know, both dead and alive. In both explanations, what is contacted is not simply one's own mind. We are in contact with other mysterious dimensions of reality. The same conclusion might be drawn from reincarnation studies. ESP, as in telepathy and clairvoyance, is looked upon by many today not as the power to *go out* into external reality, but as the power to *go in* to something like a collective unconscious. Thus parapsychology offers some of the best evidence not only for altered states of consciousness but for the existence in reality itself of dimensions which correspond to these states.

A Brief Theological Conclusion

As far as I can see, theology has scarcely begun to assess and come to terms with this modern movement, although it has begun dialogue with Hinduism and Buddhism in similar areas. My few concluding remarks, therefore, are tentative. They may be taken as areas for future research.

Theology should warn members of this new movement that we should be careful of dropping the values of the ego. Few have been more insistent on this point than Martin Buber, and rightly so. How can I have an I-Thou relation without ego? How can I love, that is, have compassion, active care, charity, without struggling in the ego area? There is a saying that a moving pendulum never stops in the middle. As we move to new insights, many have a tendency to rush to the other extreme. Fifty years from now, some new spiritual movement may begin which accents ego. Even today, we know that we cannot live without technology, without order, without ego planning. The new consciousness explosion may forget this as it offers its message, even while using the latest technological gadgetry. I cannot see an I-Thou relation in charity and love which does not involve ego level operation. Self-transcendence should come only after one has developed a fully responsible ego. Else, as Maslow noted, the result will be an irresponsible and unethical "low nirvana." Finally, the absolute elevation of group consciousness over the individual has ominous overtones.

Another point which theology must emphasize is the distinction between God and consciousness. Already some in the new movement speak of cosmic consciousness, without qualification, as God. For example, Peter Koestenbaum writes: "If we call the stream of consciousness God, then this God is not a person and does not have personal attributes." It has, however, "a soothing, cosmic, protecting character." "To be an individual is to alienate ourselves from the vastness of being. To be an individual means to reject God. The individual that we are is not to be found in the stream of consciousness that runs through us. Our individual ego is constituted by this stream and observed and witnessed by it. The sense of universality runs through the ego but it is not the ego."[35] This may be acceptable in a qualified sense. But will the ordinary person make the needed qualifications, i.e., that "not a person" really means "transpersonal," and that "the stream of consciousness" is only a metaphor for a transcendent God? Morris Berman writes: "This larger Mind is comparable to God and is what perhaps some people mean by 'God,' but it is still immanent in the total interconnected social system and planetary ecology." In other words, this larger mind is not God in the Christian sense, although process theologians might dispute this assertion.

With regard to consciousness and God, one could make at

least four types of statements: (1) our consciousnesses are literal fragments of God; (2) consciousness, which we all share, is God; (3) consciousness *in* which we all share is God; (4) consciousness in which we all share is a reflection of God. Only the last statement, I believe, adequately preserves the Christian concept of the transcendence of God.

Conclusion

Most of the works which I have cited believe that we are in the midst of a paradigm clash and paradigm change. It may be one of the great turning points of history, if we last long enough. Parapsychology not only plays a part in this movement. It plays a prominent part. Theology must investigate the consciousness movement in depth. In our present study we have shown how a first important step is taken by theology through a dialogue with parapsychology.

Not a few moderns are rightly cautious of fads and movements filled with an immature optimism. However, the chief point of this book has not been optimism but truth. I have presented what I believe to be overwhelming evidence which points to contact with dimensions of reality where we are not the isolated egos we often think. Furthermore, as with Teilhard and others, the most coherent view of the cosmos reveals that we are enfolded in a psychic universe in which we operate together with a mysterious Otherness, Absolute Mind and Love. Many today share this vision, and the resultant optimism comes not from wishful thinking but from critical reflection. I share the vision of those who believe that we are witnessing the birth of a new "story" for mankind in our time, a story which involves not only man and his history, but the entire evolving cosmos. Psychic phenomena may be seen as a kind of bridge between the secular and the sacred. In order to understand religion in depth we need some understanding of where the psychic and the sacred meet.

Notes

PREFACE

1. Reprinted in *The New York Times,* December 21, 1974, p. 27.

CHAPTER I

1. Michael Maloney, *Scientist as Subject* (Cambridge, Mass.: Ballinger, 1976), p. 19. Renée Haynes, past president of the Society for Psychical Research, mentions a girl who was blind from birth but who received her sight at seventeen through surgery. At first all she could see was a frightening kaleidoscope of light and color. It is not surprising that many people find it so hard to perceive something completely new after working energetically to perceive an older ordered stereotype: *The Seeing Eye, The Seeing I* (London: Hutchinson, 1976), p. 39.

2. Alan Gauld, *The Founders of Psychical Research* (N.Y.: Schocken Books, 1968), a solid study of the origin of parapsychology in Britain and the United States. "Spiritualism" in contrast is more dogmatically oriented. A good account is found in Geoffrey K. Nelson, *Spiritualism and Society* (N.Y.: Schocken Books, 1969).

3. *Ibid.,* p. 100.

4. *Ibid.,* p. 142. For an example of Myers' method, see his *Human Personality and Its Survival of Bodily Death* (N.Y.: Longmans, Green, 1903) and its abridgement in Susy Smith (New Hyde Park, N.Y.: University Books, 1961).

5. For a typical investigation of fraud in séances, see Trevor Hall, *The Spiritualists. The Story of Florence Cook and William Crookes* (N.Y.: Helix Press, 1962). An attempt is made to show deceit on the part of Crookes, a psychic investigator and prominent British physicist (1832–1919). This attempt has been criticized recently. Similarly, see Ronald Pearson, *The Table-Rappers* (N.Y.: St. Martin's Press, 1972), a survey of Victorian spiritualism, but with a bias leading to a too easy dismissal of inexplicable data.

6. Gauld, p. 329.

7. See Dennis Brian, *The Enchanted Voyager. The Life of J.B. Rhine*

(Englewood Cliffs, N.J.: Prentice-Hall, 1982); also Joseph B. Rhine, *Extra-Sensory Perception,* revised edition (Boston: Bruce Humphries, 1964); D.S. Rogo, *Parapsychology. A Century of Enquiry* (N.Y.: Dell Publishing Co., 1975); *Psychic Exploration. A Challenge for Science,* John White, ed. (N.Y.: G.P. Putnam & Sons, 1976); *Handbook of Parapsychology,* Benjamin B. Wolman, ed. (N.Y.: Van Nostrand Reinhold, 1977); Norma Bowles and Fran Hynds, *Psi-Search* (N.Y.: Harper & Row, 1978); C.E.M. Hansel, *ESP and Parapsychology: A Critical Re-Evaluation* (Buffalo: Prometheus Books, 1980, 2nd ed.).

8. J.G. Pratt, *A Decade of Research with a Selected ESP Subject: An Overview and Re-Appraisal of the Work with Pavel Stepanek* (N.Y.: ASPR, 1973), p. 28.

9. "Psi Information Retrieval in the Ganzfeld: Two Confirmatory Studies," *JASPR,* 70, 2, April 1976, 207–217.

10. "Has Science Developed the Competence to Confront Claims to the Paranormal?" in *The Signet Handbook of Parapsychology,* Martin Ebon, ed. (N.Y.: New American Library, 1978), p. 483.

11. See, for example, *Science and the Paranormal,* George O. Abell and Barry Singer, eds. (N.Y.: Charles Scribner & Sons, 1981). Articles by Gardner, Asimov, Randi and Sagan are included. One thinks of what Thomas Goldstein in *The Dawn of Modern Science* (Boston: Houghton Mifflin, 1980) has written: "Although modern science has profited incalculably from this self-imposed limitation of the focus of research (and attendant methodological clarifications), it is evident that such progress was achieved at a heavy price. Precision was gained at the expense of an intrinsic largeness of view; the elimination of all that is unverifiable (and of much that was no more than fantasy) at the expense of a sensitive open-mindedness toward psychic phenomena or toward a realm of existence that may be reached only by unhampered speculative thought, sometimes merely by a kind of groping intuition" (pp. 170–171).

12. Dennis Rawlins, "STARBABY," *FATE,* October 1981, pp. 67–98. On CSICOP see also Theodore, Robert and W. Teed Rockwell, "Irrational Rationalisms: A Critique of *The Humanist's* Crusade Against Parapsychology," *JASPR,* 72, 1, January 1978, 23–34.

CHAPTER II

1. Herbert Thurston's work, *The Physical Phenomena of Mysticism,* edited by J. H. Crehan, S.J. (Chicago: Regnery Company, 1952), remains an excellent source for this material. D. Scott Rogo's *Miracles: A*

Parascientific Inquiry into Wondrous Phenomena (N.Y.: The Dial Press, 1982) is an excellent modern study.

2. *Portrait of a Parish Priest. St. John Vianney, the Curé d'Ars* (Westminster, Md.: Newman Press, 1958). See also Mandor Fodor, *An Encyclopedia of Psychic Science* (Secaucus, N.J.: The Citadel Press, 1966), s.v. "Curé d'Ars."

3. See Renée Haynes, *Philosopher King. The Humanist Pope, Benedict XIV* (London: Weidenfeld and Nicolson, 1970).

4. *Signs and Wonders* (N.Y.: Desclee, 1966), p. 177.

5. *Ibid.,* p. 180.

6. See *An Encyclopedia of Psychic Science,* s.v. "Fox"; Earl W. Fornell, *The Unhappy Medium* (Austin: University of Texas Press, 1964); and D. Scott Rogo, *The Poltergeist Experience* (N.Y.: Penguin, 1979), p. 58.

7. On PK experiments, see Gertrude Schmeidler, "Research Findings in Psychokinesis," in *Advances in Parapsychological Research,* Vol. I, *Psychokinesis,* edited by Stanley Krippner (N.Y.: Plenum Press, 1977), pp. 79–132; D. Scott Rogo, *Minds and Motions. The Riddle of Psychokinesis* (N.Y.: Taplinger, 1978), and subsequent references in this chapter.

8. *The Magic of Uri Geller* (N.Y.: Ballantine Books, 1975). On magicians who have studied Geller, see Charles Panati, *The Geller Papers* (N.Y.: Houghton Mifflin, 1976), pp. 151, 243.

9. *Psychic,* June 1974, p. 14.

10. Manning's own story is found in *The Link* (N.Y.: Ballantine Books, 1974). For his subsequent history, cf. Walter Uphoff, *New Psychic Frontiers* (London: C. Smythe, 1977, 2nd ed.).

11. "Pk Effects Upon Continuously Recorded Temperature," *JASPR,* 67, 4, October 1973, 325–340.

12. "Probable Psychokinetic Effects Produced in a Clinical Thermometer," in *Psychoenergetic Systems. The Interactions of Consciousness, Matter and Energy,* edited by Stanley Krippner (N.Y.: Gordon & Breach, 1979), pp. 35–40.

13. *The Metal Benders* (Boston: Routledge & Kegan Paul, 1981). See also *Research in Parapsychology 1980,* edited by William G. Roll and John Behoff, esp. pp. 32–42.

14. J. G. Pratt and H. H. J. Keil, "Firsthand Observations of Nina S. Kulagina Suggestive of PK Upon Static Objects," *JASPR,* October 1973, pp. 381–390.

15. "Spring in Leningrad: Kulagina Revisited," *Parapsychology Review,* July–August 1973, pp. 5–10.

16. "Kinetic Effects at the Ostensible Location of an Out-of-Body Projection During Perception Testing," *JASPR,* July 1980, pp. 319–329.

17. "Distortions in the Photographs of Ted Serios," *JASPR*, April 1981, pp. 143–153.

18. Walter and Mary Jo Uphoff, *Mind Over Matter* (N.Y.: Weiser, 1980).

19. *The Poltergeist* (N.Y.: New American Library, 1972), pp. 104ff.

20. Hans Bender "Modern Poltergeist Research," in *New Directions in Parapsychology*, John Beloff, ed. (Metuchen, N.J.: Scarecrow Press, 1975).

21. Iris M. Owen with Margaret Sparrow, *Conjuring Up Philip: An Adventure in Psychokinesis* (N.Y.: Harper & Row, 1976). For a similar case in England see J. Batcheldor, "Report on a Case of Table Levitation and Associated Phenomena," *J Soc PR*, 1966, 43, and Diana Robinson, *To Stretch a Plank* (Chicago: Nelson Hall 1981), pp. 133ff.

22. Martin Ebon, editor, *Exorcism: Fact not Fiction* (N.Y.: New American Library, 1974), pp. 6ff.

23. Martin Ebon, "Exorcism Beyond the Chaos," *Psychic*, October 1974, p. 52.

24. Juan Cortes in *The Case Against Possessions and Exorcism* writes, "A supernatural explanation of the facts may be accepted only when every natural explanation is impossible or has proven to be so." This position is extreme. We may never, in most cases, be able to rule out, as at least possible, a natural explanation.

25. *Psychiatric News*, June 3, 1977, pp. 28–31.

26. *The Poltergeist Experience*, p. 250.

27. *Xenoglossy: A Review and Report of a Case* (N.Y.: American Society for Psychical Research, 1974), pp. 75–79.

28. *Magic and Mystery in Tibet* (Baltimore: Penguin Books, 1971), pp. 314ff. This mind-creature is called a *tulpa*. It tends to free itself of its maker's control. In a modern study, *The Story of Ruth*, by the psychotherapist Morton Schatzman (N.Y.: Putnam's, 1980), Ruth had an obsessive vision of her father, and even of herself, which followed the laws of optics and perspective. However, only once were any of her hallucinations seen by others. Her husband, perhaps through telepathic exchange, spoke to the hallucination of his wife, thinking it was there.

29. This seems to be the position of Gonzalo Gonzalez, "God and the Devil: Conquest of Dualism," *Theology Digest*, Spring 1978, pp. 19–22, and of Fr. J. Edgar Bruns, "Toward a New Understanding of the Demonic," *The Ecumenist*, January–February 1966, pp. 29–31. Jesus spoke of Satan many times in the Gospels, as, for example, when he said, "I saw Satan falling like lightning from heaven." The Gospels also speak of Jesus' struggle with Satan in the temptation in the desert.

Gonzalez does not claim that Satan is only a personification in the New Testament writings, but he does claim that Satan is not a central truth of the Christian faith. The Council of Lateran IV in 1215 solemnly declared that God created everything that exists, whether visible or invisible, angels or devils. However, if one employs the generally accepted principles of hermeneutical research, it is clear that the Council was not making its central theme the existence of Satan but that whatever existed was created by God and is good. That is what is central to the faith. Satan himself does not appear in the Apostles' Creed. It has often been pointed out that in the earlier parts of the Old Testament Satan was a messenger from God who tried to test people under God's orders. Bruns points out that in Mesopotamian literature there was a mythical monster of chaos called Tiamat, and in Canaanite literature called Leviathan. In Hebrew writings "Leviathan is never portrayed as anything but a monster; this indicates that it was conceived of as being a force, though a force which rebelled against its Creator and therefore was endowed with some kind of instinctive will." Jesus, as a figure of his own period in which belief in a personal Satan was widespread, gave no indication that he held that Satan was only a force. Yet a Christian is not bound to hold all that Jesus held. He was a person living in culture-bound time and place. For example, Jesus believed that David wrote a psalm which we know was not written by David; Jesus probably believed that Jonah was a real historical figure, a point which most exegetes today would not agree upon. Returning to Gonzalez, we might note that his approach is not sensational and his conclusions seem to me to be rather balanced. (1) No matter what import we accord to official teaching, the existence or non-existence of evil spirits is clearly not central to our faith. Even Paul VI's Allocution (November 15, 1972) says merely that "refusing to admit the devil's existence means departing from biblical and ecclesiastical teaching" but not abandoning Catholic faith. (I am making a distinction here between traditional *teaching* and *formal dogmatic* interpretations of revelation.) (2) The preceding does not mean that we have demonstrated a non-existence of the devil. (3) Even granting that the devil exists, the problem of evil is much wider. Some Christians seem to think that the existence of the devil is as important to Christianity as the existence of God. This is absolutely false. Both Gonzalez and Bruns see the devil as *at least* a personification of all those malefic forces which contain a certain excess of evil that is inexplicable to our reason. The conclusion that this force is embodied in a personal being is secondary in the hierarchy of truths connected with our Christian faith. Fr. Richard McBrien in his simple but brilliant synthesis, *Catholicism,* writes, "Evil, like miracle, is a *power.* So intense and so focused may this power be that it can be personified as *Satan....* That such evil is often collective and at the same time very personalized is also evident. *What* this evil is at its core is not so clear. To the extent that the Church has addressed itself officially to the question, the official magisterium has affirmed the existence of the devil and of evil spirits, has acknowledged their negative effect on the course of history, and has insisted that they like all creation . . . come under the sovereignty of God" (Vol. I., p. 329). Karl Rahner, whose subtle presentations are summarized at risk of distortion, says that what the Church teaches is "the existence in the world of evil which is not absolute and which cannot be identified with human evil." Evil in the world has a certain depth which is not simply attributable to man . . . but is something which can be overcome only by God's eschatological act in Christ (*Encyclopedia of Theology,* s.v. "Demonology"). While the doctrine of the devil is not in the forefront of the hierarchy of Christian truths, still the doctrine of the devil cannot be trivialized. Man's calamitous situation is not one that is constituted solely by human freedom. A created freedom which is supra-human and antecedent to the history of human freedom contributes to this world situation (*ibid.,* s.v. "Devil"). Whitehead called evil "the brute motive force of fragmentary purpose, disregarding the eternal vision." Berdyaev called it "an uncreated freedom which precedes being and is submerged in the irrational sphere." The word "uncreated" seems to offer unnecessary ideas of dualism here, but the point seems to be that the mystery of the existence of evil is irrational, i.e., insoluble. Personally, instead of calling Satan a "person," I would prefer to call it "a creature." If personal means the ability to know and love, nothing seems to be less personal than Satan. That Satan is an individual creature has been the Church's continual position. Some recent challenges may cause us to approach the question from fresh perspectives. If one checks the words "nothing" and "nothingness" in Barth's *Church Dogmatics* or in Tillich's *Systematic Theology,* one is immediately at the heart of the mystery of evil.

30, Cf. *Xenoglossy,* p. 79; also Stevenson and Erlendur Haraldsson, "A Communicator of the 'Drop-In' Type in Iceland: The Case of Runolfur Runolfsson," *JASPR,* January 1975, esp. p. 58.

31. An excellent example of the difficulty in interpreting a possession case is found in an exorcism case in Earling, Iowa in 1928. A forty-three year old woman had suffered possession phenomena since she was fourteen. The exorcism was performed by Theophilus Riesinger, O.F.M. in the church of Rev. Joseph Steiger. The woman was of a

fervent, religious type. She would become unconscious during the exorcism ceremony. Many witnesses saw her levitate to a wall above a door, from which position she had to be pulled down. She could correctly distinguish between an unblessed and a blessed object. She understood and replied, according to the reports, in English, German and Latin. She vomited forth vast quantities of foul excrement and other substances even though for twenty-three days she took only liquid nourishment through injections. Apparently unconscious and often with her mouth and eyes closed tight, "independent voices" as well as barkings, etc. were heard. A malicious dialogue went on between, as was claimed by the voices, Beelzebul, Judas, Jacob, the woman's deceased husband, Mina, his mistress, and the exorcist. Fr. Steiger and other priests who attended the exorcism sessions subsequently experienced strange poltergeist manifestations on return to their own abodes. Tested previously for years by specialists, she was declared normal. A stench filled the room, especially as the "spirits" departed.

This case contains many of the details which I have called criteria for genuine possession. However, a reading of the accounts leaves me a bit uneasy about its interpretation. Judas' appearance seems strange, as well as his replies. "Do you not regret that you committed such a despicable act?" (that is, in committing suicide). Judas replies, "Let me alone. Don't bother me with your fake God. It was my own fault." A demonic Judas calling such an act a fault seems out of character. Is there coloring here by the reporter, Fr. Steiger or Fr. Theophilus? The main demon barks out that it is Beelzebub. Yet it distinguishes itself from "Lucifer, the prince of devils." Further, it states that it once belonged to the "seraphic choir," again a term which in its normal usage in laudatory. The demons say they cannot desist from the possession for two reasons: (1) Lucifer will not permit it, and (2) sufficient atonement has not yet been made to God's justice." Again the phraseology seems out of character. Finally, it was revealed at the exorcism ceremony that the girl's father had attempted "incest" with her. A number of cases of split personality have had a similar sexual episode involved, and in these cases guilt feelings seem to have been strongly repressed by powerfully operative. D. Scott Rogo says that a new effort is being made to investigate the case. For the exorcism see Martin Ebon, editor, *Exorcism, Fact or Fiction?* pp. 212–250; Robert W. Pelton, *Confrontations with the Devil* (N.Y.: A.S. Barnes, 1979), pp. 184–204; D. S. Rogo, *The Poltergeist Experience,* pp. 205–209.

For the recent case of Arne Johnson in Connecticut whose defense at his trial for murder rests on "possession," see Gerard Brittle, *The*

Demonologist. The Extraordinary Careers of Ed and Lorraine Warren (Engle-wood Cliffs, N.J.: Prentice-Hall, 1980).

32. Doug Boyd, *Rolling Thunder* (N.Y.: Random House, 1974); for examples from East and West, see D. Scott Rogo, *Miracles*, p. 152, and "Psychic Weather Control," *Fate*, pp. 79–85; Alan Vaughan, *Patterns of Prophecy* (N.Y.: Dell, 1976), pp. 192ff.

33. See Thurston, *The Physical Phenomena of Mysticism, passim;* Rogo, *Minds and Motion*, pp. 69ff.; D. D. Home, *Incidents in My Life* (N.Y.: University Books, 1973); Brian Inglis, *Natural and Supernatural* (London: Hodder and Stoughton, 1977), pp. 225–239.

34. Erlendur Haraldsson and Karlis Osis, "The Appearance and Disappearance of Objects in the Presence of Sri Sathya Sai Baba," *JASPR,* January 1977, pp. 33–43; on similar results from a second visit, see *Parapsychology Review,* March–April 1982, p. 19.

35. Cf. Renée Haynes, *The Hidden Springs. An Inquiry into Extra-Sensory Perception* (Boston: Little, Brown, 1972, revised ed.), pp. 128ff.; *Life, Death and Psychical Research,* edited by J. D. Pearce-Higgins and Rev. G. Stanley Whitby (N.Y.: Doubleday, 1973) pp. 125 ff. Morton Kelsey, *Healing and Christianity*, p. 86, says that personal psychic power is never spoken of in Jesus' healings. But this would have been impossible at that time.

36. "Psychical Research and Religion," *The Christian Parapsychologist,* March 1982, p. 141.

CHAPTER III

1. "Two Essays in Analytical Psychology," *Collected Works of C. G. Jung,* Vol. 7 (Princeton, N.J.: Princeton U. Press, 1966), esp. pp. 30–40, 64–79, 90–113. For introductions to Jung, see Frieda Fordham, *An Introduction to Jung's Psychology.* (N.Y.: Viking, 1966); Jolande Jacobi, *The Psychology of C.G. Jung* (New Haven: Yale, 1971); Calvin Hall and Vernon Nordby, *A Primer of Jungian Psychology* (N.Y.: New American Library, 1973).

2. "The Psychological Foundations of Belief in Spirits," *Collected Works,* Vol. 8, pp. 301–308.

3. "The Shadow," *Collected Works,* Vol. 9, part 2, pp. 8–10.

4. "The Syzgy: Anima and Animus," *Collected Works,* Vol. 9, Part 2, pp. 11–22.

5. Joseph Campbell, *The Hero With a Thousand Faces* (Princeton, N.J.: Princeton U. Press, 1968), pp. 3–46.

6. "The Self," *Collected Works,* Vol. 9, Part 2, pp. 23–71.

7. "Psychology and Alchemy," *Collected Works,* Vol. 12, pp. 12, 17.

8. On Jung's methodology, see Robert C. Smith, "Empirical Science and Value Assumptions: Lessons From C. G. Jung," *Journal of Religion and Health,* 16, 2, 1977, pp. 102–109; Peter Homans, *Jung in Context* (Chicago: U. of Chicago Press, 1979).

9. "The Symbolic Life," *Collected Works,* Vol. 18, p. 706.

10. Morton Kelsey, "Jung as Philosopher and Theologian," *The Well-Tended Tree,* Hilde Kirsch, ed. (N.Y.: Putnam's, 1971), p. 194.

11. Vincent Brome, *Jung. Man and Myth* (N.Y.: Athenaeum, 1978), reduces the collective unconscious to "the gene pool" of instinctual coding. This position is irreconcilable with parapsychological data.

12. Pierre Teilhard de Chardin, *The Phenomenon of Man* (N.Y.: Harper and Row, 1959), pp. 299ff.

13. *The Phenomenon of Man,* pp. 71–76; Christopher Mooney, S.J., *Teilhard de Chardin and the Mystery of Christ* (N.Y.: Harper and Row, 1967); Emile Rideau, *Teilhard de Chardin: A Guide to His Thought* (N.Y.: Harper and Row, 1967).

14. Teilhard de Chardin, *Science and Christ* (N.Y.: Harper and Row, 1965), pp. 22ff.

15. Teilhard de Chardin, *The Vision of the Past* (N.Y.: Harper and Row, 1966), p. 227.

16. Modern thought calls this "punctuational." See Steven M. Stanley, *The New Evolutionary Time Table* (N.Y.: Basic Books, 1981).

17. *Science and Christ,* p. 179; Rideau, pp. 77ff.

18. *Science and Christ,* pp. 26–30, 41–46, but also 79.

19. Teilhard combined the teleological approach with the cosmological approach in this phrase "the Prime Mover Ahead": *Phenomenon of Man,* p. 271.

20. Michael Novak, *Belief and Unbelief* (N.Y.: Macmillan, 1965), pp. 146–147. On Teilhard, see Henri de Lubac, S.J., *The Religion of Teilhard de Chardin* (N.Y.: Desclee, 1967), pp. 178–182. For parallel approaches, see Hoimar Ditforth, *The Origins of Life: Evolution as Creation* (N.Y.: Harper and Row, 1981); John F. Haught, *Nature and Purpose* (Washington, D.C.: University Press of America, 1980); Richard Swinburne, *The Existence of God* (N.Y.: Oxford, 1979), pp. 131ff; Stanley Jaki, *The Roads of Science and the Way to God* (Chicago: U. of Chicago Press, 1978); Arthur R. Peacocke, *Creation and the World of Science* (N.Y.: Oxford, 1978).

21. Teilhard de Chardin, *Christianity and Evolution* (N.Y.: Harcourt Brace Jovanovich, 1974).

22. *Christianity and Evolution,* p. 85.

23. Teilhard de Chardin, *The Heart of Matter* (N.Y.: Harcourt Brace Jovanovich, 1979), p. 212.

24. *The Heart of Matter,* p. 201.

25. Teilhard de Chardin, *Human Energy* (N.Y.: Harcourt Brace Jovanovich, 1962), pp. 141ff; *How I Believe* (N.Y.: Harper and Row, 1967), pp. 47ff.

26. Rideau, *Teilhard de Chardin,* p. 451.

27. Teilhard de Chardin, *The Future of Man* (N.Y.: Harper and Row, 1964).

28. Karl Rahner, "The Experience of God Today," *Theological Investigations,* Vol. XI, 1974, p. 161. Teilhard puts the same point as follows: "It is *precisely because* he is at once so deep and yet so akin to an extensionless point that God is infinitely near, and dispersed everywhere. It is *precisely because* he is the center that he fills the whole sphere.

CHAPTER IV

1. Greenwich, Conn.: Fawcett Publications, 1974.

2. Plainfield, N.J.: Logos International Press, 1976.

3. Notre Dame, Indiana: Ave Maria Press, 1974. See pp. 161ff.

4. Notre Dame, Indiana: Ave Maria Press, 1977. See pp. 68ff McNutt later left the priesthood.

5. See the helpful treatment on this point in Morton Kelsey, *Encounter with God* (Minneapolis: Bethany Fellowship, 1972) pp. 56ff. However, that the two systems are not very different, if seen in depth, and that St. Thomas used a neo-Platonic creation doctrine with an Aristotelian scaffolding is shown by J. Thibault, S.S.S., in *Creation and Metaphysics. A Genetic Approach to the Existential Act* (The Hague: Niehoff, 1970), pp. 63–70. See also Benedicta Ward, *Miracles and the Medieval Mind* (Philadelphia: University of Pennsylvania Press, 1982). pp. 3ff.

6. Dr. Howard Schapker of Jersey City State Teacher's College has shown in an unpublished Ph.D. dissertation at Fordham University that the Roman Catholic modernist crisis was related, in part, to this division. Much of what the so-called "modernist" George Tyrrell wrote from an "Augustinian" perspective was read with "Aristotelian" eyes.

7. "Some Biological Effects of the Laying On of Hands and Their Implications," *Dimensions in Wholistic Healing,* Herbert A. Otto and James W. Knight, eds. (Chicago: Nelson-Hall, 1979), pp. 199–212.

8. "The Laying On of Hands," *The Signet Handbook of Parapsychology* (N.Y.: New American Library, 1978), p. 119.

9. "Paranormal Effects on Enzyme Activity," *Proceedings of the Parapsychological Association,* 1968, 5, 15–16. My comments are also based on a taped cassette from Big Sur.

10. Charles Panati, *Supersenses* (N.Y.: Quadrangle, 1974), p. 91. An enzyme is a protein which acts as a biochemical catalyst. Estebany increased the rate of the reactions of the enzymes.

11. Stanley Krippner, Alberto Villoldo, *The Realms of Healing* (Millbrae, Cal.: Celestial Arts, 1976), pp. 101ff.; Robert N. Miller, "Methods of Detecting Healing Energies," in *Future Science* (N.Y.: Doubleday, 1977), pp. 431–444; Edwina Cerutti, *Olga Worrall. Mystic with the Healing Hands* (N.Y.: Harper & Row, 1975), pp. 130ff., where other experiments are also described. For a photograph see Robert N. Miller, Ph.D. Philip B. Reinhardt, Ph.D., "Measuring Psychic Energy," *Psychic,* June 1975, p. 47.

12. This and the previous experiment are reported in *Parapsychology Bulletin,* Jan.–Feb. 1980, p. 2.

13. Dean Kraft, *Portrait of a Psychic Healer* (N.Y.: Putnam's, 1981), pp. 181–185.

14. See Dolores Kreiger, *The Therapeutic Touch: How To Use Your Hands To Help or Heal* (Englewood Cliffs, N.J.: Prentice-Hall, 1979); Patricia Heidt and Marianne Borelli, *Therapeutic Touch: A Book of Readings* (N.Y.: Springer, 1980). On the work of Dr. Lawrence Le Shan, see Joyce Goodrich, Ph.D., "A Psychic Healing Training and Research Project," in *Healing: Implications for Psychotherapy,* James L. Fosshage, Ph.D. and Paul Olsen, Ph.D., eds. (N.Y.: Human Sciences Press, 1978), pp. 84–110. The Japanese scientist Dr. Hiroshi Motoyama has found PK power in Francis McNutt, *Science and the Evolution of Consciousness* (Brookline, Mass.: Autumn Press, 1978), p. 124.

15. "Faith Healing and Psychic Healing: Are They the Same?" *Journal of Religion and Psychical Research,* Jan. 1981, p. 22, from author's abstract.

16. Cited in Peter Maddock, "London Parascience Conference, 1978," *Parapsychology Review,* May–June 1979, p. 19; see also Renée Haynes, "Miraculous and Paranormal Healing," *ibid.,* September–October 1977, pp. 25–28.

17. Cf. Raymond E. Brown, S.S., *Jesus God and Man* (Milwaukee: Bruce, 1967), pp. 61ff. His position is that the exact predictions of the resurrection were written in after the resurrection itself and that the disciples, therefore, were not basing their reactions to Jesus on an anticipated conviction about resurrection. This is a common exegetical position today.

18. L. Howard Maxwell, *The Origins of New Testament Christology* (Downers Grove, Ill.: Intervarsity Press, 1976), p. 46. The point has been questioned by the German exegete H. Conzelmann, among others, but it seems to stand as a solid point. (Neither Raymond Brown, *op.*

cit., p. 89, nor Edward Schillebeeckx, O.P. places "Abba" in so central a position while affirming Jesus' uniqueness. Cf. John P. Galvin, "The Uniqueness of Jesus and His 'Abba Experience' in the Theology of Edward Schillebeeckx," *Proceedings of the Catholic Theological Society of America,* June 1980, pp. 309–314.)

19. Maxwell, *ibid.,* p. 45. See Joachim Jeremias, *The Prayers of Jesus* (Naperville, Ill.: Allenson, 1967), pp. 108–115.

20. Karl Barth spoke of God as "the One in three ways of being": *Dogmatics in Outline* (N.Y.: Harper & Row, 1959), p. 42. Karl Rahner, S.J. writes, "But one could also, for instance, instead of speaking of three persons, speak of three distinct ways of being there (in the economy of salvation) and three different ways of subsistence (immanently) for the one God." *Encyclopedia of Theology* (N.Y.: Seabury Press, 1975), p. 1763, col. 2.

21. "Miracles and Early Christian Apologetics," in *Miracles,* C. F. D. Moule, ed. (London: Mowbray, 1965), p. 214.

22. *Jesus the Christ* (N.Y.: Paulist Press, 1976), pp. 90–91. However, Kasper's treatment of miracles deserves reading. "God can never replace this-worldly causality. If he were on the same level as this-worldly causes, he would no longer be God but an idol. If God is to remain God, even his miracles must be thought of as mediated by created secondary causes." No amputated limb, for example, has ever suddenly reappeared.

23. *On Being a Christian* (N.Y.: Doubleday, 1976). p. 233.

24. Paul is probably citing an early Christian hymn. For a recent, different interpretation of this hymn, see James D. G. Dunn, *Christology in the Making* (Philadelphia: Westminster Press, 1980), pp. 114ff.

25. See Renée Haynes, *The Hidden Springs* (Boston: Little, Brown, 1972), pp. 128ff.; *Life, Death & Psychical Research,* Canon J. D. Pearce-Higgins and Rev. G. Stanley Whitby, eds. (N.Y.: Image Books, 1973); Morton T. Kelsey, *Healing and Christianity* (N.Y.: Harper and Row, 1973).

26. *Science and Christ* (N.Y.: Harper & Row, 1965), p. 61.

27. From John S. Lawton, *Miracles and Revelation* (London: Littleworth, 1959), p. 227.

28. "The Handsome Heart," *Poems and Prose of Gerard Manley Hopkins,* W. H. Gardner, ed. (Baltimore: Penguin Books, 1953), p. 46.

29. Philadelphia: Fortress Press, 1964, pp. 76, 165.

30. Walter Kasper in *Jesus the Christ, op. cit.,* writes, "The theological question about miracles is only well-formed when it does not look for a 'gap' within physical causality as it has been discovered, but asks about the general system of causality. In scientific terms, however,

problems about the nature of this system of causality can only be described as a never-ending task and a question which in principle cannot be answered by scientific methods. The question of the ultimate nature of this system of causality is therefore not a scientific question, but the philosophical and theological question of the meaning of existence as such" (pp. 93–94). Karl Rahner, S.J., who sees God as the Holy Mystery who is the *Ground* of the world and *not an object* like other objects in the world, sees a special intervention "of God as simply a concrete embodiment of God's general grounding of the world. This is not a "God of the gaps": *Foundations of Christian Faith* (N.Y.: Crossroad, 1978), p. 87. John H. Wright, S.J. brings out the same point by using Teilhard's idea of "the within": *A Theology of Christian Prayer* (N.Y.: Pueblo Publishing Co., 1979), pp. 43ff.

31. L. Monden, *Signs and Wonders, op. cit.,* pp. 226–228. See also the case of Pierre Rudder in whose leg about an inch of new bone formed (pp. 240ff.).

32. Philadelphia: Westminster Press, 1971, p. 110.

33. On group PK in Canada, England, and elsewhere, see Rogo's *Minds & Motion, op. cit.,*ch. 8; on its religious implications, see *The Haunted Universe* (N.Y.: New American Library, 1977), ch. 3, and *Miracles, op. cit.,* pp. 284-314.

34. Cited in S. Krippner, *The Realms of Healing, op. cit.,* p. 264.

35. *Miracles and Pilgrims. Popular Beliefs in Medieval England* (London: Dent & Sons, 1977), p. 99.

36. Rockford, Ill.: Tan Books and Publishers, 1977. Citations are from pp. 295–297.

37. *We Are All Healers* (N.Y.: Harper & Row, 1973), p. 63.

38. Spiritism differs from Spiritualism in America. Spiritism comes mainly from South America (ultimately perhaps from Africa). The form prevalent among the intellectual classes in South America is called Kardecism. It is named after Allan Kardec (1804–1869), a Frenchman who developed the theory behind it in his work, *The Spirits' Book.* It is not a scientific study such as found in parapsychology. Kardec claimed that his theory rested on his experience, but it has become coded in a dogmatic list of beliefs, such as the following: (a) Man is an incarnate soul. (b) This soul was not created at the time of birth. (c) It has had other lives on earth and others will follow. (d) Contact between incarnate and discarnate persons has been taking place since man appeared on earth for the first time. (e) The psychic faculty known as mediumship is the method devised by nature to establish this enlightening and necessary contact. (g) Primitive people all over the world are well educated in these simple facts of life. Until recently

the Catholic Church in South America had been verbally attacking the Spiritist movement. Recently upon word from Rome this attack has ceased. Spiritists run hospitals there and do much good.

39. *Phenomena of Materialization* (N.Y.: Arno Press, 1920).

40. See D. Scott Rogo, *An Experience of Phantoms* (N.Y.: Dell Publishing Co., 1974), pp. 170–174. On the work of Sir William Crookes, see Brian Inglis, *Natural and Supernatural* (London: Hodder and Stoughton, 1977), pp. 253ff. On Icelandic materialization cases, see Einer Nielsen, *Solid Proofs of Survival* (San Francisco: H. G. White, 1950).

41. Susy Smith, "Seattle's Psychic Wonder," in *True Experiences in Communicating with the Dead* (N.Y.: New American Library, 1968), pp. 60–75. The reader is cautioned as I have found no other source for this experiment.

42. See D. S. Rogo, *Minds and Motion, op. cit.,* pp. 49ff.; Diana Robinson, *To Stretch a Plank: A Survey of Psychokinesis* (Chicago: Nelson-Hall, 1981), pp. 121ff.; W. G. Roll, *The Poltergeist, op. cit.,* s.v. "apports."

43. "The Appearance and Disappearance of Objects in the Presence of Sri Sathya Sai Baba," *Journal of the American Society for Psychical Research,* January 1977, pp. 33–43.

44. Henry K. Puharich, M.D., "Psychic Research and the Healing Process," in *Psychic Exploration,* John White, ed., (N.Y.: Putnam's, 1976), pp. 333–348; John Fuller, *Arigo. Surgeon of the Rusty Knife* (N.Y.: Pocketbooks, 1974).

45. *Psi-Healing* (N.Y.: Bantam Books, 1976), pp. 266ff.

46. George W. Meek, *Healers and the Healing Process* (Wheaton, Ill.: Theosophical Publishing House, 1977).

47. *Ibid.,* pp. 151ff.; Lyall Watson, Ph.D., *The Romeo Error* (N.Y.: Dell Publishing Co., 1976), pp. 215ff.

48. *Healers and the Healing Process,* pp. 125–127.

49. *Song of the Siren* (N.Y.: Harper & Row, 1975), p. 241. One of the best studies of the entire field of healing is by Krippner and Villoldo, *The Realms of Healing, op. cit.*

CHAPTER V

1. *Patterns of Prophecy* (N.Y.: Dell Publishing Co., 1973), pp. 17–18.

2. Martin Ebon, *They Knew the Unknown* (N.Y.: New American Library, 1971), p. 53.

3. Jeane Dixon, *A Gift of Prophecy* (N.Y.: Bantam Books, 1965), p. 6.

4. *Ibid.*

5. *Patterns of Prophecy,* p. 19. The insight originated with Stanley Krippner. John F. Kennedy knew of this cycle.

6. Denis Brian, *Jeane Dixon. The Witnesses* (Garden City, N.Y.: Doubleday & Company, 1976), records remarkable hits. James Bjornstad, *20th Century Prophecy. Jeane Dixon, Edgar Cayce* (N.Y.: Pillar Books, 1976), cites many errors.

7. Jeane Dixon, *The Call to Glory* (N.Y.: William Morrow & Co., 1971), p. 173. In *The Nation Tattler,* December 29, 1974, her distinction is between "psychic prediction" and "prophecy." Here she says that prophecy is for her a state that lasts seven days. The specific prophecy is given on the fourth day (p. 21). She claims the future has been shown her to 2037.

8. Allan Angoff, *Eileen Garrett and the World Beyond the Senses* (N.Y.: William Morrow, 1974), pp. 28ff.

9. *National Enquirer* June 12, 1979, p. 32. Normally, I would not cite *National Enquirer* as a source for parapsychological evidence. However, remember that we are considering anecdotal evidence. This report and the others cited give specific names, they were made publicly, two were notarized, and they were never challenged to my knowledge. I had intended to present anecdotal evidence from Louisa Rhine's *Hidden Channels of the Mind* or *The Invisible Picture.* However, none are as specific as the ones I mention here.

10. *National Enquirer,* December 11, 1979.

11. *National Enquirer,* April 19, 1977, p. 60.

12. *National Enquirer,* July 22, 1975, p. 37.

13. Edgar Mitchell, *Psychic Exploration, op. cit.,* p. 165; Louisa E. Rhine, *Hidden Channels of the Mind* (N.Y.: William Morrow, 1961), p. 84.

14. *Psychic Exploration,* p. 165; D. Scott Rogo, *Parapsychology,* p. 99.

15. Joseph Rhine, *The Reach of the Mind* (N.Y.: William Sloane Associates, 1947), pp. 69ff.; J. Gaither Pratt, *Parapsychology. An Insider's View of ESP* (N.Y.: Dutton, 1968), pp. 154ff.; Louisa E. Rhine, *Mind Over Matter* (N.Y.: Macmillan, 1970), p. 190, and *ESP in Life and Lab: Tracing Hidden Channels* (N.Y.: Macmillan, 1967), pp. 86ff.

16. *Psi-Search, op. cit.,* p. 59.

17. *Psychic Exploration,* p. 165.

18. Montague Ullman, M.D., and Stanley Krippner, Ph.D., with Alan Vaughan, *Dream Telepathy* (N.Y.: Macmillan, 1973), pp. 174ff.; *Psi-Search,* pp. 59–61.

19. *ESP and Parapsychology: A Critical Reevaluation* (Buffalo: Prometheus Books, 1980), pp. 141–167.

20. N.Y.: Harper & Row, 1975, p. 41.

21. Naomi A. Hintze and J. Gaither Pratt, Ph.D., *The Psychic Realm: What Can You Believe?* (N.Y.: Random House, 1975), p. 50.

22. *Premonitions: A Leap into the Future* (N.Y.: Warner Books, 1973), pp. 258–267.

23. "Backward Causation," *Parapsychology Review,* January–February 1977, pp. 1–5. See also B. Brier and M. Schmidt-Raghavan, "Precognition and the Paradoxes of Causality," *Philosophy of Science and the Occult,* Patrick Grim, ed. (Albany: S.U.N.Y., 1982), pp. 207–216.

24. "Theories of Psi," in *Extrasensory Perception,* Stanley Krippner, ed. (N.Y.: Plenum Press, 1978), p. 255.

25. *Hidden Channels of the Mind,* p. 177.

26. *Man and Time* (N.Y.: Doubleday, 1964), pp. 290ff.

27. William Johnston, *The Still Point* (N.Y.: Harper & Row, 1970), pp. 79–80.

28. Dr. Charles T. G. Rogers, "God's Power in the Holistic Health Paradigm," *Journal of the Academy of Religion and Psychical Research,* July 1979, p. 116.

29. See Jean Levie, S.J., *The Bible. Word of God in the Words of Men* (N.Y.: Kenedy, 1962), pp. 232ff.; James Burtchaell, C.S.C., *Catholic Theories of Biblical Inspiration Since 1810* (N.Y.: Cambridge U. Press, 1969), pp. 263, 267.

30. Fr. Richard McBrien in *Catholicism* writes, "Revelation has its origin and foundation outside the human subject, but if it happens at all, it happens within the consciousness of the human subject" (p. 242). Karl Rahner, S.J. adds that one cannot hear another's word "without confronting it with the rest of what is already present in one's mind and consciousness": *Theological Investigations* (Baltimore: Helicon, 1966), Vol. V, p. 28. He adds that the hearing of the message is "hearing by means of categories already possessed from elsewhere ... however much these horizons themselves may be altered by this hearing": *Theological Investigations* (Baltimore: Helicon, 1969), p. 73. Avery Dulles, S.J. writes, "The biblical authors, in the New Testament as well as in the old, were badly mistaken about many matters, not only scientific and historical, but also moral and doctrinal": "The Meaning of Revelation," *Theological Folia of Villanova University Speculative Studies* (Philadelphia: Villanova University Press), 1975, pp. 151–179.

31. See Dan O. Via, Jr., *What Is Form Criticism?* (Philadelphia: Fortress Press, 1969).

32. See Norman Perrin, *What Is Redaction Criticism?* (Philadelphia: Fortress Press, 1969).

33. *The Two Edged-Sword* (Milwaukee: Bruce, 1956), p. 302.

34. The following data are from Boyce M. Bennett, Jr., "Vision and Audition in Biblical Prophecy," *Parapsychology Review,* January–February 1978, p. 7. See also "Vision and Audition in Biblical Prophecy as Illuminated in Recent Research on Human Consciousness," in *Psi and*

States of Awareness, Betty Shapin and Lisette Coly, eds. (N.Y.: Parapsychology Foundation, 1978), pp. 101 130.

35. Robert P. Carroll calls the failure of predictive prophecy "cognitive dissonance." He considers the efforts made to come to terms with it and believes it led to the decline of prophecy: *When Prophecy Failed: Cognitive Dissonance in Prophetic Traditions* (N.Y.: Seabury, 1979), pp. 175, 198.

36. Boyce Bennett, Jr., *op. cit.*, believes that when "the hand of the Lord" was upon Ezekiel, he was in what we would call an altered state of consciousness. In the ASC there would be right hemisphere dominance characterized by primary process thought, more intuitive and imaginative. One is reminded here of Julian Jaynes in *The Origin of Consciousness in the Breakdown of the Bicameral Mind* (N.Y.: Houghton Mifflin, 1977). However the treatment is free of the reductionist element found in Jaynes. On paranormal phenomena in the prophets, see J. Lindblom, *Prophecy in Ancient Israel* (Philadelphia: Fortress Press, 1962, reprint 1973), pp. 197ff.; Kurt Nussbaum, "Abnormal Mental Phenomena in the Prophets," *Journal of Religion and Health*, 1974, 13, 3, pp. 194–200. On Jesus' prophetic characteristics, see David Hill, *New Testament Prophecy* (Atlanta: John Knox Press, 1979), pp. 58ff.

37. *Jesus God and Man* (Milwaukee: Bruce, 1967), pp. 61ff.

38. Norman Perrin, *Jesus and the Language of the Kingdom* (Philadelphia: Fortress Press, 1976); Robert H. Stein, *The Method and Message of Jesus* (Philadelphia: Westminster, 1981).

39. Jesus' statement in Mark 13:32, "But of that day and hour no one knows, not even the angels in heaven, nor the Son, but only the Father," is variously interpreted by scholars, either as an avowal by Jesus of a total lack of knowledge, or of a lack of knowledge only of the exact day and hour coupled with an expectation of imminence, or else the statement is seen as an addition by the early Church to account for the delay of the parousia.

40. *The Theology of Revelation* (N.Y.: Herder & Herder, 1966), p. 69.

41. See Martin Ebon, ed., *Doomsday* (N.Y.: New American Library, 1977), pp. 148–162; T. F. Glasson, *His Appearance and His Kingdom* (London: Epworth, 1953); see also Bryan W. Bell, *A Great Expectation. Eschatological Thought in English Protestantism to 1660* (Leiden: Brill, 1975).

42. See Mary Ellen Carter, *Edgar Cayce on Prophecy* (N.Y.: Paperback Library, 1968), pp. 63, 197; Alan Vaughan, *Patterns of Prophecy, op. cit.*, pp. 173ff.

43. This and the previous predictions are found in *Patterns of Prophecy*, pp. 208, 218.

44. Henry C. Roberts, ed., *The Complete Prophecies of Nostradamus* (Oyster Bay, N.Y.: Nostradamus Co., 1947), p. 336. See also *Patterns of Prophecy*, pp. 209ff. Rene Noorbergen, who also worked on *Jeane Dixon—My Life and Prophecies*, has tried to plot out a timetable of events in the future war while using Nostradamus in *Nostradamus Predicts the End of the World* (N.Y.: Pinnacle Books, 1981). One can do no better than to read Nostradamus himself to see how enigmatic his oracles are.

CHAPTER VI

1. Glenn D. Kittler, *Edgar Cayce on the Dead Sea Scrolls* (N.Y.: Warner Paperback, 1970), pp. 147, 192.

2. Irving Litvag, *Singer in the Shadows* (N.Y.: Popular Library, 1972), pp. 16, 30ff.

3. *Ibid.,* p. 160.

4. *Ibid.,* p. 208.

5. *Ibid.,* p. 110.

6. *Ibid.,* p. 258. See the fine, brief study in Rosalind Heywood, *Beyond the Reach of Sense* (N.Y.: Dutton, 1974), especially p. 110, where the passage I have cited was also presented in poem form. See also *The Psychic Realm, op. cit.,* pp. 173–190.

7. Litvag, p. 245.

8. *The Road to Immortality* (London: Psychic Press, 3rd ed. 1967), p. 177. This statement is allegedly from Frederic W. H. Myers in a script written by Miss Cummins. "Myers" claimed that discarnate beings could recapture their earthly memories if they wished, but normally they were in temporary abeyance. For a critique of Cummins, see Rodger Anderson, "The Mediumship of Geraldine Cummins," *Theta,* Autumn 1983, pp. 50-55.

9. See Stephan A. Schwarz, *The Secret Vaults of Time* (N.Y.: Grosset & Dunlap, 1978), pp. 57ff., and Jeffrey Goodman, *Psychic Archeology. Time Machine to the Past* (N.Y.: Berkley Medallion Books, 1977), pp. 31–51. For similar investigations, see David E. Jones, *Visions of Time. Experiments in Psychic Archeology* (Wheaton, Ill.: Theosophical Publishing House, 1979).

10. D. Scott Rogo, *Parapsychology, op. cit.,* p. 156.

11. *The Secret Vaults of Time,* pp. 52ff.; *Psychic Archeology,* pp. 3ff.

CHAPTER VII

1. Krister Stendahl, ed., *Immortality and Resurrection* (N.Y.: Macmillan, 1965); Pierre Benoit and Roland Murphy, *Immortality and Resurrection* (N.Y.: Crossroad, 1970).

2. Karl Rahner, *On the Theology of Death* (N.Y.: Herder & Herder,

1961), pp. 26–34; also *Encyclopedia of Theology* (N.Y.: Seabury Press, 1975), s.v. "death," pp. 330–331.

3. Celia Green, *Out-of-the-Body Experiences* (N.Y.: Ballantine Books, 1968), p. 149.

4. Herbert B. Greenhouse, *The Astral Journey* (N.Y.: Avon Books, 1974), p. 73.

5. See D. Scott Rogo, *Miracles. A Parascientific Inquiry into Wondrous Phenomena* (N.Y.: Dial Press, 1982), p. 84.

6. John McCaffrey, *Tales of Padre Pio, the Friar of San Giovanni* (Kansas City: Andrews & McMeel, 1978), pp. 24–34; also Michael Grosso, "Padre Pio and the Paranormal," in *The Christian Parapsychologist,* September 1982, pp. 218–226.

7. D. Scott Rogo, *Miracles,* pp. 100–104.

8. Karlis Osis, "Field Research in India," *ASPR Newsletter,* Summer 1975; also "Out-of-Body Research at the ASPR," *ASPR Newsletter,* Summer 1974, p. 1; D. Scott Rogo, ed., *Mind Beyond the Body. The Mystery of ESP Projection* (N.Y.: Penguin Books, 1978), p. 168.

9. Frederic W. H. Myers, *Human Personality and Its Survival of Bodily Death,* abridged edition (N.Y.: Longmans, Green, 1935), pp. 181–186; see also John White, ed., *Psychic Exploration* (N.Y.: G. Putman's Sons, 1976), pp. 376–377.

10. C. D. Broad, *Lectures on Psychical Research* (N.Y.: Humanities Press, 1962), pp. 147–152.

11. *Ibid.,* pp. 175–178; also Janet Lee Mitchell, *Out-of-Body Experiences. A Handbook* (Jefferson, N.C.: McFarland, 1981), p. 42. For a critical approach see Susan Blackmore, "Parapsychology—With or Without the OBE?" *Parapsychology Review,* 13, 6, November–December 1982, p. 2, and *Beyond the Body* (London: Heinemann, 1982).

12. Robert Crookall, *More Astral Projections* (London: Aquarian Press, 1964); D. Scott Rogo, ed., *Mind Beyond the Body, op. cit.* p. 243 on Muldoon. Rogo mentions that the parapsychologist Hornell Hart included fifteen such apparitional cases in his study (p. 25).

13. Greenhouse, *The Astral Journey, op. cit.,* p. 287; Rogo, *Mind Beyond the Body, op. cit.* p. 91.

14. Susan Blackmore, "Out-of-Body Experiences," in *Psychical Research. A Guide to its History, Principles and Practices,* Ivor Grattan-Guinness, ed. (Wellingborough, Northhamptonshire: Aquarian Press, 1982), pp. 78–89; John Palmer, "The Out-of-Body Experience: A Psychological Theory," *Parapsychology Review,* 9, 5, Sept.–Oct. 1978. pp. 19–22.

15. Janet Lee Mitchell, *Out-of-Body Experiences, op. cit.*

16. Charles T. Tart, "A Psychophysiological Study of Out-of-Body Experiences in a Selected Subject," in *Mind Beyond Body, op. cit.,*

pp. 103–133; also "Out-of-the-Body Experiences," in *Psychic Explorations, op. cit.,* pp. 349–373.

17. For another similar study, see Karlis Osis and Janet Lee Mitchell, "Physiological Correlates of Repeated Out-of-Body Experiences," *Journal of the American Society for Psychical Research,* 49, 772, June 1977, pp. 525–536.

18. Karlis Osis, "Out-of-Body Research at the American Society for Psychical Research," in *Mind Beyond Body, op. cit.,* pp. 162–169. Susan Blackmore criticizes these experiments, claiming that the results were marginal and that positive conclusions rested only on those parts of the experiments when Tannous' confidence was high. Still, how are these parts of the experiments to be explained? "Parapsychology—With or Without OBE?" *op. cit.,* p. 5.

19. Karlis Osis and Donna McCormick, "Kinetic Effects at the Ostensible Location of an Out-of-Body Projection During Perceptual Testing," *Journal of the American Society for Psychical Research,* 74, 3, July 1980, pp. 319–329.

20. Karlis Osis and Donna McCormick, "Insider's View of ESP," *ASPR Newsletter,* July 1978, p. 18.

21. A. Hilary Armstrong, *St. Augustine and Christian Platonism* (Phila.: Villanova U. Press, 1967), p. 12; also Otto Pieper, *Death and Immortality* (N.Y.: Herder and Herder, 1969), p. 114.

22. For a detailed study of such texts, see Andrew T. Lincoln, *Paradise Now and Not Yet* (London: Cambridge U. Press, 1981), esp. pp. 51, 63–69, 79.

23. See F. Gordon Greene, "St. Teresa of Avila. Christian Mysticism and Out-of-Body Consciousness: A Discussion of Parallel Experiences," *Theta,* 10, 3, Autumn 1982, pp. 59–62.

24. Michael Grosso, "Some Varieties of Out-of-Body Experience," *Journal of the American Society for Psychical Research,* April 1976, esp. p. 181, and "Plato and Out-of-Body Experiences," *ibid.,* Jan. 1975, pp. 61–74.

25. Michael Grosso, "Padre Pio and the Paranormal," *The Christian Parapsychologist,* September 1982, esp. p. 222.

CHAPTER VIII

1. *Life After Life. The Investigation of a Phenomenon—Survival of Bodily Death* (Atlanta: Mockingbird Books, 1975).

2. Atlanta: Bantam/Mockingbird Books, 1977.

3. *Deathbed Observations by Physicians and Nurses* (New York: Parapsychology Foundation, Inc., 1961).

4. Introduction by Elisabeth Kübler-Ross, M.D. (New York:

Avon Books, 1977). See also "Deathbed Observations by Physicians and Nurses: A Cross-Cultural Survey," *The Journal of the American Society for Psychical Research* 71, 3, July 1977, pp. 237–259.

5. " 'Life After Death?' 'Yes, Beyond a Shadow of Doubt,' Says the Eminent Dr. Kubler-Ross," *People*, Nov. 24, 1975, p. 66.

6. In the United States the messengers were either relatives or religious figures. In India, quite a few of the dying saw "Yamdoots"— in Indian folklore the messengers of Yama, the god of death. The authors see these figures as different only in name and interpretation from the Western religious figures. Cf. *At the Hour of Death*, p. 41.

7. "Near-Death Experiences: Their Interpretation and Significance," in *Between Life and Death*, Robert Kastenbaum, ed. (New York: Springer, 1982), pp. 73–88. "Depersonalization in the Face of Life-Threatening Danger: An Interpretation," *Omega* 7, 1976, pp. 103–114. "The Experience of Dying," *Psychiatry* 35, 1972, pp. 174–184.

8. New York: Nelson, 1978.

9. New York: Coward, McCann and Geoghegan, 1980 (cf. pp. 193ff. for a critique of Rawlings similar to my own). Also, "Further Studies of the Near-Death Experience," *Theta* 7, 2, Spring 1979, pp. 1–3, and "Religiousness and Near-Death Experiences," *Theta* 8, 3, Summer 1980, pp. 3ff.

10. Ring takes issue with Rawlings on the idea of "selective recall" of events and "repression" of the more negative visions. He notes: Moody and Sabom also had interviewed patients immediately after cardiac arrest and they record no "hellish" experience. (Ed.: But Moody in his second book, *Reflections on Life After Life*, pp. 28ff., describes a realm of depressed, bewildered spirits.) Ring also says that in LSD induced states, which have similarities to NDE states, there is no selective recall or repression. And, finally, patients seem to separate these negative experiences from the core experience. They are seen to be hallucinationary visions and *qualitatively* different from the core experience. But Ring admits that the issue here is still open.

11. New York: Harper and Row, 1982. Also, "Physicians Evaluate the Near-Death Experience," co-authored with Sarah Kreutziger, *Theta* 6, 4, 1978, pp. 1–6.

12. "The Psychology of Life After Death," *American Psychologist*, 35, 10, 1980, pp. 911–931; "Accounting for 'Afterlife' Experiences," *Psychology Today*, January 1981, pp. 65–75; also, see the exchange with John Gibbs and Ian Stevenson, *American Psychologist*, November 1981, pp. 1467–1482. The first two articles are unusually sarcastic and filled with careless generalization for an article in a scholarly journal. This is allowed, it seems, as long as the treatise is an attack on parapsychology.

13. Siegel is a specialist in hallucinations. Cf. *Hallucinations: Behavior, Experience and Therapy*, eds. R.K. Siegel and J. West (New York: Wiley, 1975), esp. pp. 111–161.

14. *The UFO Handbook*, ed. Allan Hendry (New York: Doubleday, 1979), pp. 154ff.

15. In *Hallucinations*, Siegel emphasizes that while 72 percent of the people studied shared images and the "form constants," which, as I have mentioned, were a feature, "no consistent patterns or directions of movement were seen" (p. 111). He mentions image changes, e.g., a dolphin changes into a diver, the red color appears often as well as cartoon-like characters. David Myers in his otherwise excellent *The Human Puzzle, Psychological Research and Christian Belief* (New York: Harper and Row, 1978), p. 85, has accepted Siegel's general thesis and has reprinted that geometric tunnel diagram. Also, Carl Sagan in *Broca's Brain* presents a position similar to Siegel's.

16. *Life After Death*, eds. Arnold Toynbee and Arthur Koestler, "Psychedelics and the Experience of Death" (New York: McGraw-Hill, 1976), pp. 182–202.

17. See *Realms of the Human Unconscious* (New York: Viking, 1975), pp. 158–161. *The Human Encounter with Death* (New York: Dutton, 1977), pp. 41–62. For books appearing since Siegel's articles, see *LSD Psychotherapy* (Pomona Cal.: Hunter House, 1980), pp. 79–89, and Stanislaw and Christina Grof, *Beyond Death* (London: Thames and Hudson, 1980), pp. 26–30. See the excellent presentation of David Crownfield, "Religion in the Cartography of the Unconscious: A Discussion of Stanislaw Grof's *Realms of the Human Unconscious*," *JAAR* 44, 2, 1976, pp. 302–313.

18. *Beyond Death*, p. 31.

19. *The Human Encounter With Death*, p. 110.

20. *The Varieties of Psychedelic Experience* (New York: Delta, 1966), esp. pp. 144–150. Cf. also Lester Grinspoor and James Bakalar, *Psychedelic Drugs Re-Considered* (New York: Basic Books, 1979), pp. 95ff.

21. Cf. pp. 180–185.

22. G.S. Kirk, *Myth. Its Meaning and Function in Ancient and Other Cultures* (Berkeley: University of California Press, 1970), p. 270.

23. New York: Random House, 1961, p. 302. Jung said that many never drink the cup of life to the lees. These, when they are old, keep looking back. "It is particularly fatal to such people to look back. For them a prospect and a goal in the future hold out the promise of a life beyond, which enables a mortal man to live the second half of life with as much purpose and aim as the first." "Everything old in our unconscious hints at something coming." "Everything psychic is pregnant

with the future": C.G. Jung, *Psychological Reflections,* eds. J. Jacobi and R.F.C. Hull (Princeton: Princeton University Press, 1970), pp. 327, 331.

24. *The Well-Tended Tree,* ed. Hilde Kirsch, "Jung as Philosopher and Theologian," Morton Kelsey, p. 195. The pragmatic coloring echoes William James with whom Jung corresponded.

25. *The Image of an Oracle* (New York: Helix, 1974), p. 359.

26. *New York Times,* November 25, 1968, p. 25. Carl Rogers, after his wife had a NDE and after reading Moody, says he has a new openness toward death; cf. *A Way of Being* (New York: Houghton-Mifflin, 1980), p. 88.

27. D.E.H. Whiteley, *The Theology of St. Paul* (Philadelphia: Fortress, 1964), p. 97.

28. Michael Grosso, "The Mirror of Transformation," *Theta* 6, 1, 1978, p. 7. See also his excellent article, "Toward an Explanation of Near-Death Phenomena," *The Journal of the American Society for Psychical Research* 75, 1, January 1981, pp. 37–60. Some of his positions are close to my own, but I read his article only after completing this essay.

29. George Kuykendall, "Care For the Dying: A Kübler-Ross Critique," *Theology Today,* April 1981, pp. 37–49, warns about this danger in this excellent article. The main point of the article is that Kübler-Ross' stages are more *a priori* and hortatory than empirically based.

30. "The Dying Patient's Concern with 'Life After Death,' " in *Between Life and Death,* ed. R. Kastenbaum (New York: Springer, 1979), pp. 45–60. See also *A Collection of Near-Death Research Readings,* Craig Lundhal, ed. (Chicago: Nelson-Hall, 1983), pp. 160–164.

CHAPTER IX

1. G.N.M. Tyrrell, *Apparitions,* rev. ed. (N.Y.: Collier Books, 1953), p. 35.

2. *Psychic Exploration,* John White, ed. (N.Y.: Putnam's, 1974), p. 378.

3. Raynor Johnson, *The Imprisoned Splendour* (Wheaton, Ill.: Theosophical Publishing House, 1953), p. 197.

4. D. Scott Rogo, *An Experience of Phantoms* (N.Y.: Dell, 1974), pp. 30–41.

5. *Ibid.,* pp. 219–222.

6. Naomi Hintze and J. Gaither Pratt, *The Psychic Realm: What Can You Believe?* (N.Y.: Random House, 1975), pp. 230–233.

7. See Elizabeth E. McAdams, Ph.D. and Raymond Bayless, *The*

Case for Life after Death (Chicago: Nelson-Hall, 1981), pp. 41–43. A copy of this rare pamphlet is at the American Society for Psychical Research.

8. *An Experience of Phantoms,* pp. 23–25; *Psychic Exploration,* pp. 383–384. A reprint from the original proceedings of the Society for Psychical Research may be found in *Theta,* Summer 1979, pp. 17–19. Tyrrell in *Apparitions* mentions that the dogs, a retriever and a skye terrier, reacted, at times, with terror to the apparitions (p. 157).

9. Fred Gettings, *Ghosts in Photographs. The Extraordinary Story of Spirit Photography* (N.Y.: Harmony Books, 1978). See also Hans Holzer, *Psychic Photography* (N.Y.: McGraw-Hill, 1969). On thoughtography, see Jule Eisenbud, "Psychic Photography and Thoughtography," in *Psychic Exploration,* pp. 314–331.

10. Karlis Osis, Ph.D., "New Equipment for ASPR Research on Apparitions," *ASPR Newsletter,* July 1982, p. 1.

11. See Rodger Anderson and Wilma Anderson, "Veridical and Psychopathic Hallucinations: A Comparison of Types," *Parapsychology Review,* May–June 1982, p. 19. The authors question collectivity as a norm for "veridical hallucinations." I suspect this may be true for shipwrecked sailors who see a non-existent ship, but I have seen no evidence that they see exactly the same ship.

12. Brian C. Nisbeth, "Apparitions," in *Psychic Research,* pp. 92–93.

13. Tyrrell, *Apparitions,* pp. 53–90; H. Richard Neff, *Religion and Psychic Phenomena* (Philadelphia: Westminster, 1971), pp. 131–134.

14. D.S. Rogo, *An Experience of Phantoms.* p. 171.

15. *Ibid.,* p. 172.

16. *Ibid.,* p. 173.

17. Ian Stevenson, "Apparitions: Research Approaches Past and Present," in *Research in Parapsychology,* William G. Roll and John Beloff, eds. (Metuchen, N.J.: Scarecrow Press, 1981), p. 2.

18. Rudolf Bultmann, *The Theology of the New Testament* (London: SCM Press, 1952), Vol. I, pp. 44ff.; *Kerygma and Myth. A Theological Debate* (N.Y.: Harper & Row, 1961), p. 41. "If the event of Easter Day is in any sense an historical event additional to the event of the Cross, it is nothing else than the rise of faith in the risen Lord . . ." (p. 42).

19. For a careful treatment, see Hans C.C. Cavallin, *Life After Death. Paul's Argument for the Resurrection of the Dead in I Cor. 15* (Lund, Sweden: W.K. Gleerup, 1974).

20. Edward Schillebeeckx, *Interim Report on the Books Jesus & Christ* (N.Y.: Crossroad, 1981).

21. Hans Küng, *On Being a Christian* (Garden City, N.Y.: Doubleday, 1976), pp. 350–362; also *The Christian Challenge* (Garden City, N.Y.: Doubleday, 1979), pp. 209–227.

22. Raymond Brown, *Biblical Reflections on Crises Facing the Church* (N.Y.: Paulist, 1975), pp. 111–115.

23. Charles G. Martin, *Christian Origins and History* (London: Longmans, 1969), pp. 65–66.

24. Wolfhart Pannenberg, *Jesus—God and Man* (Philadelphia: Westminster, 1968), p. 95.

25. Karl Rahner, *Visions and Prophecies* (N.Y.: Herder and Herder, 1963).

26. Karl Rahner, *Theological Investigations*, Vol. XIII (N.Y.: Seabury, 1975), p. 210.

27. *Ibid.*, p. 212.

28. Karl Rahner and Karl-Heinz Weger, *Our Christian Faith. Answers for the Future* (N.Y.: Crossroad, 1981), p. 112.

29. Karl Rahner, *Theological Investigations*, Vol. XI (N.Y.: Seabury, 1974), pp. 310–311.

30. See Gerald O'Collins, S.J., *What Are They Saying About the Resurrection?* (N.Y.: Paulist, 1978), pp. 52ff.; Reginald Fuller, *The Formation of the Resurrection Narratives* (N.Y.: Macmillan, 1971), pp. 84–88, takes a different approach.

31. Xavier Léon-Dufour, *Resurrection and the Message of Easter* (N.Y.: Holt, Rinehart and Winston, 1971), pp. 160ff.; Fuller, *The Formation of the Resurrection Narratives*, says it contains a nucleus of historical fact (p. 113).

32. Léon-Dufour, p. 166; Fuller, pp. 109, 115. Many exegetes believe these details have been added to support the conviction that Jesus was not merely a disembodied inhabitant of Sheol. Cf. Lloyd Bailey, Sr., *Biblical Perspectives on Death* (Philadelphia: Fortress, 1979), pp. 26ff. Perhaps the question would best be left open.

33. Celia Green and Charles McCreedy, *Apparitions* (London: Hamish Hamilton, 1975), pp. 102–113; Tyrrell, *Apparitions*, pp. 63ff. Elisabeth Kübler-Ross in private correspondence has assured me that she walked down a corridor with an apparition of a patient who had died; she touched her and the patient even left her signature on a pad which is still preserved.

34. See Chapter VII on OBEs. In *Autobiography of a Yogi* by Paramahansa Yogananda (Los Angeles: Self-Realization Fellowship, 1971), it is claimed that the deceased gurus, Babaji and Lahiri, materialized and were touched. Babaji accepted "fruits and rice cooked in milk and clarified butter" (pp. 308, 349). This autobiography is undoubtedly uncritical according to our standards. Yet other such cases now known make one reluctant to reject the stories *a priori*.

35. Karl Rahner, *Foundations of Christian Faith* (N.Y.: Seabury, 1978),

p. 252; *Theological Investigations,* Vol. XIII, p. 212; E. Schillebeeckx, *Interim Report,* p. 78.

36. Herbert Thurston, S.J., *Surprising Mystics,* J.H. Crehan, S.J., ed. (Chicago: Regnery, 1955), pp. 70ff.; similarly, see Johannes Steiner, *The Visions of Therese Neumann* (N.Y.: Alba House, 1976), where her visions do not always coincide with those of Anne Catherine Emmerich's.

37. C.C. Martindale, S.J., *The Vision of Fatima* (N.Y.: Kenedy, 1950), p. 31.

38. *Ibid.,* p. 103.

39. For details see Martindale, pp. 73ff.; Costa Brochado, *Fatima in the Light of History* (Milwaukee: Bruce, 1955), pp. 176ff.

40. Louis Kondor, S.V.D., *Fatima in Lucia's Own Words* (Cambridge, Mass.: Ravengate Press, 1976), pp. 107ff.

41. *Ibid.,* p. 118, n. 4.

42. Karl Rahner, *Visions and Prophecies,* p. 104.

43. On the child motif in apparitions, see William A. Christian, Jr., *Apparitions in Late Medieval and Renaissance Spain* (Princeton, N.J.: Princeton Univ. Press, 1981), pp. 215ff.

44. D. Scott Rogo, *Miracles* (N.Y.: Dial, 1982), pp. 234–235.

45. *Ibid.,* p. 236. See the photographs of a Marian apparition in Zeitoun Egypt in 1968.

46. Morton Schatzman, *The Story of Ruth* (N.Y.: Putnam's, 1980).

47. See the discussion in Rodger Anderson and Wilma Anderson, "Veridical and Psychopathic Hallucinations: A Comparison of Types," *Parapsychology Review,* May–June 1982, p. 19.

48. Alexandra David-Neel, *Magic and Mystery in Tibet* (Baltimore: Penguin Books, 1965), p. 311.

49. For interesting and intelligent parapsychological discussions of this question, see *Life, Death and Psychical Research,* Canon J.D. Pierce-Higgins and Rev. Stanley Whitby, eds. (London: Rider, 1973), pp. 147–155, and Michael Perry, *The Resurrection of Man* (London: Mowbrays, 1975). The reader may also be interested in pursuing study of the Holy Shroud. See H. David Sox, *The Image on the Shroud* (publication pending). Sox follows the opinion of the scientist Dr. Walter McCrone that the shroud is a forgery. Kenneth E. Stevenson and Gary R. Habermas, *Verdict on the Shroud* (Ann Arbor, Michigan: Servant Books, 1981), present a refutation of this by a scientist on the team studying the shroud; unfortunately the second half of the book is marred by a Fundamentalist approach to Scripture; Ian Wilson, *The Shroud of Turin. The Burial Cloth of Jesus Christ?* (Garden City, N.Y.: Doubleday, 1978); Robert Wilcox, *Shroud* (N.Y.: Macmillan, 1977).

CHAPTER X

1. See M. Lamarr Keene, *The Psychic Mafia,* as told to Allen Spraggett (N.Y.: St. Martin's, 1976).
2. See Ian Stevenson, "Some Comments on Automatic Writing," *JASPR,* October 1978, pp. 315–332; Barbara Honegger, "A Neuropsychological Theory of Automatic Verbal Behavior," *Parapsychology Review,* July–August 1980, pp. 1–8. The author believes such writing is caused by communication from the right to the left hemisphere of the brain; cf. Ira Progoff, *The Image of an Oracle* (N.Y.: Garrett, 1964), a study of Eileen Garrett.
3. Gardner Murphy, *Challenge of Psychical Research,* with collaboration of Laura Dale (N.Y.: Harper, 1961), pp. 210–211. Elizabeth McAdams and Raymond Bayless in *The Case For Life After Death. Parapsychologists Look at the Evidence* (Chicago: Nelson-Hall, 1981) state that Hall had really known a deceased Bessie Beals but concealed this fact. This however does not radically change the point being made as is seen from the context.
4. Rosalind Heywood, *Beyond the Reach of Sense* (N.Y.: Dutton, 1974), p. 126.
5. *Psychic Exploration,* J. White, ed. (N.Y.: Putnam's, 1976), pp. 398–401; Alan Gauld, "Discarnate Survival," *Handbook of Parapsychology,* Benjamin Wolman, ed. (N.Y.: Van Nostrand Reihold, 1977), pp. 613–615.
6. Andrew MacKenzie, *Riddle of the Future* (N.Y.: Taplinger, 1975), pp. 120–121.
7. Leon S. Rhodes, "Emanuel Swedenborg: Scientist, Seer and Mystic," *JASPR,* July 1975, p. 144. See also Signe Toksvig, *Emanuel Swedenborg* (London: Faber & Faber, 1948). At times Swedenborg erred. He spoke of people from Mars, Mercury, Venus and Jupiter.
8. Laurens van der Post, *Jung and the Story of Our Time* (N.Y.: Random House, 1976), pp. 266–268. It is not clear whether the quoted section is entirely from Jung or partly from the author.
9. For ample citations from the scripts, see Gardner Murphy, *Challenge of Psychical Research,* pp. 202–270; H.F. Saltmarsh, *Evidence of Personal Survival From Cross-Correspondences* (London: Bell, 1938); W.H. Salter, *Zoar. The Evidence of Psychical Research Concerning Survival* (N.Y.: Arno Press, 1975 ed.), pp. 169–220; for a reliable popular summary see Rosalind Heywood, *Beyond the Reach of Sense,* pp. 69–91; Martin Ebon, *The Evidence for Life After Death* (N.Y.: New American Library, 1977), pp. 18–19; Ian Currie, *You Cannot Die* (N.Y.: Playboy, 1978), pp. 254–258.

10. Murphy, *Challenge of Psychical Research*, p. 251.

11. Heywood, *Beyond the Reach of Sense*, p. 90. Cyril Burt, the psychologist, estimated that Mrs. Piper's cross-correspondence sittings represented odds of 1 to 372,400 against chance! Cf. *ESP and Psychology*, ed. by Anita Gregory (N.Y.: John Wiley, 1975), p. 155. For modern cross-correspondence cases, see Martin Ebon, *The Evidence for Life After Death*, pp. 77–85, and Allen Spraggett, *The Case for Immortality* (N.Y.: New American Library, 1974), pp. 25–27.

12. W.G. Roll, "Research on Mediumship," *Theta*, Winter 1981, pp. 8–16.

13. Alan Gauld, "Discarnate Survival," *Handbook of Parapsychology*, p. 615.

14. Signe Toksvig, ed., *Swan on a Black Sea. A Study in Automatic Writing: The Cummins-Willett Scripts* (N.Y.: Weiser, 1970, revised ed.). Geraldine Cummins knew Gerald Balfour who himself knew Mrs. Coombe-Tennant. See Miss Cummins' book, *Dr. E.O. Somerville* (London: Dakers, 1952), p. 93. She wrote twenty-two books and plays, some by automatic writing. Though she did poorly on ESP tests, she once read through a ouija board the outline of a play existing in W.B. Yeats' mind. Cf. Anne Dooley, *Every Wall a Door* (N.Y.: Dutton, 1974), p. 60. His scripts were produced in broad daylight in her study.

15. Alan Angoff, *Eileen Garrett and the World Beyond the Senses* (N.Y.: Morrow, 1974). See also Ira Progoff, *The Image of an Oracle* (N.Y.: Garrett, 1964).

16. John Fuller, *The Airmen Who Would Not Die* (N.Y.: Putnam's, 1979).

17. Allen Spraggett with William V. Rauscher, *Arthur Ford: The Man Who Talked with the Dead* (N.Y.: New American Library, 1973), pp. 250ff. William Stringfellow and Anthony Towne in *The Death and Life of Bishop Pike* (Garden City, N.Y.: Doubleday, 1976) believe Ford was almost totally a fraud but admit their incompetence in psychical research. See Ford's own *The Life Beyond Death*, as told to Jerome Ellison (N.Y.: Berkley, 1971). Also on Pike see Allen Spraggett, *The Bishop Pike Story* (N.Y.: New American Library, 1970).

18. Spraggett, *Arthur Ford*, p. 249.

19. Spraggett, *The Case for Immortality*, p. 40.

20. On the "Ear of Dionysius" case see Gardner Murphy, *Challenge of Psychical Research*, pp. 252–269. For other strong cases, see Andrew MacKenzie, *The Unexplained* (N.Y.: Abelard Schuman, 1970), the Vandy case, pp. 97–116; Susy Smith, *The Life of Gladys Osborne Leonard* (N.Y.: Arno Books, 1972), the Raymond case, pp. 40–47, and the book tests, pp. 77–83.

21. Hoyt L. Edge, "Do Spirits Matter: Naturalism and Disembodied Survival," *JASPR*, July 1976, p. 298.

22. H.H. Price, "The Problem of Life After Death," *Religious Studies*, p. 458.

23. William G. Roll, "The Catch 22 of Survival Research," *Theta*, 6, 3, 1978, p. 24.

24. W.G. Roll, "Survival Research: Problems and Possibilities," *Psychic Exploration*, pp. 397–424.

25. Ian Stevenson, M.D., *Xenoglossy. A Review and Report of a Case* (N.Y.: American Society for Psychical Research, 1974).

26. Reverend Carroll E. Jay, *Gretchen, I Am* (N.Y.: Avon. 1977). (Months later Mrs. Jay secretly bought a dictionary to learn German, p. 90.) Ian Stevenson, "A Preliminary Report on a New Case of Responsive Xenoglossy: The Case of Gretchen," *JASPR*, January 1976, pp. 65–77.

27. James H. Hyslop, "The Mental State of the Dead: A Limitation to Psychical Research" (Limited Edition Books, 1972), believed that the dead are in an abnormal state while communicating, almost like a hypnotic trance.

28. Erlendur Haraldsson and Ian Stevenson, "An Experience with an Icelandic Medium Hafstein Björnsson," *JASPR*, October 1978, pp. 192–202; Erlendur Haraldsson, J.G. Pratt and Magnus Kristjansson, "Further Experiments with the Icelandic Medium Hafstein Björnsson," *JASPR*, October 1978, pp. 337–347. For a reliable popular summary see N. Hintze and J.G. Pratt, *The Psychic Realm*, pp. 209–215.

29. Herbert Thurston, S.J., *The Church and Spiritualism* (Milwaukee: Bruce, 1933), pp. 17–18.

30. Rev. Donald Bretherton, "Psychical Research and Biblical Prohibitions," *Life, Death and Psychical Research*, J.D. Pearce-Higgins, ed., p. 108.

31. Martin Ebon, ed., *The Satan Trap: Dangers of the Occult* (Garden City, N.Y.: Doubleday, 1976); Gina Corvina, *The Ouija Board* (N.Y.: Simon and Schuster, 1979).

32. Marjorie Suchocki, "The Question of Immortality," *Journal of Religion* 57, 1977, p. 288. However, this is by no means to deny for theologians the importance of other insights like those of B. Collopy, S.J., "Theology and Death," *Theological Studies* 39, 1978, pp. 22–54. His "dark model" of "a thanatology from below" evokes with great impact a bleak archetypal human experience. This type of phenomenological description is important. It keeps theologians from falling into a blithe "denial of death." As he says, "As such, the resurrection of Jesus does not serve as a shelter from the awful cost and cruelty of death. . . ."

However, it is not true that there is simply a "clueless dark," and there is "the good news."

33. Karl Rahner, *Foundations of Christian Faith* (N.Y.: Seabury, 1978), p. 436.

34. Gabriel Marcel, *De l'existence à l'être.* Roger Troisfontaines, ed. (Paris: Vrin, 1953), pp. 79–90; see also John Heaney, "Beyond Death," *Thought,* March 1975, pp. 45–46.

35. Karl Rahner, "The Life of the Dead," *Theological Investigations,* Vol. IV (Baltimore: Helicon, 1966), p. 353.

36. Edward Schillebeeckx; "Interdisciplinarity in Theology," *Theology Digest* 24 (1976), pp. 140–142.

37. Gardner Murphy and Robert O. Ballou, *William James on Psychical Research* (N.Y.: Viking, 1960), p. 274.

38. Raymond Bayless, *The Other Side of Death* (New Hyde Park, N.Y.: University Books, 1971); Paul Beard, *Living On. How Consciousness Continues and Evolves After Death* (N.Y.: *Continuum,* 1981); Neils Jacobson, M.D., *Life Without Death?* (N.Y.: Dell, 1973), pp. 328–335; Ian Currie, *You Cannot Die* (N.Y.: Playboy, 1978); Susy Smith, *The Book of James* (N.Y.: Berkley, 1974); Arthur Ford, *The Life Beyond Death* (N.Y.: Berkley, 1971).

CHAPTER XI

1. Helen Wambach, *Reliving Past Lives* (N.Y.: Bantam, 1978), an attempt to verify the evidence; *Life Before Life* (N.Y.: Bantam, 1979), regression to the fetal period; Dr. Edith Fiore, *You Have Been Here Before* (N.Y.: Ballantine, 1978), uncovering traumas as the source of this life problem but with little verification; Peter Moss with Joe Keeton, *Encounters with the Past* (N.Y.: Doubleday, 1980), by a writer and a hypnotherapist with verifications mainly through street directories and names; Morris Netherton, Ph.D. and Nancy Shiffrin, *Past Lives Therapy* (N.Y.: Morrow, 1978), the use of dream reverie to study therapeutic results; Dr. Gerald Edelstein, *Trauma, Trance and Transformation* (in press), the effectiveness of hypnotic regression as therapy.

2. Helen Wambach, *Reliving Past Lives,* pp. 41–43, 71–79.

3. Peter Moss, *Encounters with the Past,* p. 221.

4. D. Scott Rogo, "Adventures in Make-Believe," *Fate,* December 1982, pp. 77–82.

5. Ian Stevenson, M.D., *Twenty Cases Suggestive of Reincarnation,* 1974, revised ed., *Cases of the Reincarnation Type,* Vol. II, *Cases in Sri Lanka,* 1977, *Cases of the Reincarnation Type,* Vol. III, *Twenty Cases in Lebanon and Turkey,* 1980, all published at Charlottesville, Virginia by the University of Virginia Press; for an excellent summary, see Ian Stevenson, "Reincarnation: Field Studies and Theoretical Issues," *Handbook of Para-*

psychology, B. Wolman, ed., pp. 631–663. See also J. Gaither Pratt, *ESP Research Today* (Metuchen, N.J.: Scarecrow Press, 1973), pp. 140–154.

6. *Twenty Cases*, p. 345.

7. *Twenty Cases*, pp. 91–105.

8. *Twenty Cases*, pp. 259–269.

9. For other investigations, see Dr. H.N. Banerjee, *Americans Who Have Reincarnated* (N.Y.: Macmillan, 1980), and *The Once and Future Life* (N.Y.: Dell, 1979); Edward W. Ryall, *Second Time Around* (St. Helier, England: Spearman, 1974), a case with incredibly detailed memories; Francis Story, *Rebirth as Experience and Doctrine* (Kandy, Sri Lanka: Buddhist Publication Society, 1975), particularly valuable for birthmark cases; Guy Lyon Playfair, *The Unknown Power* (N.Y.: Pocket Books, 1975), cases in South America; for popular versions see Frederick Lenz, Ph.D., *Life Times. True Accounts of Reincarnation* (N.Y.: Fawcett Crest, 1979), and Martin Ebon, ed., *Reincarnation in the Twentieth Century* (N.Y.: New American Library, 1969).

10. But see the Indian parapsychologist, C.T.K. Chari, "Reincarnation Research: Method and Interpretation," *The Signet Handbook of Parapsychology* (N.Y.: New American Library, 1978), Martin Ebon, ed., pp. 313–324, and "A New Look at Reincarnation," *The Christian Parapsychologist*, December 1981, pp. 121–129. Chari, while not denying paranormal processes, sees much room for "cultural contagion" as a partial explanation of many cases.

11. A mild indication of such a focusing tendency was found in the experiments with Pavel Stepanek. It is called the "focusing effect." But this is only faintly analogous to the impersonations which we are discussing. Cf. *Cases of the Reincarnation Type*, Vol. III, p. 361.

12. F.W.H. Myers, *Human Personality and Its Survival of Bodily Death* (London: Longmans, Green, 1954 edition), Vol. I, pp. 360–368; Naomi Hintze, J.G. Pratt, *The Psychic Realm: What Can You Believe?* pp. 194ff. For a negative and critical treatment, see Rodger I. Anderson, "The Watseka Wonder: A Critical Re-Evaluation," *Theta*, Fall 1980, pp. 6–10, and continued as a debate in *Theta*, Autumn 1981, pp. 20–24. For a detailed treatment presented with the liberties of a novelist see David St. Clair, *Watseka: America's Most Extraordinary Case of Possession and Exorcism* (N.Y.: Playboy, 1977).

13. Dr. Giovanno Scambia of the Italian Psychical Research Association has investigated the case of Maria Telarico. On January 5, 1939, in the village of Siano, Italy, she suddenly became Pepe Veraldi. She was walking across a bridge where she was supposed to have committed suicide. She knew everything about Pepe but did not know her own family. "Pepe" named four murderers and acted out the death.

Then Maria lost the Pepe consciousness. Indications of verification of details followed. See also Ian Stevenson, "A Case of Secondary Personality with Xenoglossy," *American Journal of Psychiatry,* 136.7, December 1979, pp. 1591–1592.

14. "Genetic memory," if it exists, would not explain some reincarnation cases. Cf. *Twenty Cases,* p. 343.

15. Cf. H. Crouzel, "Origen and Origenism" *New Catholic Encyclopedia* (N.Y.: McGraw-Hill, 1967); J.N.D. Kelly, *Early Christian Doctrines* (N.Y.: Harper & Bros., 1959), pp. 469ff.: R.P.C. Hanson, *Allegory and Event* (Richmond, Va.: John Knox, 1959), pp. 341ff. On the Albigensians, see *Reincarnation: The Phoenix Fire Mystery,* Joseph Head and S.L. Granston, eds. (N.Y.: Julian Press, 1977), pp. 162–165.

16. Avery Dulles, S.J., *The Survival of Dogma* (Garden City, N.Y.: Doubleday, 1973), ch. 11; Piet Fransen, "The Authority of the Councils," *Problems of Authority,* John Todd, ed. (Baltimore: Helicon, 1962), pp. 43–78.

17. *Reincarnation: The Phoenix Fire Mystery,* pp. 135–140; Quincy Howe, Jr., *Reincarnation for the Christian* (Philadelphia: Westminster, 1974), pp. 85–97.

18. Barnabas Lindars, *The Gospel of John* (London: Oliphant, 1972), p. 342; Rudolf Bultmann, *The Gospel of John. A Commentary* (Oxford: Blackwell, 1971); Raymond Brown, S.S., *The Gospel According to John* (Garden City, N.Y.: Doubleday, 1966), p. 371.

19. William Barclay, *The Gospel of Matthew,* Vol. II (Philadelphia: Westminster, 1975, rev. ed.), p. 136.

20. Karl Rahner, *Theological Investigations,* Vol. V. pp. 199–211; Raymond Brown, S.S., *Jesus—God and Man* (Milwaukee: Bruce, 1967), pp. 39ff.; Bruce Vawter, *This Man Jesus* (Garden City, N.Y.: Doubleday, 1973), pp. 134ff.

21. Gabriel Moran, *Theology of Revelation* (N.Y.: Herder & Herder, 1966), p. 69.

22. Geddes MacGregor, *Reincarnation in Christianity* (Wheaton, Ill.: Theosophical Publishing House, 1978), pp. 93–94.

23. Letter to Editor, *The Christian Parapsychologist,* March 1982, p. 163.

24. Karl Rahner, *Foundations of Christian Faith,* p. 442.

25. Cf. C.J. Ducasse, *A Critical Examination of Belief in a Life After Death* (Wheaton, Ill.: Theosophical Publishing House, 1961), ch. XXI; also "Objections to Reincarnation," in *Reincarnation: The Phoenix Fire Mystery,* pp. 7–12.

26. On ancillary questions, such as what is the interval between lives or the notion of karma in the evidence, see Ian Stevenson, "Some

Questions Related to Cases of the Reincarnation Type," *JASPR,* October 1974, pp. 395–416.

CHAPTER XII

1. P.T. Forsyth, *This Life and The Next. The Effect of This Life of Faith in Another* (London: Independent Press, 1918, 1946), p. 23.

2. Cyril Burt, "Psychology and Parapsychology," *Science and ESP* (N.Y.: Humanities Press, 1967), p. 140.

3. Nils O. Jacobson, M.D., *Life Without Death?* (N.Y.: Dell, 1971), p. 334.

4. See William Johnston, *The Inner Eye of Love. Mysticism and Religion* (N.Y.: Harper & Row, 1978), p. 194.

5. Hywel D. Lewis, "Religion and the Paranormal," in *Philosophy and Psychical Research,* Shivesh C. Thankur, ed. (N.Y.: Humanities Press, 1976) p. 152.

6. Cf. C.K. Barrett, *A Commentary on the Second Epistle to the Corinthians* (N.Y.: Harper & Row, 1973); also H. Cavallin, *Life After Death,* pp. 171ff.

7. Maurice Nedoncelle, *Baron Friedrich von Hugel* (N.Y.: Longmans, Green, 1937), p. 109.

8. Karl Rahner, "The Intermediate State," *Theological Investigations,* Vol. XVII (London: Darton, Longman & Todd, 1981), p. 123.

9. See Joseph A. Bracken, S.J., "Salvation: A Personal Choice," *Theological Studies,* September 1976, pp. 410–424; Robert Gleason, S.J., *The World To Come* (N.Y.: Sheed & Ward, 1958), pp. 124–125.

10. See Franz Siebel, "Purgatory: An Interpretation," *Theology Digest,* Spring 1978, p. 41.

11. Bracken, "Salvation: A Personal Choice," p. 423.

12. Ladislaus Boros, S.J., *The Mystery of Death* (N.Y.: Herder & Herder, 1965), pp. 130–132.

13. William Thompson, "The Doctrine of Hell," *The Ecumenist,* March–April 1972, pp. 33–37.

14. Boros, *The Mystery of Death,* pp. 85ff.; *Pain and Providence* (Baltimore: Helicon, 1966).

15. Karl Rahner, "Hell," *Encyclopedia of Theology* (N.Y.: Seabury, 1975).

16. John A. Mourant, *Augustine on Immortality* (Philadelphia: Villanova U. Press, 1969), pp. 120ff.

17. Jose-Maria Gonzalez-Ruiz, "Should We De-Mythologize the 'Separated Soul'?" *The Problem of Eschatology,* E. Schillebeeckx, ed. (N.Y.: Paulist, 1969), p. 995.

18. D.Z. Philips, *Death and Immortality* (N.Y.: Macmillan, 1970), p. 74.

19. H.A. Williams, *True Resurrection* (N.Y.: Holt, Rinehart and Winston, 1972); Peter Kreeft, *Heaven, The Heart's Deepest Longing* (N.Y.: Harper & Row, 1980); George Maloney, S.J., *The Everlasting Now* (Notre Dame, Ind.: Ave Maria Press, 1980).

20. E.J. Fortman, S.J., *Everlasting Life After Death* (N.Y.: Alba House, 1976), pp. 207–211, takes an opposite position.

21. See Fortman, *Everlasting Life After Death*, p. 190.

22. For some examples, see Jane Roberts' books such as *Seth Speaks* (N.Y.: Prentice-Hall, 1972); Paul Beard, *Living On. How Consciousness Continues and Evolves After Death* (N.Y.: Continuum, 1981); Dr. Robert Crookall, *What Happens When You Die* (Gerrards Cross, England: Colin Smythe, 1978); George W. Meek, *After We Die, What* (Franklin, N.C.: Metascience, 1980); Stewart Edward White, *The Unobstructed Universe* (N.Y.: Dutton, 1940); Mary LeBeau, *Beyond Doubt. A Record of Psychic Experience* (N.Y.: Harper & Row, 1956); Susy Smith, *The Book of James* (N.Y.: Putnam's, 1974); Ruth Montgomery, *A World Beyond* (Greenwich, Conn.: Fawcett Crest, 1971); Eileen Sullivan, *Arthur Ford Speaks From the Beyond* (Greenwich, Conn.: Fawcett Crest, 1975). It would be interesting to compare the last two books which are about Arthur Ford.

CHAPTER XIII

1. Thomas Berry, C.P., "Future Forms of Religious Experience," and "Cosmic Person and the Future of Man," *Riverdale Studies,* Vol. I (Riverdale Center for Religious Research, Riverdale, N.Y. 10471).

2. Teilhard de Chardin, *Building the Earth* (Wilkes-Barre, Pa.: Dimension Books, 1965), p. 19.

3. Teilhard de Chardin, *Activation of Energy* (N.Y.: Harcourt Brace, 1971), p. 16.

4. Ewert Cousins, "Teilhard and Global Spirituality," *Anima,* Fall 1981, p. 28.

5. Bernard Lonergan, "Theology in a New Context," in *Conversion: Perspective on Personal and Social Transformation* (N.Y.: Alba House, 1978), p. 3.

6. Ursula King, *Towards a New Mysticism. Teilhard de Chardin and Eastern Religions* (N.Y.: Seabury, 1981), esp. pp. 169–191.

7. Richard S. Valle and Rolf Von Eckartsberg, *The Metaphors of Consciousness* (N.Y.: Plenum, 1981), p. 23. On paradigms, see Gary Gutting, ed., *Paradigms and Revolutions* (Notre Dame, Ind.; U. of Notre Dame, 1980).

8. Valle and Von Eckartsberg, p. 24. Cf. also K. Ramakrishna Rao, "Science and the Legitimacy of Psi," *Parapsychology Review,* Jan.–Feb. 1982, pp. 1–6.

9. Michael Novak, *Ascent of the Mountain, Flight of the Dove* (N.Y.: Harper & Row, 1978), pp. 55ff., 73ff.

10. Valle and Von Eckartsberg, p. 80.

11. See Morris Berman, *The Reenchantment of the World* (Ithaca: Cornell U. Press, 1981), p. 136.

12. Bernard Lonergan, *Method in Theology* (N.Y.: Herder and Herder, 1972), p. 265; Novak calls this "intelligent subjectivity" in *Ascent of the Mountain* (p. 98).

13. Cf. T.S. Kuhn, *The Structures of Scientific Revolution* (Chicago: U. of Chicago Press, 1970).

14. For a good survey see Charles Hampden-Turner, *Maps of the Mind* (London: Beazley, 1981).

15. Among the countless books on this subject, see H.D. Lewis, *The Self and Immortality* (N.Y.: Seabury, 1973), esp. pp. 64ff. On a high popular level see Arthur C. Custance, *The Mysterious Matter of Mind* (Grand Rapids, Mich.: Zondervan, 1980).

16. Robert Ornstein, *The Psychology of Consciousness* (N.Y.: Penguin, 1975); "The Two Modes of Consciousness and the Two Halves of the Brain," in *Consciousness: Brain, States of Awareness and Mysticism* (N.Y.: Harper & Row, 1979), pp. 19–24; with reference to theology, see David R. Crownfield, "Consciousness and the Voices of the Gods," a critical review of Julian Jaynes' book, *The Origins of Consciousness in the Breakdown of the Bicameral Mind, Journal of the American Academy of Religion,* XLVI, 2, pp. 193–202.

17. Jacob Needleman and Dennis Lewis, *On the Way to Self-Knowledge* (N.Y.: Knopf, 1976), p. 215.

18. John Wellwood, ed., *The Meeting of the Ways. Explorations in East/West Psychology* (N.Y.: Schocken, 1979), pp. 76–77.

19. Wellwood, p. 184.

20. Berman, *The Reenchantment of the World,* pp. 170, 126.

21. Ken Wilber, *The Spectrum of Consciousness,* pp. 282–283. See the summary by Wilber in Roger N. Walsh, M.D. and Frances Vaughan, Ph.D., *Beyond Ego. Transpersonal Dimensions in Psychology* (Los Angeles: Tarch, 1980), and in Wellwood, *The Meeting of the Ways,* pp. 7–28.

22. David Bohm, *Wholeness and the Implicate Order* (London: Routledge and Kegan Paul, 1980).

23. Valle and Von Eckartsberg, *The Metaphors of Consciousness,* p. 123.

24. Karl Pribram, *Languages of the Brain* (N.Y.: Brooks/Cole, 1977).

See the interview, "Holographic Memory," in *Psychology Today*, February 1977, pp. 71–84.

25. Berman, *The Reenchantment of the World*, p. 136.

26. Valle and Von Eckartsberg, *The Metaphors of Consciousness*, p. 134.

27. George Leonard, *The Secret Pulse. A Search for the Perfect Rhythm That Exists in Each of Us* (N.Y.: Dutton, 1978), p. 63.

28. Kenneth S. Pope and Jerome L. Singer, *The Stream of Consciousness* (N.Y.: Plenum, 1978), p. 84.

29. Stanislaw Grof, *Realms of the Human Unconscious* (N.Y.: Dutton, 1976), and *Beyond Death. The Gates of Consciousness* (N.Y.: Thames and Hudson, 1980); R.E.L. Masters and Jean Houston, *The Varieties of Psychedelic Experience* (N.Y.: Dell, 1966); Walter Houston Clark, *Chemical Ecstasy* (N.Y.: Sheed and Ward, 1969).

30. John Lilly, *The Deep Self* (N.Y.: Simon and Schuster, 1977) and *The Scientist: A Novel Autobiography* (N.Y.: Lippincott, 1978).

31. Robert G. Jahn, ed., *The Role of Consciousness in the Physical World* (Boulder, Col.: Westview Press, 1981). See the fine review by Evan Walker in *Parapsychology Review*, July–August 1982, pp. 18–21.

32. Peter Koestenbaum, *The New Image of the Person* (N.Y.: Greenwood, 1978).

33. See Robert C. Zaehner, *Mysticism, Sacred and Profane* (London: Oxford U. Press, 1957), and *Drugs, Mysticism and Make-Believe* (London: Collins, 1972); Joseph Marechal, S.J., *Studies in the Psychology of the Mystics* (N.Y.: Magi Books, 1964 ed.); Richard Woods, O.P., *Understanding Mysticism* (Garden City, N.Y.: Doubleday, 1980), pp. 449ff., 477ff. With regard to the possible oversimplifications of books on mysticism and physics such as Fritjof Capra, *The Tao of Physics*, Gary Zukav, *The Dancing of the Wu Li Masters* and Michael Talbot, *Mysticism and the New Physics*, see Robert John Russell's review of Zukav in *Zygon*, December 1980, pp. 440–443.

34. On the implications of animal psi, see C.W.K. Mundle, "The Psychic Powers of Non-Human Animals," in *Philosophy and Psychical Research*, Shivesh C. Thankur, ed. (N.Y.: Humanities Press, 1976), pp. 157–180.

35. Peter Koestenbaum, *The New Image of the Person*, p. 153.